By Edwin Cameron

Witness to Aids
Justice: A Personal Account

Behind Prison Walls

Unlocking a Safer South Africa

Edwin Cameron
Rebecca Gore
Sohela Surajpal

Tafelberg

Cover photograph © Mikhael Subotzky
Cover design by Marthie Steenkamp
Graphics by Phillip Johnson
Edited by Alison Lowry
Proofread by Linde Dietrich
Index by George Claassen
Photographs supplied by authors

Originally printed in South Africa
ISBN: 978-0-624 09269-8 (First edition, first impression 2025)

LSiPOD: 978-0-624-09610-8 (First edition, first impression 2025)

ISBN 978-0-624-09297-1 (epub)

'No one truly knows a nation until one has been inside its jails. A nation should not be judged by how it treats its highest citizens, but its lowest ones.'

Nelson Rolihlahla Mandela

Contents

List of Figures

Foreword by the Honourable
Mr Justice Malindi

This book uncovers our prisons more than 30 years after South Africa's transition to democracy. Its themes – punishment, imprisonment, sentencing and the horrors behind prison walls – resonate with my life experiences.

In the 1980s, during our people's growing resistance to apartheid, I was charged with treason, terrorism and murder. I was arrested and detained after the Vaal uprising that erupted on 3 September 1984. In June 1985, after long months in detention without trial, I became accused number five in the renowned Delmas Treason Trial. Twenty-two of us stood trial for resisting apartheid.

Eleven of my co-accused were acquitted. Eleven of us were convicted. The Judge, Mr Justice van Dijkhorst, sentenced me in 1988 to five years' imprisonment for statutory 'terrorism'.

I served one year on Robben Island before the fate of all those whom the Judge had convicted took a dramatic turn. In December 1989, the then Appellate Division (forerunner of the Supreme Court of Appeal), set aside all convictions and sentences. The proceedings were nullified. This was because of a gross procedural error the Judge committed in dismissing one of his two assessors.

I had by then spent four years in four different prisons. I emerged from Robben Island, joyfully, but with profoundly sad insights. I had experienced solitary confinement, detention without trial and unjust imprisonment.

1

So, I have read this book with exceptional interest and engagement. The authors plunge into the racially charged history of prisons in South Africa. They describe our democracy's pledges on prisons, which were inspired by the world's most famous prisoner, our first President, Nelson Rolihlahla Mandela.

These promises set our faces against apartheid's harsh, punitive prisons. Instead, we would have a new carceral system, based on human dignity, reform, rehabilitation and education.

Sadly, as the authors vividly describe, those promises are yet to be met. This book takes us behind the high prison walls that only a few can access and calculates in human terms the cost of our young democracy's over-reliance on mass incarceration.

Now, I am a sitting Judge in one of our country's busiest courts. I sit on the Judicial Benches that Judge van Dijkhorst once sat. Now, I sentence people to prison.

As I write this Foreword, the Judge President has assigned me to hear criminal cases. It is a matter of high importance to me as a Judge, and to all South Africans, that we, our country, can do better in how we deal with crime and with incarcerating offenders.

This book is full of practical suggestions. Without minimizing the seriousness of crime and violence, the authors strongly oppose the idea that imprisonment, by itself, holds any solution to stopping crime. They point out, instead, that we can and should do more.

Effective crime intelligence, better policing, preventative methods, intervention agencies or institutions, and more expeditious trials and prosecutions would put us on the right track. This book urges that prisons cannot be a catch-all solution to our systemic, societal problems. The authors call for creative, imaginative, practicable interventions.

The idea of a prison can be unsettling and even jarring. This book confronts our fears and misconceptions. It asks us not to look the other way. Everyone concerned about our country should be concerned about our grievous lapses in ensuring safety, in how we have failed to ensure that punishment is humane, and that effective rehabilitation is provided.

Everyone concerned about our country and these grievous lapses will benefit hugely from this book. It is written with a depth of personal engagement and critical reflection. I strongly commend it.

GCINUMUZI P MALINDI
Judge of the High Court of South Africa

Authors' Foreword:
Why a Book on Prisons, Now?

South Africa's prisons are everywhere: 243 of them, in almost every town and city across our country, cramming in the largest prison population in Africa. Some are big, some small; some well run, many not. And yet, despite being pervasive, our prisons are also nowhere.[1] We blank them out of our minds. We prefer not to think about them. We do not want to know about them, or what goes on inside them. They are an uncomfortable irritant, an unwanted speck on our consciences.

We should not feel guilty about this. We live in a dangerous society. Our country's violent crime is truly frightening. This tempts us to think that those entangled in the prison system must deserve to be there. Besides, prisons are dark, unknown, secluded places. Like abattoirs, they are designed not to be open or transparent. If you are not a prisoner yourself, it's difficult to get inside a prison, to know what happens there. Very few of us will ever gain access to a prison or even spend much time thinking about prisons.

Yet all that happens there is done in our name. We – the public, the voters, the taxpayers, the concerned community – are responsible for our carceral system, for our overreliance on mass incarceration and sentence inflation both practically (through the politicians we vote for) and morally (because without our approval or acquiescence, even just our inaction or silence, the abuses could not occur in our name).

This is why we have written this book. To invite you to know a bit more about prisons, and to reflect. And, most importantly, to consider how we – you, we, our country – can do better.

The book tries to make the history, functions and conditions of our closed, secretive prison system more visible, and to prompt forward-looking debate about how our prisons can be effectively and humanely run. It is informed by the unique exposure and personal access to prisons we three authors had while we worked together in the national prison oversight body, the Judicial Inspectorate for Correctional Services (JICS) – one of us, Edwin Cameron, as a Judge long engaged with prisons (from 1994, then, from 2009, as a Justice of the Constitutional Court, and now, since 2020, as Inspecting Judge); and two of us, Rebecca Gore and Sohela Surajpal, as law clerks and researchers at JICS.

We invite you to join us because we know we can do better with our prisons. This, in turn, can help rehabilitate prisoners and positively em-power our society. As we will show, our prisons are, for the most part, miserable, and failing in their task of rehabilitating those inside. They are crammed with remand detainees awaiting trial (over one-third of all our prisoners) and jampacked with those condemned to the over-long sen-tences and over-broad crimes that are a miscreant product of a wrong turn our first parliament took in the early days of democracy.

Overcrowding is ever present, a dangerous bane for personnel and pris-oners alike. As a result of government dysfunction, most of our prisons show signs of disrepair. Gaping faults and infrastructural degradation are left unfixed. Many prisoners endure stinking toilets and unsanitary showers that imperil public health. Unsafe boundary walls put person-nel and prisoners alike at risk of dangerous intruders and escapes. And gangs. Gangs wield unique power, both inside and outside prison walls. Violent acts of assault, torture and rape put both inmates and personnel in danger. Instead of releasing rehabilitated, law-abiding individuals once they have served their time, our prisons perpetuate criminality.

It is wrong to blame this on the approximately 40 000 correctional personnel we employ. Whose fault is it, then? It is ours, our collective fault, the fault of 'the system' that we feel unable or unwilling to change. It is we, you and I, who bear responsibility.

The good news is that, with focus and will and commitment, we have the power to fix many of these problems. We can make our prisons less appalling, less alarming places. Better prisons and smarter sentencing will help us focus on steps that truly help to contain crime, especially violent crime, and deal with its root causes.

That path takes us not (as happens now) to longer, stiffer sentences for fewer and fewer perpetrators, but to strategic crime-prevention measures, effective crime intelligence, proper police follow-up, especially detective work, more efficient prosecution and court processes, more perpetrators tried and sentenced in better-functioning courts, sent to better prisons with better rehabilitation programmes.

We do not paper over the violence, brutality, cruelty and trauma that crime and criminals inflict on all of us. We do not try to ease the responsibility or diminish the agency of those who commit crimes. It is all too real for us in a deeply unequal society where about 70 people are murdered every day. Many readers of this book are victims and survivors of these harrowing crimes. Our point is that the status quo – mass incarceration and sentencing inflation – does not help any of us. Instead, we urge reforms to the criminal justice system in general, and prisons in particular, knowing this will make society safer for all of us.

Of course, hard work lies ahead. We have to allocate the resources to refocus and implement practical solutions to curb crime – and to ensure that prisons rehabilitate, and don't merely punish. Our safety, as well as our integrity as a country, calls us to do this.

EDWIN CAMERON
REBECCA GORE
SOHELA SURAJPAL

Acknowledgements

We thank our colleagues at JICS, particularly those in the national executive, and the regional leaders, with whom each of us has worked closely – Vick Misser, Ntombizodwa Sibutha, Thembelihle Ngema, Eddie Brewis, Lennard de Souza, Velaphi Mukhari, Justine Gericke, Mike Prusent, Shadrack Sibanyoni, Sambeso Sani, Murasiet Mentoor and Alexia Katsiginis (my first law clerk/researcher at JICS).

We thank also our colleagues in NICRO (National Institute for Crime Prevention and the Reintegration of Offenders), Betzi Pierce and Lungile Ngwenya; Shaun Shelly, of Harm Reduction International, for invaluable insight into drug use and remediation; Sasha Gear, Doreen Gaura and Prince Nare at JDI-SA (Just Detention International South Africa); Nabeelah Mia from Lawyers for Human Rights (LHR), who succeeded Clare Ballard in LHR's prisons project; Professor Harry Hausler and Dr Joel Steingo of TB HIV Care, and, indefatigably, Professor Lukas Muntingh and Dr Jean Redpath of Africa Criminal Justice Reform (ACJR) at the University of the Western Cape.

Our special thanks to Professor Dirk van Zyl Smit, Dr Khomotso Moshikaro and our JICS colleague Lennard de Souza for reading the whole manuscript, and for their generously insightful comments and improving suggestions.

But, most of all, we express our debt to all our JICS colleagues, not only the executive management, but the Visitors' Committee Co-ordinators, Independent Correctional Centre Visitors, inspectors and investigators. Without your shared knowledge, experience, wisdom and insights, this book would not have come about.

A note on terminology

Contemporary terminology tends to 'correctional centres' and 'inmates' or 'incarcerated persons'. This we mostly follow; but the state of our criminal justice system impels us to being blunter – 'prisons', 'prisoners', and 'offenders'. We anonymise individuals who have been incarcerated: 'inmate X'.

There is ongoing debate on whether to capitalise the names of racial and ethnic groups. We have chosen to capitalise 'Black', 'Coloured' and 'Indian' in this book. This is an acknowledgement of the fact that, as a result of South Africa's past, these terms are not simply neutral descriptions but proper nouns denoting racial groups with unique and important histories.

1

Crime, Punishment and Prisons – A Judge's Early Exposure

The first time I entered a prison was in the icy highveld winter of 1976, soon after the Soweto uprising had occurred. That visit was an experience that changed my life and helped shape my future in ways I could not have imagined.

For the six-week mid-year university break, a Stellenbosch friend, whose father was a judge, organised a light-duty holiday job for me as a judge's registrar (or secretary). While Jan worked for his father in Pretoria, I was to temp with his father's colleague in Johannesburg.

Judges' registrars had a host of duties, all of them undemanding. From the court's registry downstairs, you had to provision your judge with stationery – civil service notepads and pens and hardcover court books. During hearings, you took your place just below your judge, between the stenographer and the court orderly. You sat there proudly, perhaps a little self-importantly, as you gazed with wonder and admiration at the advocates arguing their clients' cases. Every decree the judge granted had to be entered into your judge's hardcover court book. And each day when the judges assembled for their tea break in the judges' common room, at 11:15 am, you had to make sure they had biscuits to nibble on.

To me, the courts were a strange new world, and the judges even stranger. All of them were elderly white men, who seemed severe and humourless. Amidst this, my tasks felt important, but my future felt terrifying.

In a few months, as the recipient of a generous Rhodes Scholarship, I would leave for Oxford. What would I study (Classics – or English? Politics, Philosophy and Economics – the famous Oxford PPE? Or Law)? And, after Oxford, what would I do with my life? Pursue wealth, power? Enter politics? Deeper existential questions troubled me. Who was I? I didn't know. There was hardly time in my mind to pay attention to national questions.

The judge, Douglas Davidson, seemed easygoing enough. He was fluent in the phrases of the classical languages Latin and Greek, which he had studied at Oxford in the 1940s – a course I proposed to study myself. After a few desultory recess weeks in Johannesburg, Judge President Piet Cillié – a sinister apartheid apparatchik – assigned Judge Davidson to Circuit Court duty in Vereeniging, an industrial city 60 km south of Johannesburg.

Circuit Court was a big deal. We took up lodgings, rather grandly, in the newly built hotel situated on a bend in the Vaal River, South Africa's second-largest watercourse. The staff were deferent, also to me, for I was the Circuit judge's registrar. The chair of the local attorneys' association marked the Circuit with a special reception at his home. This caused Judge Davidson, who affected some snobbish pretensions, to roll his eyes and say, 'We have to please the locals.'

Judges wielded – still wield – power, and power exacts deference, though not always respect. At that time only the superior courts, not the magistrates' courts, could impose long sentences – limits curtailed what district magistrates and regional courts could do. All serious offences, like murder, which regional court magistrates now routinely try, were then exclusively in the jurisdiction of the High Court.

Our roster was heavy with murders, robberies and one or two rapes – but no racially and politically loaded Black-on-white or white-on-Black crimes. That winter, all the accused were Black, and, barring only the interpreter, all the court personnel were white. The public gallery was filled with relatives of the accused and the victims and witnesses.

The court sittings were held in the largest courtroom in the local magistrates' court building in the 'white' town centre of Vereeniging. This was scarcely 14 km from the resource-deprived township of Sharpeville where, just sixteen years earlier, apartheid policemen had gunned down Black protesters. To this I gave no thought, however. At the time the massacre took place, in March 1960, I had just turned seven and had freshly arrived with my sisters at a children's home in Komani (then Queenstown). Those events earned apartheid world-wide notoriety, but growing up I was only dimly aware of them; as an adult, I avoided them. The Circuit passed with no mention of Sharpeville.

Toward the end of the court roll, Judge Davidson indicated that, as part of our Circuit duties, we would be visiting Vereeniging's prison. The prison was a forbidding squat building, constructed, like all apartheid prisons, to separate Black from white. Apartheid's race classifications were minute and designed to humiliate: white, Bantu, Indian (sometimes called 'Asian'), Coloured, 'Other Coloured', even a special classification for 'Rehoboth Basters'.[2] But its main, its most prized distinction, was between whites and *the rest*: 'non-whites'. Those not white were *non*: legislatively, socially, residentially and occupationally. *Non* meant to be beneath, sidelined, excluded, set below, humbled by the brutal power of the apartheid state at the majesty of whiteness.

Filled with trepidation – and perhaps an unworthy tinge of excitement – I followed the judge. We started in the white section. Uncrowded, it had a moderate sprinkling of inmates (one, an elderly man serving a long sentence for fraud, told the judge he'd been at 'St Andrews College, Cambridge' – this impressed me, until the judge murmured, 'There's no St Andrews College at Cambridge . . . nor at Oxford').

We then moved to the 'non-white' women's section. Here an incident scorched itself on me. The prison head had ordered the women to assemble in the courtyard for the judge. The space was crowded. Rows and rows of Black women. Many were young adults, though more seemed mature,

11

in their 40s or 50s. Two or three hundred women crowded into the central square, silently, subjected to our gaze.

What heinous offences could these women, some of them mothers and grandmothers, possibly have committed? My mind, pummelled by brash confusions, had no idea. The next moment changed that. Raising his voice, Judge Davidson asked, 'How many of you are here for dagga?' It was a savvy question. There was a moment's pause and then a sea of hands went up. Almost all the women were serving prison sentences 'for dagga' (cannabis or marijuana).

Just five years before, in 1971, one of apartheid's rising right-wing ideologues, Dr Connie Mulder, had pushed through the all-white Parliament the most severe punishments ever legislated 'for dagga'. Many thought Dr Mulder was destined for higher office – prime minister, or even president. He was an articulate orator and an assertive schemer. Harsh new sentences showcasing his tough stand on drugs and drug-dealing boosted his impetus. So it was Dr Mulder who led the Bill on the Abuse of Dependence-producing Substances and Rehabilitation Centres through Parliament in May 1971.[3]

When Mulder spoke of drug use it was in near-apocalyptic terms, comparing the situation in South Africa to the tip of an iceberg whose shadowy harms had already been seen elsewhere in the world. Our country, he warned, was heading in the same disastrous direction. Echoing President Richard Nixon and United States right-wingers, he inveighed against 'the permissive society', which sacrificed sexual standards and morality to 'individual freedom'. Dagga was not harmless – it was the 'most abused substance in the world'.[4] Existing punishments were insufficient. The danger was too grave. Drugs menaced western civilisation itself. Dagga dealers were no better than cold-blooded poisoners, killing their victims slowly.

Dr Mulder not only introduced mandatory minimum sentences for cannabis use and dealing; his statute legislated far heavier penalties. He conceded that the new law was 'perhaps drastic', but that, he noted, was the point. Inconvenience was but a 'trivial price to pay to safeguard our children against an evil that could ruin their lives'. Avoiding the harsh penalties was perfectly easy. 'Nobody,' he proclaimed, 'need fear these punishments if he just resists the temptation to fill his pockets at the cost of others' misery.'

Standing in the cold wintry air in the non-white women's section of Vereeniging prison, it struck me forcefully how cruel and absurd it was to imprison those women who had held up their hands 'for dagga'. They had merely done what people in their position had done for centuries – shared the product of the profusely growing local plant *cannabis sativa*.

Dagga or cannabis (or marijuana or weed or pot or grass or ganja or Mary Jane) is a crop indigenous to southern Africa.[5] Its cultivation, distribution and use long pre-date the white settlement of Africa's southern tip. It has always grown profusely in the valleys and on the hills of south-eastern Africa, across what is now Eswatini and KwaZulu-Natal and the Eastern Cape. Dr Mulder's bogeys punished people extremely harshly who were innocent of anything bar hundreds of years of traditional use.[6]

Disturbed by what I had seen, I proceeded with Judge Davidson to the 'non-white' men's section. There a distressing confrontation awaited me.

The previous day, Judge Davidson had presided over a guilty plea to a killing. A knife fight had erupted in a tavern not far from the magistrates' court, in Sebokeng, a township adjacent to Sharpeville. A young man was arrested for being the knife-wielder. In drunken fuzziness, he had fatally stabbed his antagonist. He claimed he had acted in self-defence, but the state stood ready to call witnesses to controvert this. Those who saw what had happened pointed at the accused as the instigator.

Because the young man was charged with murder, a longstanding custom honoured by advocates assigned a pro deo counsel to him – an advocate acting without charge, 'on behalf of God'. Pro deo counsel, often the most junior practitioners (or long-in-the-tooth old counsel with no other work) did their best, but seldom was this good enough. The system was swept away when the Constitutional Court ordered that all accused charged with serious crimes should have competent state-sponsored defence.[7]

The prosecutor huddled with the accused's pro deo advocate. Eventually, he accepted the facts the state would allow to form the basis of his guilty plea. The deceased and the accused were friends. They were drinking together. Their quarrel was an unexpected misunderstanding. The accused had not intended to kill. It was all a terrible, drunken mistake. The plea did not confess to murder, but to the lesser crime of culpable homicide – the negligent killing of another human being.

Counsel and the prosecutor both rose to inform Judge Davidson that they had agreed on the facts, and that the prosecution accepted the accused's plea of culpable homicide. Judge Davidson, spared another long trial of conflicting witness accounts, delivered a short judgment in double time, accepting the accused's plea and finding him guilty. Counsel pleaded in mitigation. The prosecutor countered that casual township slayings, especially alcohol-fuelled knife fights, had to be discouraged.

Judge Davidson announced that he would impose sentence after tea. What sentence would he impose? Perhaps two or three years? I sensed, perhaps wrongly, that his mind was on other things because, over tea in the chamber adjoining the courtroom, he chatted easily about various subjects. He told me he owned a beautiful estate in Magoebaskloof, a lovely mountain area four hours' drive north of Johannesburg, where, in winter and spring, azaleas and rhododendrons in their thousands burst into bloom with immoderate profusion, in an array so lavish it took your breath away. I listened in wonder; I had never been so far north. He invited me for a weekend. Although intimidated by the thought of the long drive alone with the judge, I felt honoured and gladly accepted.

Tea done, the judge arose to return to court. At the entrance, we paused for the orderly to summon the court to order. As we waited, Judge Davidson said lightly, 'I think seven is about right for this one.' He did not ask my view, but I was shocked. Seven years? Surely not! I had no idea of comparable sentences, but, given the facts the prosecutor had accepted, this seemed harsh.

The accused clearly thought so too. After a short overview of the fight, and the need to stop this kind of thing, the judge imposed his sentence sternly: 'In these circumstances, the accused is sentenced to seven years' imprisonment.' The young man looked aghast, dismayed. Counsel must have told him he'd get a shorter sentence. He shook his head disbelievingly and showed himself unwilling to be taken down the steps to the cells. As the police took him down, he kept looking back at the judge, at me, his eyes saying there must be a mistake. But there it was: seven years.

Solemnly, the judge pronounced, 'The court adjourns' and, until the year following, the Vereeniging Circuit Court was done with its business.

As we left, the accused was in the holding cells, to be fingerprinted once more, this time for the Prisons Department's records. The warrant of committal for him to start his sentence of imprisonment would be filled out. Before nightfall, and for the next seven years, barring parole, he would be locked up.

But that was not our last encounter. The next day, the 'non-white' male prisoners at the Vereeniging prison were ordered to assemble for the judge. As we entered the quadrangle, the accused suddenly broke ranks. He ran forward and clutched my arm. 'Please,' he murmured in anguish, 'please. There's a mistake, I have children, my wife . . . please help me!'

The warders allowed the man to speak to me – they seemed reluctant to intervene, no doubt because I was with the judge – and if Judge Davidson noticed, he gave no sign. He was busy with the prison head as this incident occurred and neither of us referred to it afterwards.

Even now, after serving for twenty-five years as a judge, I doubt seven years was an appropriate sentence. But was it unreasonable? Perhaps not. If the man had appealed, an appeal court might not have imposed a lighter sentence. The accused had taken another person's life. That man, too, likely had children, a family, a spouse.

Plus, pervasively under apartheid, there was race. Progressive lawyers took white judges to task for sometimes imposing sentences that seemed to make light of assaults, rapes and homicides when these were between Black people and magnifying punishments when white people were the victims. Would Judge Davidson not have faced criticism for undue leniency, if he had imposed less? Later, when as a trial judge I bore the burden of imposing sentence, I wondered – given the man's explanation, given the facts the prosecutor accepted, and the circumstances of the drunken fight – whether seven years was not shocking.

But that day in 1976, confronted by this man in the 'non-white' courtyard, what could I possibly say to him? Thinking I had power, he was entreating me to save him. I felt helpless and bewildered. I was as shocked by the seven-year sentence as the new prisoner was. Shaking my head, selfishly concerned not to cause a scene, I replied, 'I'm sorry, there is nothing I can do.' He stepped back, aghast. The judge and I went on our way.

The visit to the prison never left me. Through Oxford, through legal practice, and through my years as a judge, the man's incredulous reaction brought home to me the shocking impact of prison. One day he was with his family, out on bail; the next he was plunged into confinement.

I thought of my father, sentenced to time in Zonderwater Prison for car theft when I was six or seven. What did prison do to him? What does it do to anyone?

Sometimes, taking away another's freedom may be unavoidable. Some people commit acts of very great destructive evil. Anthony Hopkins' movie character Hannibal Lecter, in *The Silence of the Lambs*, presents an unnerving spectre: a malevolently dangerous killer who relishes inflicting ghastly wounding, mayhem, suffering and death. Such people must be locked up, away from society. For this reason – the spectre of an irreformably evil Hannibal Lecter – I have never said, abolish prisons.

Yet, beyond extreme cases, imprisonment remains a terrible thing. Most offenders, in all societies, at almost all times in history, have been men.

16

It is still so. And almost all offenders who commit violence are men. This means that, across the world, prisons press large accumulations of males tightly together, against their will, into confined spaces and under often degrading conditions. To lock up adult men with large numbers of other adult men, with no control over diet, mealtimes, recreation or company, and with minimal or no privacy, remains an awesome and shocking thing.

That night, I dined as usual with Judge Davidson. It was our last dinner at the splendid riverside hotel. For me, the meal was uncomfortable, heavy with the weight of the day. I wasn't sure the judge had seen the convicted man run over to clutch me, so I didn't raise the issue. Instead I sat lost in miserable thought.

My thoughts were not only about the sentenced man. They were about my future. At Stellenbosch University, instead of proceeding with a law degree, I had chosen to specialise in Latin and Classical Culture; I was slated to study Classics at Oxford. Did my unease point to a future in literature because I was not robust enough for the harsh realities of law? It was only later that I realised that my disquiet was justified.

A full decade on, I again found myself inside a prison. Back from Oxford, I joined the Johannesburg Society of Advocates to start a human rights law practice. Soon, Professor John Dugard, an international law expert and outspoken critic of apartheid, invited me to join a powerful band of young anti-apartheid lawyers he'd assembled at Wits University's Centre for Applied Legal Studies (CALS). Mostly funded by American philanthropic foundations, CALS worked to advance union and employment rights, to impede or stop forced removals from homes and land, and to defend the increasingly sparse rights of protest and publication.

I plunged into this work, adding some specialities of my own – defending young white conscientious and religious objectors who refused to serve in apartheid's army; plus, more controversially, equality for gay and lesbian and transgender persons. On starting in legal practice, at the end of 1982, just before my 30th birthday, I decided: never again. Never again would I apologise for, or hide, something intrinsic to my humanhood: the fact that I was queer.

Apartheid was in decline, but its decay was angry, destructive and ruthless. Opponents of the regime were slandered, confined, tortured and sometimes murdered. Lawyers were protected by apartheid-supporting Afrikaners' pride in their inherited Roman-Dutch legal system. We had some protection, but not insulation: in September 1989, apartheid agents murdered Namibian anti-apartheid lawyer Anton Lubowski.

During this time, attorneys for anti-apartheid organisations briefed me to go to the grim Pretoria Central Prison, where white political prisoners were confined, rigidly separated from their Black comrades held on Robben Island. Their conditions were better than on the island – even apartheid foes had some white benefits. Their cells were warmer, they had better clothing and blankets, and slightly better food. Nevertheless prison authorities inflicted harsh humiliations on white prisoners.[8]

To punish their radical inclinations, government tried to cut them off entirely from the outside world. All news – newspapers, news weeklies, radio broadcasts – was strictly forbidden. The prisoners challenged this harsh ban in court. They failed. Only one judge, Michael Corbett, who would later serve as Chief Justice as apartheid ended, dissented. He urged that it was unreasonable to systematically deprive political prisoners of all current news. His colleagues disagreed and the news and current affairs ban was upheld.[9]

On a cold morning – all prisons are cold, even in summer – I met with a small band of white women. They were in prison for fighting apartheid. Jansie Lourens (spouse of the later-notorious conman Carl Niehaus), Barbara Hogan (later partner of struggle stalwart and Robben Island veteran Ahmed 'Kathy' Kathrada) and Trish Hanekom (spouse of Derek Hanekom, Mandela and Ramaphosa loyalist) sat with me in a small meeting room. Trish and Derek had been imprisoned for plotting for the ANC on their free-range, organic smallholding north-west of Johannesburg. Jansie had conspired with her spouse to blow up the Johannesburg gasworks. And, at the age of 30, Barbara Hogan – convicted of revolutionary activities when ANC pamphlets were found in her car after a visit to Botswana – had been cruelly sentenced to ten years in prison, even though her counsel, George Bizos, pleaded with the judge to impose less. She might, he said, want to start a family after prison.

My instructing attorney was the fearless anti-apartheid attorney Kathy Satchwell. The women she represented were treated slightly more leniently than the white men, but their conditions were cramped and cruel. Just as we planned to launch our challenge, the apartheid government, in secret negotiations with the ANC, began relenting on its harsh treatment of Nelson Mandela and other political prisoners. Our challenge became moot.

Yet that visit to those three women in Pretoria Central evoked memories of the women in the wintry courtyard in Vereeniging more than ten years before – different in their circumstances, different in what brought them inside an apartheid prison, yet alike in dignified resistance, alike in suffering a cruel system's unjust confinement.

Soon afterwards, I made a more dramatic prison visit. Close to Vereeniging lay the township of Sharpeville, to which I had given scant thought when I'd accompanied Judge Davidson on the Circuit Court. Now, a decade later, belatedly impelled by my Oxford experiences, I was alert with political awareness. The security police's brutal murder of Stephen Bantu Biko in September 1977, during my Oxford studies, shocked my senses, drove my reading, and painfully squeezed my thinking about what I should do back in South Africa.

By now, I knew Sharpeville. Its name signified one of apartheid's most notorious atrocities. On 21 March 1960, white policemen, surrounded by unarmed Sharpeville residents protesting angrily against the pass laws, felt entrapped inside the police station. They opened fire, heedlessly and lethally, into the crowd. The resulting carnage was appalling: 69 people were killed and 180 wounded. Most of those killed and wounded had gunshot wounds to their backs. They were not advancing on the heavily armed police – they were fleeing from them.

The ghastly killings remained deeply scored in Sharpeville's collective consciousness. Twenty-four years later, on 3 September 1984, Sharpeville was again the epicentre of brutal blood-letting. When government tried to impose a new system of local councillors on townships, residents denounced them as stooges. Huge demonstrations vehemently rejected them as empty tokens, supporters of an evil system. Across the Vaal Triangle, a mass uprising erupted.

Some of the councillors who accepted office paid a terrible price. One was the deputy mayor of Sharpeville's new local structure. His name was Kuzwayo Jacob Dlamini. On that fateful Monday, an angry crowd drove Mr Dlamini from his home. Murderously, a throng of neighbours surrounded him, and did unto him a terrible death.

As he lay dying, Mr Dlamini pointed to a young man whom he knew well. His last words were a question. In his death throes, he addressed the young man directly. 'Ja-Ja, why have you done this to me?' Ja-Ja was the well-recognised nickname of Mojalefa Reginald Sefatsa. He was arrested and arraigned as accused number one in the infamous trial of the 'Sharpeville Six' that followed.

The vivid evidence of eyewitnesses established beyond doubt Ja-Ja Sefatsa's murderous role as a hands-on perpetrator in Mr Dlamini's killing. But there was no evidence of this kind against the other five accused. They were convicted not because evidence showed they helped cause Mr Dlamini's murder. They were found guilty only because they were present at the scene, making common cause with the mob.

The trial judge, Paul Human, an 'Old Boy' of my own boys' high school in Pretoria, was unconcerned that there was no evidence that the accused's support for the murderous crowd had helped the killings. He sentenced all six to death. His final words to them, before he adjourned the court, were to incant the dread formula that English judges used in imposing the death sentence:

> The sentence of this court is that you will be taken from here to the place from whence you came and there be kept until the appointed date, and upon that day that you will be hanged by the neck until you are dead. And may God have mercy upon your soul.

The death sentences provoked global outrage and rightly so. Accused number two, Oupa Moses Diniso, presented a stark challenge to apartheid justice. There was no direct evidence that he was on the scene of the murder, or even part of the crowd. When Mr Dlamini had emerged from his house to confront the mob, he was brandishing a firearm – which may have incensed the enraged crowd even further. During his murder, the firearm went missing. It was found 47 days later. Acting on a tip-off, the police went to Mr Diniso's home and confronted him. After prevaricating, he eventually pointed the police to a firearm hidden in his ceiling. It was Mr Dlamini's. Fatefully, Mr Diniso handed it to the police.

From this sketchy framework, Judge Human thought to reason that Mr Diniso must have been on the scene, and that he must have been one of the murderers. On this tenuous analysis, he would suffer death by hanging.

The Sharpeville Six appealed. Sitting on death row in Pretoria Central must have been terrifying. While they were there, in 1987, the gallows had its busiest year ever: 164 people were hanged – more than one person every third day.[10]

Now a powerful five-judge bench of judges of the then Appellate Division (the highest court in South Africa at the time) in Bloemfontein, 400 km from Johannesburg, turned down their pleas. As a young lawyer, I was both astonished and outraged that they agreed with the trial judge that all six, including Mr Diniso, were guilty of murder and must hang.

21

More disturbing even was the case of accused number six. Theresa Ramashamola was a young woman who had been on the edge of the crowd, some distance away from Mr Dlamini's murder. Hot-bloodedly, she joined in baying for him to be killed. Her cries were indeed murderous – but did they have any impact on what was happening? The answer has to be no. It was never proven that the perpetrators, some distance away, even heard what Theresa was saying, let alone that her words instigated the murder.

Theresa's conviction was on the grounds of the doctrine of common purpose, meaning that if you join in a murderous enterprise, even if your role is to drive the getaway vehicle, you are just as guilty as the actual perpetrators. Even if you are only sitting waiting in the car, by extension you share the murderous purposes of those who physically commit the deed.

The courts not only of England but also of most American states applied this approach. Theresa's murderous calls may have fallen within the broad doctrine. Perhaps, on accepted jurisprudence, she could be said to be guilty of murder. But the death sentence Judge Human imposed on her was monstrously savage. For standing on the outskirts of a murderous mob, egging it on, she was to be hanged by the neck until she was dead.

This to me seemed an outrage against justice and ordinary human decency. Though still a junior advocate, I had a voice. I decided to speak – loudly. I also took up my pen. In speeches and scholarly articles and in opinion pieces – some republished in London – I inveighed against the sentences. I denounced, in particular, the fact that Mr Diniso was convicted on such tenuous facts, and that Ms Ramashamola was sentenced to die on the gallows.

My words helped fuel an international campaign to discredit the twisted, unfeeling judicial process that produced the shocking outcome.

My campaign angered the country's top judges. The Chief Justice, Pierre Rabie, had scholarly Latin and Greek credentials, but as a lawyer he was a dour, compliant apartheid apparatchik. He lodged a formal complaint of misconduct against me with the Johannesburg Society of Advocates, which obliged my senior colleagues to investigate what I had written and said. By a majority, they rejected Rabie's complaint.

All this led the Six's devoted attorney Prakash Diar to ask me to join the team of lawyers trying to save their lives.[11] Their hanging was scheduled. South Africa was already afire with mass protests, co-ordinated by a new anti-apartheid organisation, the United Democratic Front (UDF). The country waited with bated breath. On the afternoon before their execution, while anti-apartheid activists and liberal human rights advocates across the world waited in horror, Judge Human unexpectedly granted a stay of execution. Two prosecution witnesses, both neighbours and bystanders, now dramatically recanted what they had said in court.

This might not have helped much. In most courts, anywhere, once the accused has been convicted, a prosecution witness's disavowal of evidence they gave at the trial is just about always useless. Why? Because what matters is what the witness says in court the first time they get to testify – not what they might choose to say (or be coerced into saying) later. Their first-time evidence is what counts.

But, after the trial, prosecution witnesses have to return to their homes and workplaces. They have to live with their neighbours, with the families of those convicted.

At the trial of the Sharpeville Six, these witnesses could not possibly have known that the Six would be sentenced to hang. What they had witnessed that day in Sharpeville was undoubtedly horrific and their testimonies were vivid. Yet, apart from Ja-Ja, none of the accused had played a direct part in Mr Dlamini's killing. The thought that their fellow residents would be hanged must have filled them with horror – and with fear for themselves.

As public rage grew against apartheid, the pressure on the witnesses to recant must have become unendurable. It was nevertheless surprising that Judge Human granted a stay of execution. But the stay was only temporary.

Prakash tasked me to prepare argument for reopening the case and ex-punging the convictions and death sentences. The lives of the Six remained at risk. What if the secret talks between government and the ANC failed? It was imperative to reverse the unjust verdicts.

At that point, I had read only the judgment of the trial court, plus the judgment of the Appeal Court. The trial judgment was rather terse, while the Appeal Court focused largely on whether South Africa should continue to enforce the English-inherited doctrine of common purpose (answer: yes).

I set myself to scrutinising the eyewitness evidence, together with all the statements and documents before the trial court. Now knowing what the witnesses who later recanted had testified, I was even more surprised that Judge Human had granted the stay of execution. The reason was probably not legal or judicial. It was non-judicial. One wonders whether someone in authority spoke to him, and what was said. This may have been an occasion when *realpolitik* intervened in the South African judicial process.[12]

Night after night, even on the highly censored South African media, the clips on the government-controlled television and radio stations cried out the world's outrage at the impending execution of the Sharpeville Six. The apartheid cabinet may well have thought a judicial intervention could save them from international opprobrium, as well as local catastrophe. And Mr Justice Human may well have concluded it would be better not to have the blood of the Six on his hands.

These thoughts were all too present to me when I went to death row to meet the Six. While we drafted sworn statements to reverse their verdicts, Prakash had asked me to explain directly to the Six their prospects of eluding the hangman. My task was to make clear how difficult their case was, and how narrow their legal hopes were.

One sunny spring afternoon, I arrived at death row. Though the prisons service – like the apartheid police – had more Black than white employees,

the warders stationed at death row were whites only. A formidable obstacle course of security checks awaited me. Eventually, I was processed
through. I walked up a broad flight of stairs that ended in glass doors bath-
ing the interior with light, overlooking an inner courtyard. In the middle
of the courtyard was a duck pond. Around it, flowers were blooming in
spring efflorescence. The grass was immaculately tended. The ducks were
contentedly paddling, well fed and well nurtured. The contrast – the care
lavished on growing the garden and feeding the ducks against the bleak
process of ritualised death that was executed inside – took my breath
away.

But there was no time to reflect. I was led through another set of doors.
Jangle, unlock, jangle, lock. Then to another passage, also locked and guarded. Here the administrative offices of death row were housed. At last I was
ushered into an office. In the corner stood a wooden apparatus about two
metres high and with an adjustable arm projecting from it. I looked at
it with suppressed curiosity. It was designed to measure the height of
a human being. Next to it, on the floor, was a scale – not the familiar domestic bathroom scale, but a larger, steelier one, seemingly for industrial
purposes.

Before I could ponder how these two instruments worked, and what
exactly they were for, the Six arrived, brought in by a group of warders.
All except one were shackled and manacled. The exception was Theresa
Ramashamola. She had been brought across from the women's section,
where not long before I'd met the white women political prisoners. Because she was Black, and under sentence of death, Theresa had no contact with them.

All six smiled warmly, eagerly, keen to talk. They were hopeful, ex-
pectant of what I would tell them. Judge Human's reprieve had come just
a few hours before their gruesome death. The anguish and stress they
would have been going through were hard to imagine. Still paralysed with
anxiety, now they were also throbbing with hope. Would they go through

that ordeal again? Would the process this time culminate in a fatal, two-metre drop?

As clearly and honestly and soberly as I could, I explained how difficult it was to undo a murder conviction and sentence. The concluded trial proceeding was regarded as almost inviolate. All the same, their reprieve, and our pending hearing, had brought some hope. Although there was still a risk that they would meet the hangman, their lives might yet be saved.

I delivered my short and austere explanations in a low, intense voice. The focus with which the Six listened was the focus of life and death. My short briefing over, we still had most of the hour allocated for our consultation. We sat and talked.

For me, the two most interesting of the accused were Theresa Rama-shamola and Oupa Moses Diniso. Even now, nearly forty years later, I still think how shameful it was that five serious and till then estimable appeal judges had upheld Oupa's conviction of murder.

At one point in our conversation he asked me, 'Do you see that equipment standing there?'

'Yes,' I said. Of course. No one in the room could miss it.

'The afternoon before they were going to hang us, they measured us on it,' he said. 'They put us on the scale to see how much we weighed. Then they made us stand under that lever to check our height. From that, they were working out how far each of us had to drop.'

The thought that this could actually happen – the ghastly wait, the horrified families, the merciless procession to the platform of death, the instant where the platform gives way beneath the feet of the condemned and their bodies fall with appalling velocity until a rope snaps taut around their necks – appalled me. Spared this fate, for now, the Six had to be saved.

The legal team turned to the task of reopening their trial. Prakash decided to add a heavy hitter to the team – the heaviest hitter of all South African lawyers, Sydney Kentridge QC.[13] An internationally distinguished man, who had appeared for the defence in Mandela's first treason trial,

26

Kentridge had made his name through his redoubtable cross-examination of the police witnesses who tried to cover up the 1960 Sharpeville massacre.

He gained even more renown when he appeared for the family of Steve Biko, murdered in police custody in 1977. The tattered versions with which the perpetrators tried to cover up the killing were swept away by the powerful force of Kentridge's cross-examination. Yet the inquest's shocking revelations left the presiding magistrate, an apartheid loyalist, unmoved. He declared that no one was responsible for Biko's death. The world knew differently, however, because of the merciless light the legal process cast on the perpetrators' deeds.

After more than thirty years practising in South Africa, Kentridge moved to London, where his renown grew. He agreed to return to fight for the lives of the Six. He and I worked on the argument together in his study in his family home high on Houghton Ridge in Johannesburg. He cut out large swathes of my draft, which sought to show that the court had inherent jurisdiction to set right a patent injustice – but to my relief, he kept the essence. The whole legal team then travelled to Bloemfontein to argue the appeal before the Appellate Division.

The very same Chief Justice Rabie whom I had infuriated presided over the appeal. Now, aware that the world was watching, he had to be on his best behaviour. Media from across the world crowded into the largest courtroom. With five white men glowering at him from the bench, Kentridge set about trying to persuade the court that the two recanting witnesses rendered the entire verdict against all six unsafe.

It was never going to be easy. Late in Kentridge's argument, Rabie asked the most difficult question, one that worries any court asked to reverse a conviction by now rejecting evidence which, at the trial, was deemed persuasive. He leaned forward. 'Mr Kentridge,' he asked, 'must every conviction be reversed where a witness recants? How must the Court decide which cases to reopen?'

Sitting alongside Kentridge, I knew this was the crux – the vulnerable underbelly of our argument. If the Six succeeded, could any conviction stand? From his intelligence and experience, could Kentridge formulate a test to persuade these judges to intervene?

To my surprise, Kentridge did not engage with Rabie's challenge. He did not offer a general criterion. Looking calmly at the Chief Justice, he responded evenly, 'My Lord, the answer to that question lies in the heart of the Court.' *Lies in the heart of the court.* Recognising the quicksands into which Rabie was inviting him to tread, Kentridge asked the court, instead, to intervene, in this case, because of its unusual features and special claims.

The court did not embrace this invitation. Weeks later, as we had feared, the court dismissed the appeal. We lost the battle. Yet we had won the war. The courtroom hearing before the world's media made it impossible for government to carry out the execution. In front of the watching world, Kentridge had located the issue in the heart, not the head. Though the court ruled it was helpless, the question now was whether the apartheid state would be heartless – and reckless – enough to proceed with the hanging.

And indeed it did not. The Six lived. They were released after negotiations to end apartheid started. Having come within a whisker of death by hanging, their vivid stories became part of a clamour to reform South Africa's prisons – including doing away with the death penalty.

Why do I tell these stories? The reason is that my experiences of visiting prisons and engaging with people inside of them shaped me deeply. The apartheid prison system was cold and heartless. At its core lay a disregard for the human dignity of those most at peril of being locked up by it, those most at peril of being hanged: South Africa's Black majority.

That system became one of the changes the new order promised when democracy dawned in South Africa in 1994. Nelson Rolihlahla Mandela, fresh out of prison himself, after twenty-seven years, became president of a newly democratic country, committed to creating a just society for all. One of his cherished aims was to reform the country's prison system.

During his presidency, an entirely new statute for prisons was enacted. The 1998 Correctional Services Act promised more than mere redrafting; it envisaged a carceral system based on human dignity, reform, rehabilitation – and integration back into wounded communities.

During this time, I was a newly appointed judge. One of the first things I was told when Mandela appointed me to the High Court at the end of 1994 was that I should visit at least one prison every year. The 1959 statute conferred on all judges and magistrates, as does its successor, the power to visit prisons. That power, I was told, formed part of my duties.

This I undertook, with dread, but also with determination. I was to meet many prison officials, some dedicated, all burdened, all dealing with the complex problems of holding large numbers of people in confined spaces against their will. I was to engage with many prisoners who endured challenging and often horrific conditions of confinement. I was to see how the lofty ideals of the 1998 statute, like many other aspirations of democracy, were not fulfilled, but were translated into grimier, harsher reality.

I was even to meet some of those whom I had sentenced. One young man, in particular, has quickened my belief in the human capacity for restoration. With his permission, I use his name, Glen. Arraigned before me in 2000, during my last months in the Johannesburg High Court, his drug-fuelled crimes were horrific. But he was young. At 20, his youth counted in his favour. In addition, his remorse and regret were so profound they came to dominate the courtroom. Defence lawyer, prosecutor, court personnel and judge, no matter how case hardened, no matter how cynical, could not but know that Glen was horrified by his own actions, and that he was humbly, simply, determined to do better – if he were only given a chance.

Despite the prospect of Glen's rehabilitation, I remained uncertain of

29

the course Glen's life would take in prison and thereafter. I imposed twenty years' imprisonment.

After I moved to Bloemfontein, for my eight years in the Appeal Court, and then back to Johannesburg when appointed to the Constitutional Court, I often wondered how Glen was doing. How had the grim harshness of imprisonment affected him? Early in my term as Inspecting Judge, as lockdown took hold at the end of March 2020 during the Covid-19 pandemic, I found out. He contacted me through JICS:

> The Justice and I first met when in sentencing me he encouraged me to make the most of my situation. Between October 2000 through February 2007 I applied myself diligently and in 2005 obtained a Diploma in Youth Development having run various projects under the auspices of the social workers at Johannesburg Juvenile and later the Zonderwater Correctional facilities.

> Having completed full sentence in Pretoria in October of 2015 without any disciplinary issues I bought a house, was married, have a young son and have competed internationally as a Skydiver. Throughout the years I have remained active in sports and youth development activities and am very eager to work in the Prisons, especially at this time.

Glen started a project aiming to activate rehabilitated offenders and their communities to grow food, bake bread, provide basic amenities and promote self-sufficiency, for which I have tried to help him raise funding. Most recently, he wrote to me, in November 2024, to express gratitude 'for the influence you had on me as a person and how this shaped and healed me as a father'. 'This month marks 24 years since you spoke words of life and purpose over me at a time when I had neither.' For Glen, movingly, his crimes and his sentence added meaning and purpose to his life. Sadly, this is a feature of too few crimes and sentences.

This book explores these complexities. It recounts our high aspirations as a country, and also our failures. Most importantly, it points a path to doing better – for us all to do better – in containing violent crime, and in treating both perpetrators and victims with hope for their future, for our futures. The means to do this are at hand. It is up to us, as agents of our country's democracy and its Constitution, to grasp them.

2

Prisons in South Africa – How Did We Get Here?

[Prisons] appear so monumental in design and so intrinsic to the criminal justice system that it is tempting to think of them as permanent and fixed features . . . Meting out punishment by a calculus of time to be served seems so commonsensical today that it becomes difficult to conceive of a moment when prisons were not at the core of criminal justice.[14]

South Africans know prisons. Many of our first democratic leaders spent long years there. But we also don't know them. Prisons are mysterious and inaccessible, to the mind and to the imagination. Even so, it seems almost impossible today to imagine our country – or the world – without prisons. Yet prisons are a relatively recent development. Confining large numbers of males in close quarters inside grimly barred structures dates back only about two centuries.

Understanding the history that gave prisons to South Africa and to modern societies may help us understand how we could manage them better.

The origins of prisons

For most of human history, punishing those seen as transgressing social norms has included restricting personal freedom as well as some kind of confinement. Since ancient Greece and Egypt, people had been sold into enslavement, publicly exhibited and shamed (in stocks in the village square), confined and left to starve to death, exiled or deported.[15] Imprisonment was used mostly to detain accused persons awaiting trial or convicted persons pending the execution of their sentence.[16] The punishment itself could range from flogging and whipping or other bodily inflictions, penal servitude or enslavement, fines, deportation to colonies or exile, even to death.[17]

By the sixteenth century, in various parts of England and Europe, debtors, drifters (deemed 'vagrants') and petty offenders began to be detained in what were called 'houses of correction'. There, in theory, discipline and hard labour would rehabilitate them from their anti-social conduct.[18] In reality, local prisons were rife with disease, corruption and death; they were 'abhorrent microcosms of vice, shame, and misery'.[19]

But even then, punishment in the form of long imprisonment was uncommon. Punishment was generally a violent, public spectacle.[20] What changed? How did locking up large numbers of people for long periods in confined spaces become enmeshed in our modern conception of justice?

Towards the end of the eighteenth and the beginning of the nineteenth century, the public understanding of punishment changed. Gruesome public spectacles and violent ceremonies gradually ceased. In their place, prisons emerged, supposedly more subtle and humane, but, signally, hidden from the public eye.[21]

How can we understand this shift? Michel Foucault, the twentieth-century French philosopher, upturned conventional thinking about imprisonment. He explained that punishment moved from 'the domain of more or less everyday perception' to 'abstract consciousness'; its efficacy was seen as resulting not from 'visible intensity', but from inevitability. It was the certainty of being punished, rather than a horrifying public spectacle, that was supposed to discourage crime. The consequence, Foucault said, was that 'justice no longer takes public responsibility for the violence that is bound up with its practice'.[22]

Complex and even contradictory reasons impelled this shift. Eighteenth-century enlightenment ideals, pressure from religious reformers and economic factors contributed.[23] In some ways, modern prisons repre-sented a progressive reform of the penal system – they were a humane improvement on publicly inflicted violence, mutilation and death.[24] Re-formers in England, Europe and America hoped to transform the goals of punishment. Instead of public forms of vengeance, punishment would now seek to reform offenders.[25]

There were religious underpinnings. Replacing public punishment with rehabilitation through isolation, reformers urged that being detained in quiet reflection would help offenders repent. Early prisons were called penitentiaries (and in the United States still are), derived from the word 'penance'. Isolating the body, reformers thought, would 'allow the soul to flourish'.[26] In the 1820s, Cherry Hill Penitentiary in Philadelphia, USA, required isolation and silence.[27] Solitary confinement became a widely-used form of punishment.

The actual impulse may have been less benevolent, however. Critics explain that prisons offered states, monarchs and ruling elites a more efficient way of controlling 'lower' social classes.[28] Public executions and punishments, long relied on to instil fear and obedience, risked provoking spectator unrest and solidarity with the offender. Foucault explains this was especially so if the conviction was considered unjust – or when a 'man of the people' was put to death for a crime for which a more powerful or richer person might have been lightly punished.[29]

Prisons took away this high-stakes risk. In moving punishment away from the public domain its brutality was less obvious. Prisons also allowed ruling elites to control labour. To imprison 'vagrants' (those not formally employed) provided low- or zero-cost convict labour. Foucault doubted prisons originated so as to introduce a 'humane' alternative to corporal punishment. While their emergence at the end of the eighteenth century embodied 'the strange idea' that the response to crime had to be 'something other than death, torture, a fine, or exile', what was put in place instead was 'some kind of constraining labour to which the individual would be compelled'.[30]

After enslavement formally ended in the United States, the link between the proliferation of prisons and the need for labour emerged clearly. Prisons and formal policing ensured a steady supply of free Black labour. Although the Thirteenth Amendment to the US Constitution formally abolished enslavement,[31] gross subordination, exploitation and racial discrimination continued.[32] The amendment abolished enslavement and involuntary servitude *'except as a punishment for crime'* – a gaping hole. In her book *The New Jim Crow*, Michelle Alexander explains that through this amendment, as well as the Black Codes in the South,[33] criminalisation and punishment became central to new stratagems of perpetuating forced labour and racial segregation.[34] Bryan Stevenson, the inspiring founder of the Equal Justice Initiative, notes that Black people, 'once seen as less than fully human "slaves", were seen as less than fully human "criminals"'.[35]

After the American Civil War (1861–1865), the prison convict lease system was key to filling labour supply shortages. In the South, companies and individuals paid leasing fees to states in order 'to recruit and discipline a convict labour force'; this enabled them 'to develop their states' resources without creating a wage labour force, and without undermining planters' control of black labour'. However, the opposite occurred: 'the penal system could be used as a powerful sanction against rural Blacks who challenged the racial order upon which agricultural labour control relied.'[36]

This history accentuates how prisons, far from being natural to human order, reflect sometimes warped, and often cruel, perceived social imperatives.

Exploring and examining the origins of prisons is not an abstract exercise. Prisons deeply affect us all. They reflect but also shape the societies we live in. That we accept and understand this is vital for our future planning. Why did we start locking people up – and why do we continue to do it? Are prisons places for the safe custody and reform of 'the worst'? Or are they harm-perpetuating tools of state control, power and coercion in our democracy?

Angela Davis, a leading United States prison abolitionist and renowned civil rights activist, says it is easy to take prisons for granted as 'an inevitable fact of life, like birth and death'.[37] But history reminds us that prisons are not natural or inevitable. Locking people up is just one way – a fairly new way – of trying to punish or reform. For now, it dominates public policy and our collective imagination. To understand how we arrived here, we need further to explore how prisons in South Africa were established and employed to enforce colonial and apartheid rule.

Colonialism and prisons

Pre-colonial African societies employed various forms of punishment but incarceration of mass numbers of persons was not one of them. Pre-colonial systems of justice were not homogeneous; nor were they by any means utopian. Yet, generally, they prioritised reparation, restitution and compensation.

Jeremy Sarkin records that, as punishment, incarceration 'was unknown to Africa when the first Europeans arrived'.[38] 'Imprisonment and capital punishment were viewed as last resorts within African justice systems, to be used only when perpetrators such as repeat offenders and witches posed discreet risks to local communities.' He also links the proliferation of prisons with colonisation, noting that: 'As the history of the African prison makes clear, incarceration was brought to the continent from Europe as a means by which to subjugate and punish those who resisted colonial authority. The employment of corporal and capital punishment to stifle political oppression was the central aim of Africa's first prisons.'[39]

When Dutch seafarers and merchants colonised the southern tip of Africa in 1652, they imposed public, and painful, physical punishments.[40] Convicts were executed by firing squad and, sometimes, public crucifixion. Imprisonment was rare. Rather than being itself the punishment, confinement was generally for detaining those awaiting trial – or to extract 'confessions' through torture.[41] After the British first occupied the Cape in 1795, 'the orientation of the penal system towards physical harm began to decline' and was replaced with imprisonment.[42]

In contrast to the ideal of prison reform in Europe, prisons in the colonies still utilised 'archaic forms of punishment', including 'corporal sentences, flogging and public exhibition'. Hence, in Africa, the prison did not replace but 'rather supplemented public violence'.[43] As in other parts of the colonised world, prisons in South Africa developed differently from the system in Europe. Their proliferation was closely tied to the enforcement of racist colonial policies. In addition, the objective of reforming criminals in the colonies was premised upon 'a coercive doctrine of domination over Africans', who were 'seen as a fundamentally delinquent race'. Racial segregation and subordination thus provided a long-term – albeit unspoken – basis 'for the architectural, moral, and bureaucratic management of colonial penitentiaries'.[44]

At the Cape, the British also used imprisonment for instrumental reasons. When trade in enslaved humans was abolished in 1807 (and enslavement itself in 1834), the Cape Colony, with its expanding economy, needed a new source of cheap labour.[45] A convict labour force served this purpose. It seems hardly coincidental that in the very year trade in enslaved humans was abolished, the Cape adopted a new penal policy. This effectively replaced corporal punishments with imprisonment.[46]

It was in this very period that white South Africa's notorious pass system was introduced. Restricting the movement of indigenous San and Khoi people was a largely unsuccessful attempt to force them to work on farms.[47] Long before Nelson Mandela and other anti-apartheid activists were imprisoned there, from the eighteenth century and well into the nineteenth century, Robben Island held Khoi, Xhosa and Korana leaders who dared to resist colonial oppression.[48]

Later laws sought to force indentured immigrant labourers from England to continue working for their employers.[49] Even though the attempt to impose passes on San and Khoi people was abandoned in 1828, the prison population in the Cape rapidly grew – consisting in a large part of San and Khoi people.[50]

By the 1840s, echoing developments in Europe, 'progressive' reforms to the penal system emphasised the reformative purpose of imprisonment – but without neglecting the instrumental value of convict labour. As Florence Bernault explains, 'prisons in the Cape underwent a major reform under John Montagu, the new colonial secretary. Montagu improved the detainees' diet, supervision and access to education. Most importantly, inspired by reformers' ideals in Europe and the United States, Montagu emphasized the reformatory role of the prison.'[51]

The pass system was resurrected and expanded. Those arrested for falling foul of it, or for vagrancy and idleness and petty offences, were imprisoned in portable wooden structures. These could be moved to the sites of public infrastructure projects. The convicts housed within would work in chain gangs on roads, ports and farms.[52] Convict labour thus built colonial infrastructure.

By the 1880s, the colony had come increasingly to rely on convict labour. This was now provided to private industry on a more organised basis. After the discovery of gold and diamonds, mines made use of convict labour. The De Beers Diamond Mining Company was the first non-state corporate entity to regularly make use of convict labour.[53] For this, it paid not the labouring prisoners, but the state.[54] So successful was this system that De Beers built and staffed its very own branch prison. De Beers effectively controlled, housed and fed prisoners. By 1888, the company was 'employing' about 600 prisoners a day. Dwarfing this figure, by 1903 the government had set up a scheme which supplied De Beers with 'native labour up to a daily average of 11,000 when practicable'. This government-provided 'native labour' was mostly convict labour.[55]

In roughly the same period, prisons were, for the first time, segregated along racial lines.[56] The Cape Legislative Assembly adopted a motion (proposed by James Rose Innes, later a renowned liberal Chief Justice of South Africa) to establish a commission of inquiry into the segregation of prisons.[57] The commission recommended complete segregation, since

> the association of the Native with the European [in prison] not only crushes out of the European what little moral feeling there may be left in him, by the sense of degradation, but lowers the whole race in the eyes of the Native, destroying the respect for us without which we can never hope to succeed either as their rulers or as their preceptors, leading them by counsel and example into the higher life of civilization.[58]

Black and white prisoners were thus detained separately. They were served different food. While white prisoners were provided opportunities for skills development and rehabilitation, Black prisoners performed hard labour and were subject to physical punishment.[59] Many of the Black prisoners were detained for pass offences.[60] Often longer sentences were imposed on them, on the racist premise that Black people were less able to respond to rehabilitation or punishment.[61]

Thus, prisons, and the convict labour they provided, proved crucial to the extraction of resources that was the powering impulse of colonisation. The system also reinforced white domination and hierarchalised segregation, which was the heart of apartheid.

South Africa's four British colonial entities were unified in 1910. Their separate penal systems were merged into one national Department of Prisons. The new Prisons and Reformatories Act 13 of 1911 came into effect. While some positive reforms were introduced, the overall effect was to bring together some of the harshest aspects of the preceding systems. The statute permitted cruel treatment within prisons (including whipping, solitary confinement, dietary punishment and hard labour) and enforced strict racial segregation. The new system was tied to 'the progressive institutionalisation of racial discrimination'.

In sum, colonial imprisonment was 'imposed disproportionately against the poor, the powerless, the marginalized or those whom the repressive government deemed expedient to eliminate from society'.[62] Apartheid strikingly embodied this.

Prisons were elemental to apartheid

The colonial penal system had already criminalised Black political resistance. From 1948, racial segregation and white domination were formalised, institutionalised and more harshly enforced. Prisons were indispensable to this. From 1960, as repression deepened, political detention and imprisonment for political offences became widespread. Since prisons reflected 'a microcosm of the society outside', apartheid's prisons constituted 'an important window on the nature of the [apartheid] state'.[63]

The Lansdowne Commission on Penal and Prison Reform was a judicial commission established in 1945. It found that the 1911 statute had not established 'a new era' in prisons, but that it had been 'instrumental for maintaining the cruel and discriminatory prisons system'.[64] The commission's 1947 report embraced the broader 'civilising' mission of prisons and recommended improvements: they were a means not just to curb or punish crime but to 'ensure that the Natives in town become decent members of society, and obey European standards of morality'.[65] However, the commission did recommend prohibiting prisons from hiring out labour to outside entities.[66] Sadly, nothing came of the commission's report.

Like its predecessor, the 1911 statute, the new Prisons Act 8 of 1959 entrenched racial segregation.[67] White prisoners, though also subject to harsh conditions, received better work, better food, better treatment and better living conditions.[68] The statute established military-style prison management. Prison staff were cloaked in paramilitary status and ranks. White warders outranked Black warders.[69]

Racism pervaded the prison system and government's approach to crime, which was framed in racial terms. Disciplining Black people was considered 'part of the white man's burden'.[70]

Under apartheid, influential Afrikaner academics built on this frame-work. They espoused the seemingly progressive view that crime was caused by social rather than individual factors. Many became members of the apartheid police and prisons, and were concerned with tackling crime and social deviance amongst poor white Afrikaners. How? Through segregation. In their reasoning, Coloured and Black people were predisposed to crime. Therefore, if white people interacted freely with them, whites could become contaminated. Apartheid was thus justified by the need 'to protect poor, Afrikaner whites from unfair economic competition and from crime-related contact with lesser races . . . Thinking about crime thus became inextricable from thinking about apartheid.'[71]

Anti-apartheid activist Sonia Bunting, who was detained and charged with treason in 1956, denounced the prison system as 'antiquated, brutal, barbaric', noting that the evils of the prison system sprang from white supremacism:

> It is the whole disease of white supremacy which fosters inhuman-ity and makes for the mistreatment of African prisoners by white warders. And this is reflected also in their bad treatment by African warders and at the hands of the prisoners themselves. The prevail-ing official attitude is that the African prisoner is 'expendable', and this attitude is reflected from top to bottom of the prison hierar-chy – in matters of diet, clothing, treatment.[72]

She emphasised that brutalities, including beatings and other humiliations, were visited mostly on Black prisoners. Prisons also continued to ensure free Black labour, generally from large numbers of Black men imprisoned for petty offences. These included pass offences and failing to pay taxes.[73]

As a result of the vast web of apartheid statutes, by the 1960s and 1970s pass law violations accounted for one in every four persons imprisoned in South Africa.[74] Bunting explained that 'for the lack of a piece of paper', many people were 'deprived of their liberty and subjected to torture and punishment quite out of proportion to the nature of their offence'.[75]

Many people were held in farm prisons. Those arrested for pass law infractions could 'volunteer' as farm labour to have charges dropped.[76] They were never tried, but were taken to labour bureaus with little choice but submission.[77] After public outcry in response to an incident where a man was beaten to death on a farm, government suspended the arrangement, but only briefly. Instead the 1959 Prisons Act was amended to formalise the continuation of the system, but now guarded by strict secrecy.[78] Reporting on prison conditions became hemmed in with criminal penalties, and there were instances of whistle-blowers and writers being prosecuted.[79]

In the Cape winter of 1982, when I returned from Oxford to begin practising law, I attended a pass law court in Langa, a township of Cape Town, with Dirk van Zyl Smit, then a criminology professor at the University of Cape Town. For several hours, we sat there, watching the obviously bored magistrate processing hundreds of pass 'offenders'. Each one came before him, pleaded guilty, and was sentenced to a few days in prison – five to ten days, depending on previous convictions. The process was wretched, misery-inducing, for those subjected to it, but also for those who were watching. The men being processed were impoverished, often ill-clad against the rainy chill of the Cape winter, often hungry-looking. Most of them had come to Cape Town to seek work. This was apartheid's

'justice'. It exposed many millions of people in South Africa to imprisonment in aid of a system that sought to make them unentitled outsiders
in their own land.

A then recent decision of the Appeal Court in Bloemfontein had already
made the pass laws difficult to enforce,[80] but they soon became unenforce-
able. The all-white Appeal Court delivered a second decision that thwarted
the laws almost entirely.[81]

The noxious legacy of the pass laws lives on, however. One of the most
enduring images of the apartheid prison system is the political prisoner –
but every one of the millions of Black men and women who spent time
in police vans, police lockups or prisons because of pass laws was also
a prisoner of apartheid.[82] The Truth and Reconciliation Commission (TRC)
described imprisonment or the threat of imprisonment as a vital part of
'the chain of oppression' of opponents of apartheid.[83]

The apartheid government denied that South Africa had any political
prisoners, but this claim was derisory. Imprisoning dissidents was a 'significant permanent feature' of apartheid.[84] Most forms of active dissent
were criminalised. This impacted primarily Black resisters – but the threat
of imprisonment also kept white South African opponents in line. Apartheid laws promoted an 'ideal' notion of whiteness (in parallel with laws
criminalising queer sex) and suppressed white dissent.

In the late 1970s, young white men refusing compulsory military service in apartheid's army were locked up. Refusing to serve could entail
six years' imprisonment. As more conscientious and religious objectors
spoke out against apartheid, in 1983 the End Conscription Campaign
(ECC) was formed.[85]

In July 1988, David Bruce became the first conscientious objector to
face the maximum sentence of six years. He refused to serve in the military because he would not 'fight in defence of a racist political system'.[86]
By the late 1980s, there were over 1 000 objectors willing to go to prison.
It was no surprise that in August 1988, the ECC was the first 'white'

organisation the apartheid regime banned in more than two decades. Minister of Law and Order Adriaan Vlok described the ECC as part of the 'revolutionary onslaught against South Africa'.[87]

As a young lawyer defending white conscientious objectors, I represented Bruce, who avoided imprisonment when we won a narrow 3-2 Appeal Court victory against a strict interpretation of the sentencing provisions. But the decision came too late for another client, Dr Ivan Toms, who had received a lesser sentence since he had completed part of his military service. He had already experienced prison life in Pollsmoor. Visiting Ivan was my very first visit to Pollsmoor – an experience that became more and more forbidding as Pollsmoor became more and more overcrowded.

Political prisoners faced harsh conditions. They were denied privileges that other prisoners enjoyed, were subjected to cruelty, violence and torture, including prolonged solitary confinement, and were not eligible for amnesty or remissions of their sentences.[88] The Constitutional Court noted:

> More insidious than the physical violence and unexplained disappearances was the psychological torture, cruelty and neglect suffered by prisoners. The lights at Pretoria Central Prison were 'never, ever, ever switched off' and prisoners were under constant surveillance, refused shoes and fed rotten food.[89]

The effects of solitary confinement were extreme. One former prisoner, Zahrah Narkedien, who testified at the TRC hearings, described the pain that seven months of isolation inflicted on her as intense; she imagined the cells as coffins, each with a dead person inside, 'as if I was alive and all these people were dead'.[90]

The murder of Steve Biko, the charismatic Black Consciousness Movement leader, poignantly instances how detention behind closed doors conferred impunity on police perpetrators. In August 1977, police arrested

Biko and held him at Walmer police station. They then took him to the Port Elizabeth security police. After days of beatings and a brutal interrogation, on 7 September his captors inflicted a severe head injury. Despite this, the police kept him shackled to a grille. Two district surgeons papered over his serious injuries. On 11 September, police transported the grievously injured man, in the back of a police van, 1 200 km to Pretoria. The next day, 12 September 1977, Biko died on the floor of a cell in Pretoria Central Prison, naked and alone.[91]

The inquest magistrate ruled that his fatal head injury was probably sustained during a 'scuffle' with his captors. The TRC found otherwise – Biko's death in detention was a gross human rights violation. The police, nurses, doctors and the magistrate were complicit in his death, all contributing to the creation of a culture of impunity.[92]

Many deaths in police or prison cells were explained away under the guise of 'suicide by hanging' or 'suicide by jumping down a stairwell'. The TRC exposed these as the product of torture and state killing. The Commission's reports not only contain viscerally disturbing accounts of torture and ill-treatment – they memorialise the names of individuals (detainees and sentenced offenders) who died in detention or custody.

DEATHS IN DETENTION

DATE	NAME	PLACE	ATTRIBUTED CAUSE
1.9.63	Bellington Mampe	Worcester	Undisclosed
5.9.63	Looksmart Ngudle	Pretoria	'Suicide by hanging'
24.1.64	James Tyitya	Port Elizabeth	'Suicide by hanging'
9.9.64	Suliman Saloojee	Johannesburg	'Fell out of window'
7.5.65	Nengeni Gaga	Transkei	'Natural causes'
8.5.65	Pongolosha Hoye	Transkei	'Suicide by hanging'
9.10.66	James Hamakwayo	Pretoria	'Suicide by hanging'
9.10.66	Hangula Shonyeka	Pretoria	'Suicide'

19.11.66	Leong Yun Pin	Pretoria	'Suicide by hanging'
30.11.66	Ah Yan	Silverton	'Suicide by hanging'
9.9.67	Alpheus Maliba	Namibia/N. Transvaal	'Suicide by hanging'
11.9.68	Jundea B Tubakwe	Pretoria	'Suicide by hanging'
5.2.69	Nichodimus Kgoathe	Silverton	'Natural causes'
28.2.69	Solomon Modipane	Silverton	'Natural causes'
10.3.69	James Lenkoe	Pretoria	'Suicide by hanging'
1.6.69	Caleb Mayekiso	Port Elizabeth	'Natural causes'
16.6.69	Michael Shivute	Namibia	'Suicide'
8.9.69	Jacob Monakgotla	Pretoria	'Natural causes'
27.9.69	Imam Abdullah Haron	Cape Town	'Slipped down stairs'; multiple injuries
22.1.69	Mthayeni Cuthsela	Transkei	'Natural causes'
27.10.71	Ahmed Timol	Johannesburg	'Suicide by jumping out of window'
19.3.76	Joseph Mdluli	Durban	'Force to the neck'
25.6.76	William Tshwane	Modderbee	'Shot while trying to escape'
15.7.76	Mapetla Mohape	East London	'Suicide by hanging'
2.9.76	Luke Mazwembe	Cape Town	'Suicide by hanging'
25.9.76	Dumisani Mbatha	Modderbee	'Natural causes'
28.9.76	Fenuel Mogatusi	Johannesburg	'Natural causes'
5.10.76	Jacob Mashabane	Johannesburg	'Suicide by hanging'
9.10.76	Edward Mzolo	Johannesburg	Cause undisclosed
18.11.76	Ernest Mamasile	Transkei	'Suicide by hanging'
25.11.76	Thabo Mosala	Transkei	'Natural causes'
11.12.76	Wellington Tshazibane	Johannesburg	'Suicide by hanging'
15.12.76	George Botha	Port Elizabeth	'Suicide by jumping down stairwell'
9.1.77	Nabaoth Ntshuntsha	Leslie	'Suicide by hanging'
9.1.77	Lawrence Ndzanga	Johannesburg	'Natural causes'

20.1.77	Elmon Malele	Johannesburg	'Natural causes'
15.2.77	Twasifeni Joyi	Transkei	Undisclosed
15.2.77	Mathews Mabelane	Johannesburg	'Fell out of window'
22.2.77	Samuel Malinga	Pietermaritzburg	'Natural causes'
26.3.77	Aaron Khoza	Pietermaritzburg	'Suicide by hanging'
7.7.77	Phakamila Mabija	Kimberley	'Fell out of window'
2.8.77	Elijah Loza	Cape Town	'Natural causes'
3.8.77	Hoosen Haffejee	Durban	'Suicide by hanging'
15.8.77	Bayempini Mbizi	Durban	'Suicide by hanging'
12.9.77	Stephen Bantu Biko	Port Elizabeth	Head injuries
7.11.77	Sipho Bonaventura Malaza	Krugersdorp	'Suicide by hanging'
10.7.78	Lungile Tabalaza	Port Elizabeth	'Suicide by jumping out of window'
10.9.80	Saul Ndzumo	Transkei	'Natural causes'
17.9.81	Manana Mgqweto	Transkei	Unknown
12.11.81	Tshifiwa Muofhe	Venda	Assault by police
5.2.82	Neil Aggett	Johannesburg	'Suicide by hanging'
8.8.82	Ernest Dipale	Unknown	'Suicide by hanging'
8.3.83	Simon Mndawe	Nelspruit	'Suicide by hanging'
5.7.83	Paris Malatji	Johannesburg	Shot in the head
20.1.84	Samuel Tshikudo	Venda	'Natural causes'
??.6.84	Mxolisi Sipele	Transkei	Unknown
25.8.84	Ephraim Mthethwa	Durban	'Suicide by hanging'
6.5.85	Andries Raditsela	Johannesburg	Head injury
24.9.85	Batandwa Ndondo	Transkei	Shot by police
5.4.86	Makompe Kutumela	Lebowa	Police assault
11.4.86	Peter Nchabaleng	Lebowa	Police assault
22.10.86	Xoluso Johannes Jacobs	Upington	'Suicide by hanging'
26.3.87	Benedict Mashoke	Burgersfort	'Suicide by hanging'

24.7.87	Eric Mntonga	East London/Ciskei	Police assault
29.7.87	Nobandla Elda Bani	Port Elizabeth	'Natural causes'
12.1.88	Sithembele Zokwe	Transkei	Shot by police
26.8.88	Alfred Makaleng	Johannesburg	'Natural causes'
30.1.90	Clayton Sizwe Sithole	Johannesburg	'Suicide by hanging'
26.3.90	Lucas Tlhotlhomisang	Klerksdorp	'Natural causes'
1.6.90	Donald Thabela Madisha	Potgietersrus	'Suicide by hanging'

Figure 1: Deaths in detention under security legislation[93]
Note: Only deaths in detention under security legislation are recorded on this list. Hilda Bernstein notes that, in February 1977, the Minister of Police stated in Parliament that 130 people had died in police custody during 1976. Of these, thirteen were political detainees held in terms of security legislation.

It is difficult to estimate the true scale of political detention. An early 1960s statute, the General Law Amendment Act 37 of 1963, introduced detention without trial for 90 days. Often victims and their families simply did not know under what legislation detainees were held.[94] About 80 000 people were detained between 1960 and 1990. About four-fifths of these were released without charge. Fewer than 4% were convicted of any offence. Their conditions were especially harsh.[95] The TRC estimated that as many as 20 000 people were tortured and at least 73 killed while detained under security legislation.[96]

Deborah Marakalala was detained without trial while pregnant. She told the TRC of her assault:

I became lame from the waist downwards, as if I had pins and needles in my body, and I lost my balance and fell and messed myself. . . . Then one day I felt weak. I lost strength and late that afternoon I started vomiting. I still asked to see a doctor, but I was told the doctor would not come. On the third day I collapsed. That was the time I was actually having a miscarriage, and I was taken

to Johannesburg Hospital where they found that I did have a miscarriage.[97]

Dismally, apartheid's judges upheld government's especially harsh confinement of political detainees.[98] In *Rossouw v Sachs*, the Appeal Court
notoriously judged that political detainees held without trial for interrogation had no right to reading and writing materials since this would 'relieve
the tedium' of detention.[99] Though previously the same court had held that
ordinary awaiting trial detainees were 'entitled to all their personal rights
and personal dignity',[100] the Appeal Court concluded in *Rossouw* that
political prisoners were entitled to only 'necessities', not 'comforts'.[101]
Thus, apartheid judges drew a stark line between political detainees and
ordinary awaiting trial detainees, enabling government's harsh measures.

Emergency rule was imposed in 1985 and again in 1986, extending
state power and its tools of oppression.

Death by hanging was an 'important weapon against opponents of
apartheid'[102] and the apartheid government employed the death penalty
immoderately. Between 1976 and 1985 South Africa executed 1 154 people,[103] in what activist Paula McBride described as the 'Christmas rush
of 1988', 28 people were hanged in a single week.[104]

Implementing the death penalty was the task of the Prisons Department.[105] While awaiting execution, prisoners were kept under strict surveillance. The lights in their cells were never switched off, they were not
permitted to study or exercise, and they were deprived of letters from
their loved ones. They were routinely 'taunted with the fact of their impending death'.[106] Prisoners sentenced to death were carefully measured –
their height, weight, even the thickness of their necks – to ensure the
length of the fatal drop was calculated with precision. I had seen the
chilling contraption for myself when I'd visited the Sharpeville Six in
Pretoria Central.

Before I met the Six, an attorney briefed me belatedly one Thursday afternoon to seek an urgent stay of execution for a condemned man due to be hanged the very next morning. My attorney had taken instructions from the condemned man for a hasty belated affidavit. We swiftly drew up papers for a stay of execution which his correspondents managed to file that same afternoon at court in Pretoria.

Late that day, the registrar informed us that our urgent application would be heard at 9 pm that evening in Court One, the main court in Pretoria's Palace of Justice. I drove across to join my attorney, rigid with dread about what was impending, what would happen if our application failed.

The judge on urgent duty was Judge Eloff, later to become Judge President. It was he who, some eight years later, in the first year of democracy, invited me to apply to become a judge in his division. But this Thursday night, Judge Eloff was in no accommodating mood. He had received our papers. They were drawn up in desperation on the say-so of a desperate man. Isolated and unsupported and running out of time, neither I nor my attorney had been able to access vital background documents. Judge Eloff, by contrast, had the entire file before him.

The court assembled at 9 pm in the dismal half-light of the courtroom. When the judge's registrar called our case, I rose to argue the application. Judge Eloff wasted no time. He glared at me. 'Why are your papers so full of untruths?' he demanded. 'None of what the applicant says is true.' As the awful hearing ground on, Judge Eloff relentlessly drew the facts of the case from the file before him, one by one, and threw them at me. The condemned man, Black, had been found guilty of a double murder. The two victims, white, were an aged couple living alone on an isolated farm, some 200 km north of where a second life-and-death confrontation was taking place.

The condemned man, Judge Eloff icily told me, had acted mercilessly. He had been part of a gang. One of its members had turned witness against him. The facts were indisputable. He was the main perpetrator. The trial judge's death sentence was unimpeachable. There was no merit in our application for delay.

'But, Your Lordship,' I pleaded, 'the applicant has not been given a chance to seek leave to appeal.' Judge Eloff had a firm reply.

'No court, knowing of these facts, could conceivably grant leave to appeal.'

Yet we had another point in favour of the condemned man, sitting on death row less than three kilometres away. The execution was scheduled for 6 am the next morning – less than eight hours away.

'Your Lordship,' I said, 'the final determination whether this man should hang lies not with the courts but with the State President, Mr PW Botha. He may exercise his power of clemency. Please give us time to draft a petition seeking clemency. The responsibility for his execution should not lie with judges alone.' Judge Eloff was implacable. His answer to my last submission still, today, puts ice into my heart.

'Mr Cameron,' he said, leaning forward over the bench, 'someone must take responsibility.'

A few moments of silence passed as we waited in dread. Then Judge Eloff proceeded to deliver judgment.

'There is no merit whatsoever in these proceedings,' he said. 'The application is dismissed.'

My attorney, who was from Grahamstown Legal Resources Centre, was staying overnight in Pretoria. It was 11 pm. My route back to Johannesburg took me, driving alone, past Pretoria Central, where the condemned man was, now, at that instant, awaiting his death by noose in a few hours. I felt sick to my stomach. Sleep eluded me. In the grey light of the next morning's dawn I thought without peace or comfort of the clinical brutality of what was taking place in Pretoria. Whatever the man had done, who now stood with his feet upon a platform that would abruptly give way beneath him, could never merit what we, his executioners, the system of justice, were now ceremonially practising upon him.

How does one mend this history? Our country has tried.

(Re)making prisons for democracy

Apartheid's abuses impelled a fresh start in democratic South Africa. The Constitution promised a penal system premised on human dignity. Pursuing this vision, the Mandela Parliament embraced a novel approach to crime and punishment. Reforming prisons and humanising prisoners were central to Mandela's vision. He, the world's most famous prisoner, now the first democratically elected president of the Republic, would usher in these reforms. His lofty aspirations were supported by former political prisoners who were now parliamentarians, judges, politicians, policymakers and other key figures in the democratic dispensation. Their collective experiences of the harshest aspects of apartheid prisons informed their thinking on how to develop a just and humane criminal justice system.

The Constitution's founding values enshrine human dignity, the rule of law and the advancement of human rights and freedoms. The Bill of Rights includes a wide array of rights that courts have the power to enforce: right to life (section 11); freedom and security of the person (section 12); freedom from slavery, servitude and forced labour (section 13).

The right to human dignity is entirely non-derogable, even in emergency. Renouncing the treatment of prisoners under apartheid, rights afforded to arrested, detained and accused persons expressly include the right to 'conditions of detention that are consistent with human dignity, including at least exercise, and the provision, at state expense, of adequate accommodation, nutrition, reading material and medical treatment' (section 35, in particular, section 35(2)(e)).[107]

Section 35(2)(e) of the Bill of Rights seeks to guard against recurrence of apartheid's brutal treatment of prisoners. History impelled the drafters. The provision expressly enshrines a right to reading materials. This 'immortalises the notorious decision in *Rossouw v Sachs*',[108] while the entitlement to 'medical treatment' recalls its denial to Steve Biko and South African Communist Party leader Bram Fischer; the latter was diagnosed with terminal cancer while serving imprisonment for life. The provision constitutionalises the *residuum* principle of the common law – prisoners retain all their rights *except* for those necessarily and justifiably limited by the fact of prison itself.[109]

Perhaps because of the exploitation of prison labour under colonialism and apartheid, South Africa's Constitution, unlike the Thirteenth Amendment to the Constitution of the United States of America, makes no exception in prohibiting slavery, servitude or forced labour for prisoners.[110] And when labour in prison is relevant for skills development of sentenced inmates, there are supposed to be safeguards in place.[111]

Instead of prisons as punishment, the 1994 White Paper on the Policy of the newly named Department of Correctional Services and the 2005 White Paper on Corrections in South Africa conceived corrections as a 'societal responsibility': 'people who leave correctional centres [should] have appropriate attitudes and competencies enabling them to successfully integrate back into society as law-abiding and productive citizens.'[112] In addition, '[t]he period of incarceration should be used to nurture and re-build the relationships between the offender, the community, and society at large.'[113] The White Paper acknowledged the shift from a prison system based on retributive justice to a correctional system committed to restorative justice.[114] And it underscored the importance of rehabilitation as a 'holistic phenomenon' merging 'social responsibility, social justice, active participation in democratic activities, empowerment with life skills and other skills' plus 'a contribution to making South Africa a better place to live in'.[115]

In 1996, the correctional service was demilitarised.[116] The new statute Parliament adopted shifted decisively from apartheid's punitive laws and mode of imprisonment. The Correctional Services Act of 1998 sought to embody this. 'Prisoners' became 'inmates' and 'prisons' became 'correctional centres'. 'Corrections' are the 'services and programmes aimed at correcting the offending behaviour of sentenced offenders in order to rehabilitate them'.[117] The goals of the correctional system are 'to contribute to maintaining and protecting a just, peaceful and safe society', to detain 'all inmates in safe custody whilst ensuring their human dignity' and to promote 'social responsibility and human development of inmates'.[118]

The Act, Regulations[119] and B-Orders[120] further specified constitutional rights in correctional centres and treatment of inmates.[121] And a signal innovation was added, intended to pierce the closed institutional culture of apartheid prisons. This was the Judicial Inspectorate for Correctional Services (JICS), a new, independent oversight body, to be headed by a judge or retired judge. The new statute tasked JICS to monitor, inspect and report on conditions in prisons and the treatment of prisoners.[122]

As an emblem of this commitment to a transformed justice system, the Constitutional Court was deliberately built on top of, and inside, the foundations of an apartheid-era pass law prison – the Old Fort, on Braam-fontein Hill in Johannesburg. When the justices hear argument in the court chamber, 150 000 bricks from the prison, the stone-hard relics of apartheid's carceral practices, surround them. Location and structure combine to represent the quest for dignity and humanity.

The first hearing in the new Constitutional Court challenged the death penalty. The court's judgment became internationally renowned. *S v Makwanyane* unanimously struck down the death penalty, on the grounds that it violated the rights to equality, human dignity and life. The court unequivocally affirmed the human dignity of inmates, even those guilty of the most heinous crimes. The court explained that under the new legal order, the rights of 'social outcasts and marginalised people' ought to be protected. This was because 'only if there is a willingness to protect the worst and the weakest amongst us' can all of us 'be secure that our own rights will be protected'.[123]

Three decades later, these visionary hopes have yet to be fulfilled.

When the late Dr Alex Boraine, deputy chair to Archbishop Desmond Tutu in the TRC, spoke at the commission's special hearings on Prisons, he warned that there may well be many in our society who feel that we ought to be talking much more about crime and about the victims rather than prisoners. That is very understandable against the background of widespread crime but nevertheless it would be quite tragic in our society if the pendulum swung so far so that we couldn't care about prisoners and about their protection.[124]

Have we let the pendulum swing? Our next chapter turns to this question.

3
Democracy's Disgrace –
Mass Incarceration

South Africa committed itself to prison reform when the interim Constitution took effect in a new democracy in 1994. Like other golden promises of that era, fixing prisons was embodied in impressive legislation. The pledge of human dignity and human rights, and to doing things differently, infused the statutes. The Correctional Services Act of 1998, scrapping the grim apartheid-era Prisons Act of 1959, was crammed chock-full of good intentions and bright promises.

What has come of these well-meant intentions and what has been achieved? The answer to these questions is: not enough. Our prison system is far from honouring the constitutional and statutory promises of dignity and equality. The statutory commitment to restorative justice and education, to rehabilitation and reintegration, has been overshadowed by long, punitive sentences in harsh conditions. Many inmates cannot afford bail and are detained for lengthy periods, sometimes for years on end, while awaiting trial.[125] Many prisons are dilapidated and nearly all are overcrowded. Rehabilitation programmes are not always accessible. Some parole boards are dysfunctional. In many prisons, corruption is pervasive. So, too, are assault, cruelty, sexual violence and even torture (including extended solitary confinement).

The old Prisons Act, which strictly racially segregated prisoners, may be gone, but inmates are still overwhelmingly – almost entirely – Black and Coloured. This reveals how a new governing elite, despite being largely Black themselves, continues overwhelmingly to imprison Black people. Crucially, though, incarcerated Black and Coloured people are overwhelmingly poor – there is an undeniable class dimension to our prisons.

Official responses to complaints and perceived indiscipline are sometimes brutal. Conditions are gravely unpleasant and, too often, undignified. Even the best prisons, which boast efficient management and dedicated staff, are dark places. These realities are difficult to square with our brave democratic hopes.

Despite our heavy reliance on prisons, South Africa remains one of the most dangerous societies in the world. According to the Global Peace Index, the world's leading data-driven analysis of its kind, in 2024 this country was ranked 127th least peaceful out of 163 countries.[126] The year 2023 recorded South Africa's highest murder rate in two decades.[127] Though most victims of murder are men, violence men perpetrate against women is pervasive. Nearly seven women a day are murdered in our country, usually by their intimate partners – yielding one of the highest femicide rates in the world.[128] Children, too, are abused and killed. On average, 33 children are violently attacked each day and at least three of them die.[129]

It is important to explore how we got here. At the very time South Africa embraced democracy, constitutionalism and human rights, an unhappy misalignment of local and international events led to a wrong turn. To counter crime, we imprudently embraced sentence inflation and mass incarceration. The results have been disastrous – both for human rights and for our safety as a people.

A closer look at the post-apartheid crime wave

Given how police and prisons were used to enforce apartheid, South Africans might have recoiled at these institutions playing a major role in post-apartheid society. But events intervened before any meaningful reckoning. Just as democracy began, a surge in violent crime seemed to threaten the promise of the new order. Reform of criminal justice collided with fear of crime. Across class and racial lines 'soft' approaches to crime and criminals became unpopular. In response, the new political elite embraced more prisons and more prisoners imprisoned for longer periods.

But how real was the post-apartheid crime wave? There is no straightforward path to finding an answer to this question, and accurate comparative statistics are difficult to measure. The answer, however, is: probably not very real.

Before democracy, crime statistics excluded a huge part of South Africa's people. Firstly, for ideological reasons the 'independent' Bantustan homelands, where 10 million South Africans lived, were not represented in South African national statistics.[130] A second problem relates to whether reports of crime to police under apartheid were a reliable indicator of actual crime levels. We don't really know. Anine Kriegler and Mark Shaw point out that 'a range of individual, social and institutional factors determine whether a given incident will be identified as criminal, reported to or detected by the police, and correctly recorded in the official statistics' and that '[t]hese factors can all change, especially in the context of major political and economic changes'.[131]

What we do know, however, is that the statistics that are available to us do not show a post-apartheid spike in crime. Between 1991 and 2000, prosecutions dropped by nearly one-quarter, and convictions by nearly one-fifth.[132] In fact, the numbers of persons the criminal justice system processed and convicted decreased.[133] This may be because the system's efficacy decreased. But it is likely that crime rates did in fact decrease.

Here, the murder rate is key. Murder rates are among the most reliable indicators of violent crime rates. Why? Because they do not depend on reports to police. They can be independently evaluated against mortuary records. In short, it is hard to hide bodies.

Murder rates in South Africa seem to have increased since the 1950s. They peaked in 1995 (approximately 27 000 or 65 murders per 100 000 people)[134] and then they steadily decreased until 2011 (approximately 15 600 murders or 30 murders per 100 000 people).[135] Then – two years after Jacob Zuma became president – a catastrophe intervened. The Zuma government appointed cronies to a range of pivotal state institutions. It deliberately laid waste to crime intelligence, policing, crime control and the National Prosecuting Authority (NPA).

The result was a significant increase in all forms of crime.

South Africa's recorded murder rate per 100 000, 1911-2015

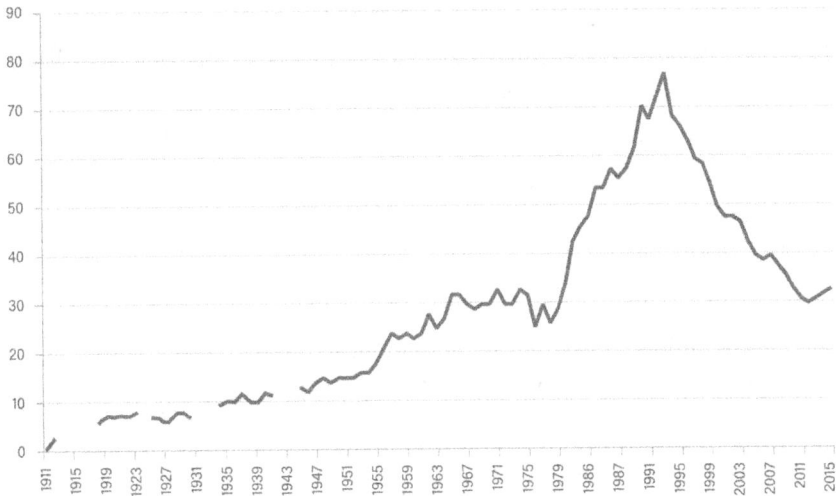

Figure 2: South Africa's recorded murder rate per 100 000 (1911–2015)[136]

Far from a spike in violent crime, the evidence suggests that democracy brought with it, at least at first, more peace and safety, not less. Yet South Africans, Black and white, urban and rural, township and suburban, became preoccupied with fear of crime.[137] Why?

No doubt, uncertainty, fears of racial integration and 'swart gevaar'

59

(white fears of dangers Black people supposedly embody) played a role. As Kriegler and Shaw explain, '[f]or many South Africans, concerns about crime [were] made to stand in for bigger concerns about reconciliation, the fabric of social life and the prospects for the post-apartheid state.'[138]

But it is also true that despite the fall in the murder rate, violence levels *were* high at the time of the transition. Between 1990 and 1994, as negotiations stopped and started, there was what the TRC called a 'dramatic escalation in levels of violence in the country'.[139] The TRC received 9 043 statements on killings and 'over half of these (5 695) occurred during the 1990 to 1994 period'; other sources found that 'from the start of the negotiations in mid-1990 to the election in April 1994, some 14 000 South Africans died in politically related incidents'.[140]

The KwaZulu-Natal conflict between Mangosuthu Buthelezi's apartheid-trained and -provisioned Inkatha Freedom Party (IFP) forces and ANC supporters and operatives contributed grievously to the killings. Violence during pre-democracy negotiations reached a peak by election month, April 1994.[141] The police responded lethally against protesters, the white right wing launched random terrorist attacks against Black South Africans, the IFP carried out sustained, brutal attacks against civilian targets, and ANC and UDF groups also engaged in violence.[142]

Much of the violence was political, often either perpetrated or aided by apartheid forces and their allies. Post-transition levels of violence remained high, though overtly political violence decreased. In the 1995–1996 period, nearly 27 000 people were murdered. So, though rates of violent crime and especially murder began to decrease after 1995, at the transition and immediately afterwards, South Africans were fearful – and eager for stronger state responses.

South Africans were also, legitimately, worried about the capability of the new state, particularly its security apparatus. The institutions of criminal justice remained weighed down by public perceptions that they were tools to enforce apartheid rather than instruments to deliver protection to all. Also, the state security apparatus, 'while monstrously efficient in defending white rule through "insertion" or "fire force" policing', was 'too under-resourced and under-skilled to take on conventional policing functions'.[143]

Contrary to the myth of apartheid institutional efficiency, policing under apartheid was 'more for control than for crime prevention'.[144] This created a trust deficit in newly democratic South Africa: 'large sectors of South Africa's population, particularly Black South Africans, regarded the police force as racist, oppressive, and illegitimate.'[145] Urgent reform was imperative, but also difficult. The police were restructured repeatedly, losing experienced, senior members (especially detectives),[146] and shrinking – decreasing by almost 20% in size between 1994 and 1999. They were 'poorly led, poorly trained and thoroughly bewildered by the transition to democracy'.[147]

Added to this, many South Africans were averse to some of democracy's forward-looking steps. As we noted in Chapter 2, in June 1995 the Constitutional Court, in striking down the death penalty, acknowledged that the 'level of violent crime in our country [had] reached alarming proportions', so much so that it posed 'a threat to the transition to democracy'.[148] While the court was unanimous that state executions had to end, a great majority of South Africans, Black and white, supported the death penalty. The President of the Constitutional Court, Justice Chaskalson, while acknowledging the tension between constitutional rights and public opinion, explained the issue thus:

> If public opinion were to be decisive there would be no need for constitutional adjudication. The protection of rights could then be left to Parliament, which has a mandate from the public, and is answerable to the public for the way its mandate is exercised, but this would be a return to parliamentary sovereignty, and a retreat from the new legal order established by the 1993 Constitution. By

the same token the issue of the constitutionality of capital punishment cannot be referred to a referendum, in which a majority view
would prevail over the wishes of any minority.[149]

Yet abolition stoked fears that without the deterrence of death, violent
crime would only get worse. Government, desperate for legitimacy, felt
it needed to act. So began democratic South Africa's calamitous experiment with mass incarceration.

The 'war on crime' and the 'war on drugs'

Feeling it had to act – or at least to be *seen* to act – the new government
looked westward, to the United States. Modelling policy on international
best practice seems savvy, but the country South Africa looked to was very
far from embodying best practice. Like South Africa, the US began systematically increasing prison populations (mass incarceration) and increasing the power and centrality of penal institutions (expanding the
carceral state) in an era of relatively liberal reform.[150]

In fact, as we noted in Chapter 2, carceralism has often developed in
direct response to progressive reforms impelled by issues of class and
race.[151] In the 1960s and 70s, civil rights legislation in the US sought to
ensure racial equality and franchise for African Americans in the South
with several pro-poor economic reforms.[152] As in South Africa, these reforms were introduced when fear of crime was high – notwithstanding
that violent crime was in fact steadily declining.[153] Public fear led President Lyndon B Johnson to declare a nationwide 'war on crime'.[154]
'Crime will not wait while we pull it up by the roots,' he proclaimed in
1965. 'We must arrest and reverse the trend towards lawlessness.'[155]

The war on crime expanded federal government's power in law enforcement, pumped millions (billions in today's currency) into building
and modernising the states' criminal justice apparatus – especially the

police – and gifted police 'new military-grade weapons and surveillance technologies'. Powers relating to surveillance and control of 'low-income urban communities' (poor Black communities) were also expanded.[156]

Concentrating efforts on this so-called war on crime drew focus and funds away from another war – the 'war on poverty'. Civil rights victories were undermined by a funding-rich, powerful criminal justice apparatus that disproportionately targeted Black Americans.

Johnson's successor exacerbated this. President Richard Nixon defunded Johnson's jobs, training and welfare programmes in Black communities but expanded Johnson's criminal justice interventions in those same communities. And Nixon started a new war: 'the war on drugs'. Drugs were 'public enemy number one'.[157] He also introduced harsher sentences and incentivised prison construction.[158]

Surveillance, drug raids and police on the beat increased dramatically. Tactics included aggressive undercover police squads.[159] For some drugs, there were new mandatory minimum sentences. While offences associated with white youths were decriminalised, at the same time, urban youth of colour were labelled 'potentially delinquent' and 'superpredators'. Long sentences were imposed on repeat offenders, even for petty crimes.[160]

The Reagan presidency (1981–1988) intensified the war on crime and the war on drugs. 'The most draconian legislative policies' on 'domestic surveillance, the criminal code, and mandatory minimum sentences' were introduced. Police were further militarised, raids increased, and harsher penalties were enacted for drugs more commonly used by Black Americans. These measures enjoyed cross-party support, from Republicans and Democrats.[161]

Attempts at reform and social movements challenging mass incarceration have faltered in the US.[162] These policies remain largely in place today, sanctified by Republican and Democrat officials alike, and by the Supreme Court.[163] The current climate in America has turned much chillier for reform.[164]

The war on drugs was exported worldwide, with severe effects.[165] From as early as the 1960s, the United States exerted pressure on other countries to adopt similarly punitive approaches, especially on drug use. The wars on crime and on drugs increased the American prison population enormously. In the century before Johnson's war on crime, the sum total of all people ever incarcerated in America's prisons was 184 901.[166] In 2024, the United States had the highest prison population in the world: 1.9 million people are currently incarcerated, with 5,7 million still entangled in the criminal justice system through parole or probation or other links to correctional facilities. At least 79 million people have criminal records and 113 million people have an immediate family member who has been incarcerated.[167] Disproportionately, they are Black or Latino. Plus, one in five inmates (more than 360 000) are incarcerated for drug-related offences.[168]

It is here that South Africa's democracy found its blighted model.

In the heady freshness of democracy, we at first embraced a holistic, social approach to crime prevention. There was even talk of a general amnesty for prisoners.[169] This approach treated crime as a societal ill caused by a range of socio-economic factors: crime was treatable by socio-economic interventions – including welfare, education, community policing, and economic empowerment.[170] The impulse to focus on the root causes of crime and violence was not sustained, however. And, at least since the late 1990s, democracy has seen a wholesale shift to harsh law enforcement. Cabinet's Justice, Crime Prevention and Security cluster at one time included the ministers of Social Development and Education, all working together to implement a comprehensive approach. This is no longer the case. Now, only the ministers directly involved in security and criminal justice are included. Even outside cabinet, relationships between their departments 'are weak' – and the departments responsible for welfare, education and health play a 'minimal' role.[171] Bodies that promoted social approaches to crime prevention, like the Secretariat for Safety and Security, were 'downgraded and marginalised'.[172]

Instead of innovation, South Africa embraced a punitive approach. President Mandela, under pressure to respond to fears of crime in the newly united democratic South Africa, engaged in 'war on crime' rhetoric, stating in Parliament in 1995:

> The situation cannot be tolerated in which our country continues to be engulfed by the crime wave which includes murder, crimes against women and children, drug trafficking, armed robbery, fraud and theft. We must take the war to the criminals and no longer allow the situation in which we are mere sitting ducks of those in our society who, for whatever reason, are bent to engage in criminal and anti-social activities.[173]

The false claim that constitutional rights contributed to crime by favouring criminals only disoriented political thinking. In 1999, Justice Minister Penuell Maduna acknowledged public worry that 'the new democratic order is more sympathetic to human rights concerns of criminals and less sensitive to the plight of victims of crime and the general sense of insecurity that continues to besiege our country'. In the same year, Safety and Security Minister Steve Tshwete took war-talk a step further. Criminals, he said, 'have obviously declared war against the South African public . . . We are ready . . . to make them feel that die tyd vir speletjies is nou verby (the time for games is now over).'[174] Increasingly dehumanising terminology became current. The police were encouraged to use extreme force, and there were calls to reinstate the death penalty.[175]

Prisons are the ultimate symbol of the state's coercive power.[176] Prisons serve to signal a government tough on crime. Rhetoric became policy. Symbols became a reality. Parliament adopted a noxious concoction of laws to keep more people in prison for longer. These included tough new bail laws, which required exceptional circumstances for release on bail for certain serious crimes.[177] Periods before prisoners could be considered for release on parole were protracted.[178] And magistrates in the lower courts received increased sentencing jurisdiction.[179] The sentencing powers of district courts expanded from one to three years' imprisonment, and the sentencing powers of regional courts ballooned from ten to fifteen years' imprisonment. We cover sentencing inflation in the next section.

In addition, huge resources were lavished on criminal justice, particularly the police. In 2000, the South African Police Services (SAPS) adopted a National Crime Combating Strategy. This framed the strategic orientation of SAPS squarely within war-on-crime thinking. Dr Guy Lamb explained how 'criminals were referred to as "enemies"; serious and violent crime was to be eliminated through aggressive policing and by apprehending and imprisoning criminals'. SAPS expanded its budget, defied efforts at demilitarisation and adopted a more aggressive, brutal style of policing:

[F]rom the early 2000s, the SAPS established further specialised paramilitary policing bodies that could be swiftly deployed to react to incidents of public disorder, violence, terrorism and natural disasters 'where normal policing was not adequate'. . . . 'War rooms' were later established with a view to delivering a more effective, integrated and co-ordinated crimefighting response.[180]

In 2010, the Police minister announced that the police 'services', SAPS, would now be 'the Force', and that

military ranks, insignias and salutes would be reintroduced to 'ensure clear lines of command and control while instilling a sense of discipline among the [police] members . . . [in order] to fight crime, and fight it tough and smart'.[181]

SAPS claimed these measures were introduced 'to inspire public confidence and lift police morale', but commentators saw them as evidencing the political elite's 'ethos of punitivism', combined with government's notion that SAPS needed to be more forceful to respond more effectively to violent crime.[182]

The prison service, too, received a massive increase in funding. Initially, the Prisons Department had ambitious plans to build several new, low-cost public-private partnership prisons as well as super-maximum security prisons in every province.[183] The plans were plagued by irregularities and in the end only three new prisons were built, with all three running suspiciously over budget. Two privately run prisons were built, Kuthamu Sinthumule and Mangaung, and one state-run super-maximum prison, Ebongweni, in Kokstad.[184] Apartheid's death row in Pretoria was renovated at great expense to create the Kgosi Mampuru II C-Max facility.

Despite this major funding, the prison service, like the police, struggled to deliver services effectively, to transform, to demilitarise and to act consistently with human rights.[185]

South Africa's own 'war on drugs' resonates unsettlingly with that of the United States. Apartheid's minimum sentences for dealing in cannabis and other drugs have led to the imprisonment of numerous inmates and fuelled gang violence.[186]

What have we gained from this 'tough-on-crime' approach? As we were finalising this book, our prisons incarcerate 164 885 people.[187] Of these, 104 089 have been sentenced and 60 796 (almost 37%) are awaiting trial. We imprison more people than any other country in Africa – and we have the 12th highest prison population in the world (of those countries that collect and publish reliable statistics).[188] The country's 243 prisons barely manage. Personnel cannot cope. Nor can those we incarcerate.

And yet, amidst these misdirected efforts, our crime rates continue to soar.

Sentencing inflation: mandatory minimums

The most grievous aspect of South Africa's wrong turn in the war on crime is mandatory minimum sentencing.[189]

South Africa's initial flirtation with mandatory minimum sentences took place in 1971, as we highlighted in Chapter 1. Echoing Nixon's rhetoric, apartheid ideologue Dr Connie Mulder introduced harsh sentences for cannabis and other drug-related offences. The Abuse of Dependence-producing Substances and Rehabilitation Centres statute limited judges' sentencing discretion by prescribing vastly increased sentences for even trivial drug offences. These did nothing at all to curb the use of cannabis or other drugs – but the human impact was severe. Even under apartheid, the judiciary expressed opposition to the measures.[190]

As we explained earlier, democratic South Africa did not renounce the Nixon-Mulder approach. Sadly, the democratic government sustained it. How did we stumble into error? In 1996, Minister of Justice Dullah Omar appointed a Law Reform Commission committee to consider sentencing policy. Before the Commission could report Parliament intervened, however, adopting the Criminal Law Amendment Act, in 1997, dunking the criminal justice system into the pool of harshest options.[191]

The statute limited judges' discretion by prescribing minimum sentences for specified serious crimes. Although minimum sentencing laws may provide greater consistency in sentences, in South Africa, like the United States, the blunt objective was to guarantee harsher sentences and, particularly, 'to encourage courts to impose life imprisonment more often'.[192]

The legislation made life sentences mandatory for: premeditated murder; murder of a law enforcement official, or a potential state witness; murder connected to a rape or robbery with aggravated circumstances; rape committed more than once and gang rape and rape of a minor under sixteen. A 15-year sentence was mandatory for first-time offenders convicted of murder, under circumstances that would not otherwise merit a life sentence; for robbery; for certain drug-related offences; for weapons-related offences; for offences relating to extortion, fraud, forgery, and theft. These last four are not intrinsically violence-linked at all – yet they were bundled helter-skelter into the sentencing package. And 20-year sentences were prescribed for repeat offenders, plus 25 years for third- or further-time offenders.

The new sentences came with severe, even cruel, trimmings. Minimum sentences cannot be suspended. Time spent awaiting trial does not count towards time served. Judges must find 'substantial and compelling circumstances' to be able to alleviate the harsh prescripts.

The new sentences were justified as *temporary* – a transient response to a temporary problem in post-apartheid South Africa. Designed 'to tide us over our transition period' and to 'restore confidence in the ability of the criminal justice system to protect the public against crime', they were to operate for only two years.[193] The promise was that thereafter a more flexible framework would replace them. No consideration was given to the impact of the sentencing regime on the inevitable increase in the number of prisoners and the limited capacity of our prisons.[194] And, like other supposedly temporary measures, they became permanent.

After two years, Parliament extended the statute. Then again. And again – until 2007, when legislated mandatory minimum sentences became *permanent*.[195]

A constitutional challenge failed. The Constitutional Court determined that the legislation preserved the discretion of courts provided 'substantial and compelling circumstances' could be found. The statute thus steered 'an appropriate path . . . respecting the legislature's decision to ensure that consistently heavier sentences are imposed', while also 'promoting "the spirit, purport and objects of the Bill of Rights"'.[196]

Parliament even tried to extend mandatory minimum sentences to children over sixteen. At this, the Constitutional Court jibbed, albeit only by a majority of seven to four. In a judgment I wrote for the majority, the Court held that the Constitution requires that child offenders be treated differently: they must be afforded 'some leeway of hope and possibility'.[197] Although children may commit heinous crimes, they should be incarcerated as a last resort and only for the shortest appropriate period of time.[198]

This ruled out what the court called a 'supervening legislatively imposed determination of what would be "appropriate" under a minimum sentencing system'.[199]

The overarching debate took place on a false premise: that a post-apartheid crime wave demanded harsh sentences. Though violent crime rates were high, there was, as we have shown, no monstrous crime wave. In fact, murder rates had begun decreasing in 1997 already, when minimum sentences were first adopted. They had decreased even further each time Parliament extended the legislation.

What has been the impact of the mandatory minimum sentencing regime on our prisons? As predicted in the early 2000s, the prison population, especially those serving longer sentences, soared after the adoption of mandatory minimum sentences.

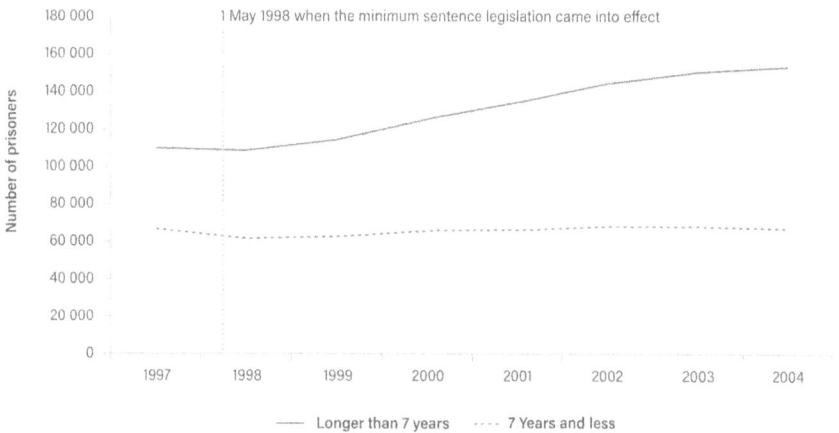

Figure 3: Effects of minimum sentences on sentenced offender population (1997–2004)[200]

Figure 5 (opposite): Overview of the length of sentences of sentenced inmates as at 31 March 2021[201]

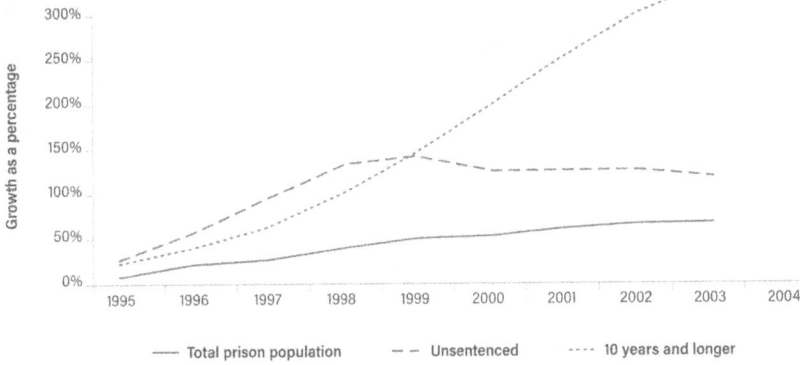

Figure 4: Growth in the prison population (1997–2004)

In 1997, 29 376 inmates were serving sentences of more than seven years and this jumped to 67 081 in 2004.[202] Experts explain that '[m]uch of the blame for the increase in the size of the prisoner population has been placed at the door' of the mandatory minimum sentencing regime.[203] Two decades later, a significant portion of our sentenced inmates continue to serve longer sentences in massive volumes:

Number of Sentenced Inmates by Length of Sentence (as at 31 March 2021)

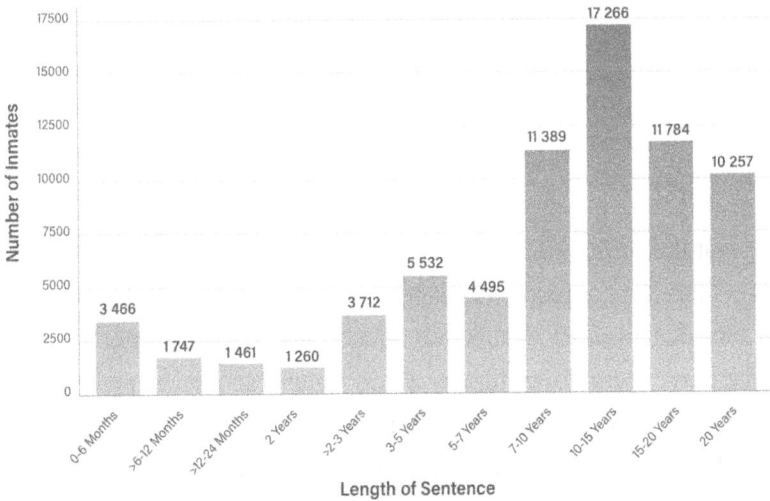

Over the years, the full impact of mandatory minimum sentences and the stricter parole regime hit home. Inmates have to serve a bigger chunk of their sentence before they become eligible for parole – four-fifths (previously, one-third); while 'lifers' (those serving a life sentence) have to serve 25 years (previously, 20 and, before that, 15). Longer sentences than ever before, on a greater proportion of prisoners.[204]

The brutal excess of our carceral policies is most evident in the number of lifers in our prisons, a category mandatory minimum sentences expanded radically. The number of inmates sent away for life surged extraordinarily: in 1996, there were 518 lifers. In March 2024, JICS recorded that our prisons held 18 795 lifers (with only 3 270 of these eligible for parole).[205]

Number of lifers since 1996

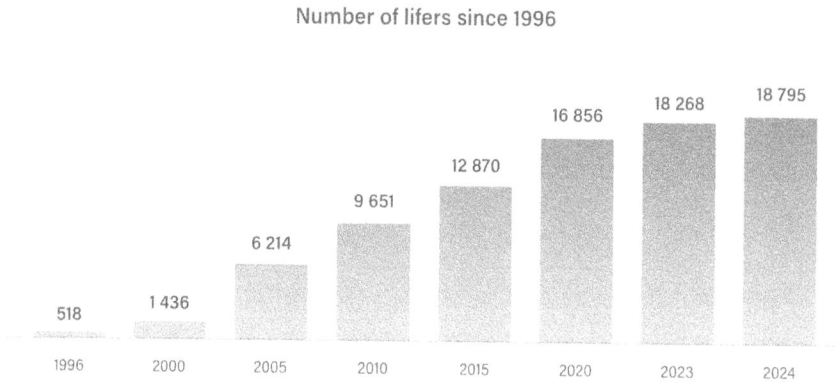

						16 856	18 268	18 795
				12 870				
			9 651					
		6 214						
518	1 436							
1996	2000	2005	2010	2015	2020	2023	2024

Figure 6: The exponential increase of inmates serving life sentences (1996–2024)[206]

Many put their trust in longer sentences to prevent crime. This seems intuitive – harsher consequences surely steer potential criminals away from their intended misdeeds. Dangerous offenders are removed from society and incapacitated from doing further harm. Longer sentences prevent future crimes, incapacitate dangerous criminals by locking them up where they cannot harm others, and ensure effective rehabilitation.

Sadly, little of this is reliable. Post-apartheid South Africa offers dismal proof that crime containment based on harsh punishment – through compulsory lengthy sentences – does not work.[207] Consider the facts. In 2024, after more than a quarter-century of minimum sentences, violent crime remains staggeringly high in South Africa – and has risen since 2011.

The weighty evidence points in the opposite direction. Harsher sentences do not make us safer. Longer sentences do not deter crime. In fact, they 'are not effective for community safety' and 'cause far-reaching harm to individuals, families and communities'.[208] Evidence in South Africa and elsewhere consistently shows that length of sentence alone has little effect on crime rates.[209]

In sum, longer sentences do not lead to a meaningful reduction in crime. The converse is also true, and important: reducing sentences does not lead to an increase in crime.[210] Why? The reason is that long sentences do nothing about the underlying *causes* of crime. They do not address poverty, inequality, unemployment, substance abuse, or misogyny fuelling gender-based violence. Nor, as importantly, do they bring greater certainty of conviction and punishment. They enhance only long imprisonment.

What *does* curb crime are other, better-directed, savvier interventions: effective crime intelligence, early detection, policing, prosecution and other forms of prevention that target the socio-economic roots of crime. We discuss these interventions in further detail in Chapter 6.

Most experts agree that it is *certainty* – not *severity* – of punishment that deters crime.[211] Increasing the length of sentence does not discourage individuals from committing a crime that they otherwise would have risked committing. Most offenders, including violent offenders, do not think they will be caught. And, anyhow, they do not know what the prescribed punishment is.[212]

What difference does it make that the statute requires that you be imprisoned for five years or ten years for murder, or for life, if you do not know the sentence? Or, worse, if you suspect, often rightly, that you will never be sentenced at all? Grievously, that is the case in South Africa today.

Between April 2023 and March 2024, SAPS recorded 27 590 cases of murder.[213] Over that period, the NPA finalised only 3 764 murder cases – and 3 025 led to convictions.[214] These are rough figures. Convictions in 2023/24 are generally for earlier murders. But, given that the total number of murders in South Africa has risen above 27 000 over the last few years, this still approximates a mere 11% conviction rate.

This arithmetic leads to a dismal conclusion: almost 90% of murders go unpunished. *Almost nine out of ten killers in South Africa are never sentenced to prison.* If minimum sentences worked, and long sentences inhibited crime, this would not be so. Instead of punishing more murderers and violent offenders, we send a smaller and smaller number to prison for longer and longer. This is an exercise in self-misleading futility.

What about incapacitating and rehabilitating criminals? These purposes can be served just as well – if not better – without imposing inordinately long sentences. Prison may incapacitate a criminal at the beginning of their sentence and perhaps some years later. Less so after twenty years. Why? Research shows that people are less and less likely to commit crime as they age, and especially after they pass adolescence and early adulthood.[215] Long sentences serve no purpose when advancing age already makes the prisoner far less prone to committing crime.

Longer sentences also do not improve rehabilitation. How much better can you rehabilitate an inmate in twenty-five years than in twenty? Or fifteen? Or ten? Inmates serving long sentences lose connection to the outside world. This makes them less likely to reintegrate successfully. And often, because release is either uncertain or so far off as to seem unattainable, inmates have little to work towards. Those serving long sentences tend to lose hope. A particular frustration for families and inmates – which adds to this loss of hope – is our haltingly effective, often ineffective and becalmed, parole process.

Correctional officials consistently tell us that long-sentence inmates are generally most frustrated, least amenable to rehabilitation and more susceptible to social and psychological problems.[216] Prison conditions make this worse. Prisons are overcrowded, full of inmates serving longer and longer sentences. There are simply not enough rehabilitation, education and training programmes.

In 2023, JICS paid an unannounced visit to a prison in Gqeberha. We found a well-managed, generally impressive prison, headed by an evidently engaged and concerned official. The official seemed to know and engage freely with every inmate we encountered. The official shared with us their vision of rehabilitation but said they lacked the means to implement it. For example, a programme that taught inmates to sew uniforms was under-staffed and under-resourced; out of 503 inmates, the programme could cater to only nine.

Overall, little prospect exists for genuine betterment of the self in prison. Instead, long sentences may prove to be training grounds for criminality – especially when gangs offer a sense of relative safety, belonging and purpose to prisoners who otherwise have little sense of security and reason for hope.

The grievous truth is that mandatory minimum sentences were overhurriedly adopted on misinformed premises. Perhaps their main effect is to enable South Africa's political elite – including us, who are writing and reading this book – to feel that we are *doing something* to keep people safe. In truth, decades of mandatory minimums have done nothing of the sort.

What they may do is satisfy our thirst for retribution or vengeance. Victims may understandably seek retribution – yet some research suggests that victims report greater satisfaction and less trauma after participating in restorative justice programmes, rather than leaving them to derive gratification from purely punitive approaches.[217] We discuss the potential of restorative justice programmes in more detail in Chapters 5 and 6.

Still, however understandable the thirst for retribution, it cannot be bottomless – especially not at the cost of cramming people into our prisons, causing sometimes unspeakable suffering to those we detain, dispropor- tionately impacting poor Black and Coloured people, imposing a massive financial burden on the state, depriving people of their liberty and their families of breadwinners, and diverting focus from alternative approaches.

At the heart of this is a fearful paradox. Despite these drastic measures to 'contain' crime, since 2011, when President Zuma's destruction of state capacity began to take hold, crime has steadily increased – especially vio- lent crime. Police recorded over 27 000 murders between April 2023 and March 2024.[218] This is a grim return to the murder levels of 1995.[219]

YEAR	NUMBER OF MURDERS PER YEAR	MURDERS PER 100k
2010/2011	15,940	32
2011/2012	15,609	30
2012/2013	16,213	31
2013/2014	17,023	32
2014/2015	17,805	33
2015/2016	18,673	34
2016/2017	19,016	34
2017/2018	20,336	36
2018/2019	21,022	37
2019/2020	21,325	37
2020/2021	19,972	34
2021/2022	25,181	43
2022/2023	27,272	46
2023/2024	27,590	44

Figure 7: South Africa's recorded murder rate per 100 000 (2010–2024)[220]

The criminal capture of our state security apparatus under Zuma's presidency, combined with incompetence, corruption and institutional dysfunction, means that we are not arresting or convicting more criminals. Prisons advocate Claire Ballard notes that we send fewer people to prison now than we did in 1995: 'In 1995 people were being sentenced to terms of imprisonment at a rate of almost 290 people per 100,000. In 2014 that figure was 210.'[221] But, Ballard points out, over the 20 years between 1995 and 2015, the number of inmates serving sentences longer than 20 years increased 5,25 times; numbers of those serving sentences of 15–20 years increased 4,8 times and 10–15 years 3,5 times. The number of inmates admitted to serve custodial sentences is *decreasing*. Instead, we are cramming our prisons with prisoners serving longer sentences, with less chance of parole. Indeed, *the rate at which sentenced prisoners are being released is slowing down.*[222] And, more sadly even, the minimum sentences wrong turn was not our last mistake.

Importing the supermax

In the late 1990s, democratic South Africa embraced a new kind of prison. This was part of government's response to public pressure about crime as well as the Department of Correctional Services' worries about prison violence and escapes. Another factor was the explosion of inmates serving life sentences (lifers) because of mandatory minimums.[223] For a solution, government turned to the idea of a super-maximum security prison. Not just a maximum prison. A *supermax*. Designed for tighter control and security than even a maximum security prison, supermaxes are intended for the most dangerous offenders, for escape risks and for those who have seriously violated prison rules.[224]

Two supermaxes were created: Ebongweni, in Kokstad, KwaZulu-Natal (to house 1 440 inmates) and Kgosi Mampuru II C-Max, in Pretoria (to house 281 inmates). Both were modelled on US facilities:

Then minister [of Corrections] Mzimela spent part of his years in exile (early 1960s through early 1990s) in the United States, where he met up with his future advisors, Golz Wessman and Sishi Mthabela. When Ebongweni was still at a conceptual stage, both Wessman and Mthabela returned to the United States on a study tour, including to a supermaximum security facility in Colorado. Once the idea for Ebongweni was approved, a team including architects was also dispatched to the United States to study supermaximum-security prisons.[225]

Ebongweni's model was Marion in Illinois, the first federal supermax. Though Marion has been copied worldwide, it has been chillingly reported to have 'a history of violence, mistakes, and inflicting serious damage on prisoners'.[226]

At the time, government hoped to build a supermax in every province, but sharp criticism from the South African Human Rights Commission (SAHRC) and civil society blunted its enthusiasm.[227] Only C-Max and Ebongweni were created.

Why the critique? There is certainly pragmatic appeal to separating dangerous inmates and those who pose a threat of violence or escape. Yet supermaxes are difficult to reconcile with the fundamental right to dignified conditions of detention. Supermaxes are built with single cells, allowing minimal movement and almost no interaction with other inmates, personnel or families.

Our own inspections of C-Max and Ebongweni were haunting. The pastel-coloured hallways and corridors are eerily quiet. No rowdiness, movement, or the noise of people talking, shouting, laughing or arguing. (Also, the rich reek of cannabis that wafts by on so many prison visits is strikingly absent.)

Every cell has a solid steel door. Only a post-box-sized slot, uncomfortably at waist height, affords a view out. Officials pass meals through the narrow gap. As we walked through, anxious pairs of riveted eyes followed us. Inmates called to us or waved their fingers through the slot to attract our attention. We crouched to meet their gaze, the inmates forced to kneel on their side. It was evident that they were desperate for some – any – contact.

Both prisons are clean, well maintained (unlike many others) and functional. They are never overcrowded. Yet the daily regimen is bleakly austere. Twenty-three hours a day, alone in each small cell. A bed, a toilet and a small sink. There is barely enough room to pace more than a few steps.

Exercise is one hour a day – alone – in an exercise cage. The enclosures we saw had no equipment (we saw one deflated soccer ball). Inmates rarely receive visitors. They are sent to Ebongweni from across the country, and few relatives can afford to travel to Kokstad, a small town 255 km south of Durban, on the Eastern Cape border. Visits, when they happen, are generally behind a glass barrier. Sometimes inmates are offered books, though not often enough. Inmates told us: 'this place is not for everyone'; 'people go mad'; 'they stop talking the way they used to and do strange things'.

Imagine no physical contact – no touch – with another human being for three years.

JICS has concluded that this amounts to unlawful solitary confinement.[228] Solitary confinement is confinement of prisoners for 22 hours or more a day *without meaningful human contact*. The United Nations Mandela Rules, a set of international human rights law standards on incarceration, prohibit solitary confinement for longer than fifteen days. That constitutes prolonged solitary confinement – which may constitute torture, or cruel, inhuman or degrading treatment or punishment.[229]

Ebongweni's inmates are kept in these conditions for at least six months. After this, conditions are slightly alleviated as they progress through a three-year 'behavioural modification programme'.

Make no mistake: we recognise that at least some of those locked up in C-Max and Ebongweni have the capacity – have proved themselves to have the capacity – to do terrible injury to others. Some have tried to escape from less-secure prisons. But the conditions we witnessed go beyond those needed for confinement. They violate the Constitution, the statute and international standards.

JICS has urged the department to relent on these conditions. The interventions we propose are not radical. We do not say – yet – that C-Max and Ebongweni must be shut down, but we urgently counsel alleviation of conditions. More exercise time. More contact – even if gradually introduced – with other prisoners, and with visitors. More telephone calls. More access to books: the C-Max books trolley, we were told, rolls by only every fortnight, and the number of books inmates can take is restricted – though at the end of November 2024, the new head of Ebongweni super-maximum prison, requested a delivery of books from JICS's book donation project. As we were finalising this chapter, NICRO was making arrangements to deliver a chunk of the book donations accumulated at JICS's head office in Centurion to Ebongweni.[230]

South Africa's two supermaxes are dismal emblems of our democracy's failed response to criminal justice quandaries. Confronted with thorny issues, we have embraced the harshest, most punitive and repressive responses – which are the least efficacious. This fails the high aspirations of our constitutional democracy while ignoring practical ways out.

What are our constitutional democracy's prisons like?

Writing in the late 1990s, when human rights aspirations on prison reform ran into a wall of public panic about crime, international prisons authority Dirk van Zyl Smit explained that the history of our prison system embodies both change and continuity.[231] Since 1994, commitment to humane prison reform (change) has been undercut by short-sighted tough-on-crime policies, mismanagement, sentencing inflation and mass incarceration, as well as violence and poor standards of treatment and conditions in prisons (continuity). We are stuck in a vicious cycle of more crime and more punishment. And it makes us no safer.

The country's 243 prisons are crammed and overflowing. As we write, our national prisons overcrowding rate is at 54% – in other words, there are over 50% more people in prison than our prisons were built to hold.[232] To put it in starker terms, there are about 50 000 more inmates than our prisons have beds to accommodate.[233] On the whole, large, urban prisons are worse. This has a terrible impact on the quality of life inside: overcrowded spaces, with less cleanliness, water, bedspace, exercise. The department's resources are spread thinly, endangering security. Impossible burdens are imposed on personnel and infrastructure.

At Durban Medium Correctional Centre at Westville, we visited a cell built for about 20 inmates. No fewer than four times that many – 81 humans – were crammed inside. They were not remand detainees, who one might hope can expect imminent change. These were inmates who had been sentenced. An adjacent cell accommodated 67 inmates. A third cell housed 63, all diagnosed with mental wellness issues. Their conditions of incarceration were not conducive to their mental wellbeing.

Seeing how they serve out their sentences, day after day, was a shocking experience. Bunk beds were stacked three or four levels high. Some were forced to sleep on the floor. The cells were cramped, with no ventilation, little natural light and terrible leaks. Inmates in each cell shared a single shower and a single toilet. These were filthy: cracked tiles, exposed concrete, and mould on the ceiling and walls. When we inspected, there was no running water – apparently a frequent problem. As a result, the toilets did not flush and the cells stank of urine.

Inmates received only the statutory minimum of one hour of exercise a day. This meant that they spent 23 hours a day in cramped, dark, dingy, stinking cells.

The Western Cape province has a reputation for relatively better governance, but its nationally managed prisons are hardly better. Pollsmoor Medium B once housed prominent anti-apartheid activists – including Nelson Mandela, Walter Sisulu and Ahmed Kathrada. The prison was then already notorious for violence. This remains. On entering, broken lights, paint-chipped walls, leaking water pipes, and the palpable stench of urine and cannabis greeted us.

Pollsmoor has long been subject to control by gangs, with endemic violence,[234] including pervasive sexual violence. Broken light bulbs make deadly weapons – the shards used as weapons or mercury for drugs. This means darkness shrouds the prison.

Confirming my own judicial findings in 2015 (related in Chapter 4), JICS's inspection found an overcrowding rate of 115% (meaning more than double capacity).[235] So many bodies forced to live, work, play, sleep and wash in the same cramped space. All this contrasted with the beauty of the Silvermine nature reserve nearby, the Norval Foundation's sculpture gardens across the road, and the lovely Steenberg wine farm.

On leaving, you cannot but ask how these worlds coexist.

Remand cells are often worse. More than a third of those we imprison are awaiting conviction or sentence. They have not been found guilty of any crime, or sentenced, but harsh bail laws, inefficiencies in our court processes and inability to afford legal representation mean long periods of time in prison. Some who are granted bail cannot afford to pay it. This means they remain incarcerated only because they are poor. Even though a judge or magistrate has decided they do not present a threat to the community, will appear for their trial and are entitled to be released, they remain in prison.

Sometimes, the bail amount keeping them inside is piteously low. In a national survey that JICS undertook for its own enlightenment in March 2023, through its prison monitors (formally known as independent correctional centre visitors (ICCVs)), JICS recorded 4 594 inmates incarcerated despite being granted bail of less than R1 000. And 2 215 had awaited trial for longer than two years.[236] Shockingly, five detainees had been awaiting trial for more than ten years. As we explain in Chapter 6, the statute empowers prison officials to approach courts with requests to reconsider these bail amounts and to reconsider long periods of pre-trial detention.[237] The department reports that its officials attempt to use these legislative powers, but are often shot down by the courts.[238]

The conditions for remand (awaiting trial) detainees can be awful. Officials tell us that remand cells are often in worse condition because detainees do not think they will be held there long, and so feel no responsibility to maintain or clean the cells. And while unsentenced, prisoners also do not have access to the same education, rehabilitation and work programmes as other inmates. As they wait for months and even years for their trial, remand detainees lose hope. Suicide, attempted suicide and self-harm are apparent.

In 2021, we entered a prison to investigate the suicide of an awaiting trial detainee at Johannesburg Correctional Centre (almost universally known as 'Sun City'). While waiting for the investigators to arrive, we saw a large SAPS truck pull up and offload the 'new' awaiting trial detainees. One by one, these persons – now branded as prisoners and to be identified by prison number – alighted. They were dressed in their own clothes, which gave us a snippet of their individuality before being submerged in an orange wave of uniforms. Some wore shoes, and some did not. While the correctional officials were rounding them up, one quickly stuck their hand in a dustbin, perhaps looking for food. They were then lined up for health checks. At that moment, our colleagues arrived.

The investigation required us to enter the cell – the single cell where the inmate had been found hanging from the door grille with a waist belt tied around his neck. We obtained the prison file and photographs. We interviewed various correctional officials and nurses. What lodged itself in our memory was the death certificate, which stated that he was born in Diepkloof in the early 1990s – part of the 'born free' generation. As a remand detainee, he died innocent, never proven guilty. Did we, our democratic society, fail him?

In the winter of 2023, we visited the remand section at Vryheid Correctional Centre. There we met remandees who had been incarcerated for years without being convicted or sentenced – one was first detained in 2015, another in 2018. The cells were appalling – all of them overcrowded. One cell, designed to accommodate between 20-25 inmates, had 41 inmates. The bathrooms were filthy, among the worst we've encountered. They smelled strongly of effluent and urine. Our report begged the prison head simply to go to a shop to buy household cleaning materials and to permit the prisoners inside to clean. We don't know if she did. Inmates seemed to have no books or television. Officials confirmed what the inmates told us – that they were almost never allowed out to exercise.

Often those awaiting trial will experience all this only for the charges against them to eventually be withdrawn. This means large numbers of innocent till proven guilty people are detained for weeks, sometimes months or even years, in horrific conditions. Even short periods of pre-trial detention can have huge socio-economic costs, disrupting work, robbing families of their breadwinners and causing extreme distress.[239] What would months in prison mean for you? Your family and loved ones? Your livlihood? And wellbeing?

The human cost also costs the state. Large numbers imprisoned while awaiting trial are a burden on the public purse. The department estimates that it costs R12 125 per month to accommodate each and every remandee.[240] There is an opportunity cost – this funding could be better used elsewhere.

With overcrowding this bad, it is difficult for the department to ensure adequate safety and security. In the Eastern Cape, a cluster head (area commissioner) told us simply: 'A maximum-security prison cannot be overcrowded.' And yet, he grimly noted, St Albans prison, notorious for gang violence, was both overcrowded and under-staffed. So many officials had been stabbed while on duty that they were taking longer and more sick leave. The head of centre complained that, as a result, she did not have enough officials to securely staff the prison. Officials had placed the entire prison on lockdown – meaning little or no privileges, visits, time outside cells, or tuck-shop purchases for inmates.

Far more frequent than inmate-on-official violence (JICS handled 13 complaints of this nature between April 2023 and March 2024), though, is violence between inmates (1 260 complaints over the same period) and official-on-inmate violence (427 complaints).[241]

Violence by officials on inmates is particularly troubling because of the power imbalance. And rarely are there consequences for an official. JICS has tried to end impunity by activating prosecutions of officials accused of violent assault. These can be brutal. Officials have used batons, cricket bats, pieces of hosepipe, electric shock shields, and dogs against inmates.[242] To cover their tracks, officials may deny inmates adequate medical attention after assault. Or prisons' medical staff may be complicit.

The department's emergency response teams (ERTs), responsible for carrying out searches and intervening when violence or disorder erupts, can be especially aggressive. JICS finds it hard to hold officials accountable and our findings and recommendations during investigations are not binding. The department, SAPS and the NPA are slow to take action against officials implicated in misconduct. The result? A culture of impunity, abuse and violence persists.

On 31 August 2023, Judge Ellem Francis delivered a historic judgment in a case Llewellyn Smith and others brought against the Department of Justice and Correctional Services.[243] With representation from Lawyers for Human Rights (LHR), the prisoners testified that they had been tortured and had suffered terrible injuries when officials at Leeuwkop prison, north of Johannesburg, beat them up. JICS's investigation found that torture (or at the very least assault) had taken place and it shared its report with LHR. After a long trial, Judge Francis found resoundingly for the prisoners. His findings, against which the department is currently appealing, largely depict the state of our prisons everywhere:

It is rather sad and disturbing that some of the events that took place during the dark days of Apartheid continued to take place in our beloved country at correctional facilities where some of the people in charge have learnt from their former masters about how to treat inmates who do not toe the line. It is also shocking that some officials would gang together to come up with a version in an attempt to mislead the courts about what really happened at their facility. It is rather disturbing that such conduct by officials occupying higher positions continues to carry on. This case is a typical case of mob justice that still plagues our country only that in this case the officials wanted and had applied mob justice against the plaintiffs. It is also rather sad that none of the officials who had witnessed the events and would be whistle blowers came to testify to court about what they had witnessed.[244]

All this makes it hardly a surprise that efforts to rehabilitate inmates often falter. Prisons can become, as one official put it to us, 'schools for crime'. His comment echoed Foucault's theories. Prisons induct inmates into gang culture, bribery, corruption, violence, brutality and sexual assault, including rape. And many prisons lack adequate opportunities for work, training and education. Though some boast impressive libraries, schools and workshops, many are 'correctional' in name only.

When we visited Ekuseni Youth Centre in northern KwaZulu-Natal in snowy conditions in July 2023, we found a facility under the direction of two deeply engaged officials. The youthful inmates (between 16 and 25)[245] were encouraged to complete their education, read, work in the vegetable garden and learn basic computer skills. But a massive workshop, glimmering on a rise on the eastern side of the facility, previously used for skills training, lay entirely unused. Management ruefully told us that all skills programmes in the region had been suspended several years before because the department's regional executives said they lacked skilled staff to administer the programmes.

Though inmates experience the evils of mass incarceration, officials also suffer. They have no control over how many are sent to prison or how long they spend there. To us, officials near-universally bemoan long trials, unaffordable bail, delays in the parole process and over-long sentences. Often, they crave the resources to fix infrastructure issues. When they can, they proudly show off workshops, gardens and rehabilitation opportunities they try to foster. Overcrowding and poor conditions make their jobs harder and more dangerous.

Do the ends justify the means?

Can we then really claim that prisons do what they are meant to? We hope that prisons may do four things.[246]

First, *deterrence*: we assume that the threat of imprisonment deters individuals from criminal activity. Second, incapacitation: imprisonment insulates the rest of society from criminal activity by separating criminals from the rest of us and thus preventing them from doing further harm. Third, retribution: we desire severe punishment to vindicate the rights of victims and society as a whole. Finally, rehabilitation: we expect prisons to reform and transform the offender into a law-abiding citizen.

Deterrence theory is intuitively appealing. It seems fair to assume that by increasing the severity of the punishment, rational actors will be dissuaded from crimes. But, as we have mentioned, experts have found that although punishment and the risk of being caught do have a deterrent effect, 'it is the *certainty of punishment* rather than the severity of the sentence that is likely to have the greatest deterrent impact'.[247] Hence, 'if anything deters, it is the certainty, not the increasing marginal severity, of punishment'.[248] Retired US Federal Judge Nancy Gertner condemns mandatory minimum sentences.[249] As we have already explained, the gloomy reality is that there is no evidence to show that increasing sentences reduces crime.

Next, while *incapacitating* individuals does inhibit crime for the time that those prone to commit it are inside prison, the 'incapacitation' effect diminishes as we lock up more and more offenders. Dangerous offenders – especially serial offenders – should be prevented from committing crimes, but when incarceration is over-inclusive, when non-violent offenders are locked up, it does not help to further prevent crime.

In light of our high recidivism rate (the chances someone released from prison will commit another offence) of about 60% to 90%,[250] the opposite may be true. We may be *creating* criminals by incarcerating more people for longer. Our prisons are not high walls that pluck dangerous individuals from our society and keep them there. They are more like 'revolving doors': you enter the system a petty criminal and leave as a hardened criminal and gang member.

Betzi Pierce, the chief executive officer of NICRO, laments: 'People, in general, leave prison in worse conditions than before.' She adds, '[t]here is joining and rejoining prison gangs to survive prison life. And there is constant exposure to more dangerous criminals while in prison.' She plainly observes that some 'don't belong in prison. There are people who don't have a serious risk profile . . . We are exposing them to hardened criminals. And they are going to come out there and would have learnt at the best university how to do crime.'[251]

And of course, though prisoners cannot harm us while they are inside, the logic is flawed: they can harm each other. The US feminist group Santa Cruz Women Against Rape argues that prisons *contain* violence and harm rather than prevent it.[252] Imprisonment means only that rather than harming those outside, prisoners may harm or be harmed by those inside. JICS's manager of inspections and investigations, Lennard de Souza, has pointed out that JICS sometimes receives complaints from families of new inmates, who are sent demands for cash in exchange for the safety of their loved ones inside. With the rise of cyber-crime, fraud, scams and extortion are sometimes masterminded from behind prison walls. And the gangs we find inside prisons spill out into the communities outside. Prison walls are thus, in some ways, an illusion. Locking someone up is not a guarantee that they will no longer do harm outside.

Retribution has a strong emotional and historical appeal. Dating back to the Old Testament principle 'an eye for an eye', it is embodied in *lex talionis*, the law of talion or vengeance. The impulse is rooted in moral justification.

But that same emotion – the thirst for vengeance – invites a fearsome logic. How do we slake our thirst for vengeance? If the crime is terrible enough, must we not visit it with a horrific enough punishment? This accounts for the cruellest of history's punishments. We are left with the sombre question: should the state, which represents our aspiration to just order, be the instrument of horrific punishment? Most societies have decided: No. In South Africa, as a response to our history, we formed a social contract – through the Bill of Rights and Constitution – to ensure that punishment is measured against the standard of human dignity.

Even if embracing retributive and vengeful instincts is warranted, there is the danger of disproportionate and excessive forms of punishment.[253] Put differently, justice for victims requires accountability for blameworthy conduct, yes, but not necessarily through the grotesque and harsh prison system.

And does every victim want retribution? Would we not be better served by expanding our idea of what constitutes justice to include ideas of restitution and reparation?

Finally, if not retribution, at least *rehabilitation*. Rehabilitation is embedded in our vision for a humane post-apartheid prison system. The statute defines 'corrections' as the 'provision of services and programmes aimed at correcting the offending behaviour of sentenced offenders in order to rehabilitate them'.[254]

With current overcrowding, caused mainly by inmates who are awaiting trial (more than 30% of the entire prison population), and those serving long sentences, security overshadows rehabilitation. As a result, education, vocational and social reintegration programmes (available only to sentenced inmates) take a back seat[255] – as we saw, vividly, in the huge but unused workshop at Ekuseni. And in many, if not most, small or rural prisons, like Stanger, Vryheid, Elliotdale and Mqanduli correctional centres, there are no books, no school or opportunity to pursue tertiary education at one's own cost, and no skills training programmes at all. Inmates at these prisons may have access to social workers, but they have little opportunity to learn skills that may help them.

Violence is ever present. JICS receives numerous complaints of assaults (official-on-inmate, inmate-on-inmate and inmate-on-official) and excessive use of force. Plus, gangs wield power and rule with violence (including sexual violence) in our prisons. Jonny Steinberg's book *The Number* vividly details the origin, history, proliferation, structures, rituals and traditions of these gangs (specifically, the notorious 26s, 27s and 28s).[256] His research also described how prison gangs are not limited to the inside of prisons – their operations extend beyond prison walls onto streets and into neighbourhoods.

People are dying in our prisons. In JICS's 2023/24 reporting period, 505 deaths occurred from what were reported to us as natural causes.[257] Meanwhile, there were only 123 deaths from unnatural causes. These numbers are slightly higher than those of the last few years.[258] The leading causes of unnatural deaths vary. Some are at the hands of officials or fellow inmates, gang wars, suicides, burn wounds, or medical overdoses, but most are reported as the mysterious category 'unknown other'.[259]

Professor Pamela Schwikkard, an expert in the law of evidence and criminal procedure, observes that some of these deaths eerily remind us of deaths in state custody during apartheid.[260] But, in contrast with apartheid, these deaths are now met with 'a low level of public or political response'.[261]

The fact is: our prisons are not rehabilitating inmates. And on release, even those with the best intentions are thrown into the same socio-economic circumstances that made them turn to crime. Often they are left with decimated family and support structures after their time in prison, and with a criminal record they may struggle to find work. Given this, it is unsurprising that South Africa has such a high recidivism rate.

The conventional rationales for imprisonment seem unconvincing in South Africa. Our democracy's wrong turn on crime in 1997/1998 failed us all. For a long quarter-century, it has failed to keep us safe from violent crime. It has caused conditions of detention that defy justification, and difficult working conditions for officials.

How do we fix it? Can it be fixed? It is these questions we now invite you to consider. But first we interrogate our role in prisons oversight.

4

Prisons Oversight – Who Guards the Guards?

Democracies like South Africa place a premium on open justice, particularly in criminal trials – open courtrooms, access to records, publicly available, reasoned judgments that are commented upon and criticised. Prisons are a sharp contrast. They are the endpoint of an almost always open criminal process – yet they are dark, grim, closed-off places. They are run in the public interest, and devour public funds – yet are blocked off from the public, who know little about what goes on inside. Democracies commit themselves to criminal justice – but we are 'practically barred from evaluating the punishment itself'.[262]

Prisons oversight seeks to pierce this veil. Nelson Mandela's oft-quoted insight guides us: 'No one truly knows a nation until one has been inside its jails. A nation should not be judged by how it treats its highest citizens, but its lowest ones.'[263]

In JICS, oversight of prisons fulfils one of Mandela's promised aspirations. Oversight tests the depth of our commitment to human rights. This chapter considers the rationale, history and efficacy of prisons oversight. We ask – who guards the guards?

Why does prisons oversight matter?

Franz Kafka's short story *In the Penal Colony* (1914) casts unsettling light on what prisons oversight might mean.[264] A new commandant of a penal colony invites a nameless traveller to observe a machine that inflicts brutal punishment on the condemned. An officer accompanying the traveller supports the machine. Proudly, he points out the machine's intricacies. The condemned man is stripped naked and strapped onto a battery-powered bed. Then, with sharp needles, an engraver and the harrow slowly inscribe the crime he has committed on his body. Enjoying mass public support, the machine used to be well maintained, but the public has lost interest. The officer disapproves of the new commandant's opposition to the machine and the 'new mild approach' he prefers. The traveller is aware of how inhumane the execution is, but at first remains silent – he is, after all, an outsider. But, as the gruesome process takes hold, he can no longer contain himself, and blurts out his horror: 'I am opposed to this.' The officer's response is a surprise: he releases the condemned man. Instead, he places himself in the machine. The machine malfunctions and viciously kills him. The condemned man is free, the machine is destroyed, and the traveller leaves a reformed penal colony.

Kafka's tale evokes seeing and being seen. How do we penetrate faraway places where power is wielded for punishment? Can oversight – the traveller – prevent abuses? Can it foster reform? An interpretation of Kafka's tale suggests that reforms are unlikely when prisons are shut off from public scrutiny.[265] When the public can enter the high prison walls, however, to see, to speculate, to question, to challenge, to propose humane conditions, reform might happen.

A sobering insight is suggested by the story. However well intentioned prison officials may be, change from within is hard. Closely linked, another insight is that *external* oversight of how we punish is essential.

How can Kafka's traveller help us understand our own vast, unknown, often cruel, penal colonies? American law professor Michele Deitch lucidly explains prisons oversight as an independent, external mechanism to ensure, at minimum, collecting and disseminating unbiased, accurate, first-hand information for the purpose of reform, primarily through on-site access.[266] Its objectives spring from the tenets of democracy: transparency – to make the hidden visible; and accountability – to ensure that prisons adhere to basic human rights and that abuse attracts consequences.[267] Our Constitutional Court echoes this: '[I]ndependent oversight is based on the premise that transparency and accountability are key features of a democracy, which requires . . . that the exercise of executive power be checked by a body that is independent of that power.'[268]

Oversight seeks to engage the public in the 'long and difficult discussion of what we, as a society, can reasonably expect of prisons'.[269] By spotlighting abuses, prisons oversight sparks a dialogue between government and the public.[270] Oversight seeks to ensure that government is held to account. In addition, by exposing the state of prisons and blemishes in our criminal justice system, it serves as a litmus test for our country's human rights record.

For prisons oversight to be effective, elementary functions are essential – reporting, regulating, auditing, investigating, monitoring and accrediting.[271] And all this must be independent of prisons administration.

Oversight serves primarily those incarcerated and their loved ones. But the public, the media, judges, policymakers, lawyers and correctional officials also benefit from transparency and accountability.[272] By trying to create safer and more humane conditions of confinement, prisons oversight aims to ensure that prisons better serve *all*.

Origins and expansion of oversight

Prisons inspectorates were conceived at the same time as the modern prison. In 1735–1736, William Hay, an English writer and member of parliament, introduced a bill to improve the dismal state of penal institutions. His draft statute included prison inspections.[273] Sadly, his ideas were never enacted. Nearly 40 years later, in the 1770s, John Howard, horrified by what he saw when inspecting local gaols, embarked on a journey to inspect prisons across England and Europe.[274] In *The State of the Prisons*, he explained that: 'The care of a prison is too important to be left wholly to a gaoler' – who might be paid for his work, but is 'often tempted by his passions, or interests, to fail in his duty'. Howard concluded emphatically: '*To every prison there should be an inspector appointed.*'[275]

In 1791, Parliament in London at last passed a statute that expressly included provision for judges to visit, inspect and report on the treatment and conditions of prisoners.[276] In 1835, an act was passed authorising the appointment of inspectors. There followed proper formalisation of a system of prisons inspectorates.[277]

The Inspectorate of Prisons for England and Wales currently operates as an independent reporting inspectorate. The Prison and Probation Ombudsman investigates complaints and prisoner deaths. And the Independent Monitoring Boards of private citizens monitor detention to confirm that it is fair, just and humane.

Rory Stewart, an articulate former prisons minister in the UK (2018–2019), instituted the 10 Prisons Project, pledging to reduce violence and drug usage. 'Prisons,' he points out, 'are isolated places, from which people often emerge more dangerous than when they entered.' Remedying this requires '*fierce independent inspections*, more willingness to admit mistakes, and a better balance of compassion and discipline'.[278] Stewart continues to push for reforms, including more openness.[279] Prime Minister Keir Starmer, and his newly appointed Prisons minister, James Timpson, have indicated a firm commitment to reform.[280]

Inspectorates have gained acceptance worldwide.[281] Oversight may even 'be the norm for prison leadership and management in the 21st century'.[282]

Internationally, the Optional Protocol to the Convention against Torture and Other Cruel, Inhuman or Degrading Treatment or Punishment (OP-CAT) requires States Parties to set up a National Preventive Mechanism

(NPM)[283] – a body or bodies to prevent torture and other cruel, inhuman or degrading treatment by conducting regular visits to places of detention.[284] More than 90 states, including South Africa,[285] have ratified OPCAT.

Developing Npms on a global scale has enhanced prisons oversight and made it the general standard. The NPM is a welcome innovation in South Africa, since its mandate extends beyond prisons. It covers all places of detention where torture or cruel, inhuman or degrading treatment or punishment may occur – including children's homes, police cells, mental health facilities, places of detention for undocumented immigrants and military barracks.

Its requirements are not novel. The European Committee for the Prevention of Torture and Inhuman or Degrading Treatment or Punishment (CPT) visits and inspects conditions in prisons and other places of detention. It is the Council of Europe's specialised independent monitoring body. In New Zealand, the Office of the Inspectorate has a team of independent inspectors to check on fair, safe, secure and humane treatment of those detained.[286] In Canada, the Office of the Correctional Investigator, an independent ombudsman, deals with complaints, investigates conditions in prisons and reports its findings on both individual and systemic issues.[287] It also makes recommendations for correctional policies and procedures.

In India, prison inspections are undertaken by the Board of Visitors, which includes official visitors (elected representatives and the Human Rights Commission) and unofficial visitors (local lay persons).[288] The board's mandate is to inspect prisons, redress complaints, observe and document prison life, improve prison conditions and prevent violations.

In Malawi, the Constitution established the Prison Inspectorate.[289] Its mandate is to monitor conditions, conduct investigations, and visit prisons. In Zambia, judges may inspect prisons at any time and may inquire into any inmate complaint or request. In addition, Zambian law allows for Visiting Justices to visit every part of the prison, access records, test the quality and quantity of prisoners' food and record the visit. Official Visitors visit a prison at least once every two months and discharge similar duties.[290] Many more African countries have established statutory oversight mechanisms.

Although the USA incarcerates vastly more persons than any other country, it is 'an anomaly on the world stage', since both federal and state prisons generally lack external oversight.[291] The absence is not uniform. The independent Correctional Association of New York State (CANY) has had statutory authority since 1846 to provide independent monitoring and oversight for state prisons.[292] In California, the Office of the Inspector General conducts independent prison visits.[293] Federally, a bipartisan bill was proposed in 2023 to establish an independent inspection regime within the Federal Bureau of Prisons – including an ombud to investigate allegations of abuse and to conduct unannounced inspections. Sadly, enactment has stalled.[294]

Prisons oversight comes to South Africa

Apartheid's prisons were deliberately hidden from public scrutiny, rendered the unseen 'gulag archipelagos'.[295] Cruel conditions were hidden behind mostly impenetrable doors. There were chinks, however. In 1964, government for the first time invited the International Committee of the Red Cross (ICRC) to inspect prisons countrywide, including Robben Island.[296]

Judges, magistrates and members of parliament could inspect prisons. Judge Hannes Fagan – who later became JICS's second Inspecting Judge – visited prisons while on Circuit.[297] Helen Suzman, the sole anti-apartheid member of parliament, regularly visited prisons, and spoke out about conditions. Both were exceptions. And reformist critics were not evenly impressed: prison visits merely fuelled a 'myth of adequate control against abuse'.[298]

As apartheid officially ended, human rights-centred penal reform finally became possible. Yet the White Paper on Corrections in 1994 did not debate independent prisons oversight. In response, the Penal Reform Lobby Group (PRLG), a group vibrantly dedicated to reforming apartheid prisons, prepared an Alternative White Paper. This highlighted the need for independent prisons oversight after apartheid. Without it, they argued, government would violate the principles of the Constitution and the values of international law.[299]

They proposed a new independent inspectorate to visit prisons, investigate prisoners' complaints, monitor investigations of crimes in prison, advise on policy issues, and establish a community-driven visitors' scheme. They precipitated change. A 1997 legislative amendment established JICS.[300]

Prisons oversight was introduced for noble reasons: 'holistic transformation of correctional services so as to promote rehabilitation within a humane and safe correctional system'.[301] Creating JICS sought to realise the requirement in the Bill of Rights that conditions of detention had to be dignified, as well as 'the principles of accountability, responsiveness and open governance'.[302]

The amendment relied on the English model, though tailored for South Africa. Unlike the English model, JICS is headed by a judge, for independence as well as political clout and prestige.[303] In addition, for costs reasons, instead of having an inspector of prisons coupled with a prison ombudsman (as in the UK), inspecting and complaints handling were combined.

The first Inspecting Judge was John Trengove (1998–1999),[304] whom Hannes Fagan (1999–2006) succeeded. Judge Fagan, the longest-serving Inspecting Judge, reflected on JICS that oversight is a 'radical departure from the previously closed system' and lauded its 'rich potential'.[305]

JICS-style oversight

JICS is an independent statutory body under the control of the Inspecting Judge.[306] It is tasked with monitoring, inspecting and reporting on the conditions in prisons, the treatment of inmates and any corrupt or dishonest practices. The Inspecting Judge's primary functions are to inspect correctional facilities, deal with complaints, hold public hearings and report on conditions. Reports are submitted to the Minister of Correctional Services as well as the Parliamentary Portfolio Committee and the National Commissioner. JICS's annual report is tabled in Parliament.

JICS's CEO, under the control and authority of the Inspecting Judge, is responsible for administrative, financial and clerical functions. In addition to inspectors and investigators, part-time on-site monitors stationed at most prisons (independent correctional centre visitors (ICCVs)) perform the core functions. ICCVs interview inmates, liaise with correctional personnel, record complaints and try to resolve them. They also function as an early warning system, alerting the Inspecting Judge to dangers or abuses (hunger strikes, uprisings, deaths). Visitors' committees aim to bolster the role of communities. They deal with unresolved complaints and promote outside interest in prisons.

JICS conducts announced and unannounced inspections, based on a National Inspection Plan. Some inspections coincide with its participation in the NPM (together with the SA Human Rights Commission[307] and other independent oversight bodies, including those for the police,[308] the military[309] and medical practitioners).[310]

The statute indispensably entails co-operation from the Department of Correctional Services. The department must report to JICS all deaths in prisons, segregation and extended segregation, the use of mechanical restraints, the use of force, assaults, torture or cruel, inhuman or degrading treatment or punishment, sexual violations, hunger strikes, attempted suicides, escapes, and matters related to dishonest practices or corrupt activities.[311] Mandatory reports send warning signals when trouble is brewing and may trigger JICS investigations.

The statute expressly obliges prison heads to assist ICCVs in performing their 'assigned powers, functions and duties'.[312] ICCVs are entitled to interview inmates in private. They must be given access to any part of the prison and to any document or record. If prison authorities refuse ICCVs' requests, the Inspecting Judge, whose decision is final, must decide the dispute.[313]

Inmates subjected to segregation or mechanical restraints may 'refer' the matter (in effect, appeal) to the Inspecting Judge, who must decide the issue within 72 hours[314] – a sadly rather notional entitlement, given the delays that dog appeals.

These provisions are extensive – but they leave JICS with no operational, managerial or executive power over the department. And the department has no obligation to implement JICS's findings and recommendations, or even to respond to JICS. Worse, the mandatory system of reports is hobbled and dysfunctional because of technological obstructions – the department has for years had no adequately functioning national reporting system. And untoward tensions between prison heads, ICCVs and inmates sometimes create obstructions.

JICS's oversight role has potential to transform correctional facilities and vindicate inmates' rights, but the conspicuous dearth of binding powers undermines its work. The statute failed to secure JICS within an independent structure. JICS depended on the department for funding. Its budget was determined by none other than the National Commissioner – whose department it is required to oversee.[315] This obvious defect – allowing the department to strangle its own oversight body through starved resources and financial and administrative controls, including support staff, IT systems and office space – led to a successful constitutional challenge brought by Sonke Gender Justice,[316] a non-governmental organisation.

The Constitutional Court ruled in 2020 that JICS lacked structural, operational and financial independence from the department – which marred also its perceived independence. The ruling struck down antithetical features of the statute. Invoking the Bill of Rights, international law and its previous decision in *Glenister II*, the court affirmed that independence is 'an inherent characteristic of a successful oversight, or watchdog, entity'. More specifically, independence is 'crucial' to 'effective oversight of correctional facilities'.[317]

Independence requires that a watchdog 'must be able to perform its functions, free from the influence of the executive body it is mandated to scrutinise'. For prisons, an oversight body must 'maintain an arms-length relationship with the Department' and 'be sufficiently insulated from undue influence and "capture"'.[318]

This was a victory for JICS's functionality. The court emphasised that oversight is vital because prisons, being 'cloistered' from society's view, are 'fertile breeding grounds for autocracy and human rights abuses'.[319] In addition, it was necessary for inmates to be confident that JICS was independent and effective: 'Without this confidence, inmates may be unwilling to report any complaints.'[320]

Parliament was given two years to fix the statute – but slow processes necessitated a request to the court, which JICS supported, for an extra year, which the court granted. The department agreed with JICS and the Public Service Administration that JICS had to be constituted as a standalone, autonomous government component. In late 2023, Parliament enacted necessary minimum amendments to the Correctional Services Act, making JICS a separate financial entity. A larger, more ambitious legislative reform, however, is still pending. This consists of a new JICS bill, which will confer enhanced powers, whose details have been painstakingly hammered out between JICS and the department. The 2024 general election proved an obstacle to its enactment and JICS's ambit and powers remain in the balance.[321]

Also in need of enhanced independence and proper regulation is the

NPM. While the establishment of the NPM is welcome, it has struggled to find its feet. Housed within the SAHRC, the NPM has no enabling legislation and thus no clear regulation of its governance, powers, budget or independence. Affiliated bodies, including JICS, participate on a largely voluntary basis. State officials do not recognise the NPM. Recently, on a joint NPM visit to Barberton prison, NPM members not affiliated with JICS found themselves barred from the prison. The impact of the NPM's work remains to be seen.

Expanding oversight – involving more judicial officers

Alongside JICS, the Correctional Services Act empowers judges and magistrates, and Parliamentary Portfolio Committee members, to visit prisons.[322] Why judges and magistrates? Because a crucial part of the judicial function is sentencing.[323] Judges should see first-hand what happens when they lock people away.

This gives extraordinary power, which is not used often enough. After President Mandela appointed me as a judge, at the end of 1994, my new colleagues informed me about a tradition – that it was part of every judge's ordinary duties to visit a prison at least once every year. I made my first visit. It was 1995, and when I stepped inside the huge Modderbee Correctional Centre, near Benoni on the East Rand, it was my first time inside a prison since my momentous visits to death row during apartheid (Chapter 1). The contrast was profound, even a relief. Modderbee was not as overcrowded as it is now, and seemed well run. I checked the clinic, the kitchen, the single cells and a few of the larger cells. I listened to prisoners' complaints, while my secretary made a note of them, for later follow-up.

Every now and then, as I trudged Modderbee's corridors alongside the acting head of the prison, the unmistakable aroma of cannabis – that almost omnipresent feature of South African prisons – wafted across our way. Indeed, it is hard to envisage how many prisons could operate without the sometimes beneficent-seeming haze of dagga.

Later, appointed to the Supreme Court of Appeal in Bloemfontein, I encouraged prison visits, though by now the idea of judges' visits as an ingrained practice was slackening. My appellate colleagues did not seem excessively enthused. I arranged two inspections: to the large prison at Grootvlei, which had been a particular focus of a commission chaired by Judge Thabani Jali (the Jali Commission), and the newly constructed private prison next door, Mangaung Maximum – which was later to become even more scandalously notorious than Grootvlei.

In 2009, now as a justice of the Constitutional Court, my efforts started anew. With the support of the then Chief Justice, Pius Nkonzo Langa (a diffident, public-spirited and conscientious person), colleagues agreed that each justice would visit up to four prisons a year. The aim was to resuscitate the notion that a judge's duties stretch beyond court decisions: they include the dark spaces where Nelson Mandela claimed a nation's integrity was judged. Sadly, that tradition seemed to have become lost in the transition from apartheid. Fewer and fewer judges were visiting prisons. The judiciary was leaving the prison system to its own devices. Persuaded that this was perilous, the Constitutional Court justices resolved to reinvigorate the tradition, not by exhorting other judges – but by setting an example themselves.

The programme started operating in 2010. Alerted to this, Sonke Gender Justice launched its One Judge, One Jail campaign.[324] There are roughly the same number of judges as prisons: 243. If every judge visits only one prison in a year, judge-supervision of prison conditions would help perk up the whole system. The Constitutional Court initiative worked, for a while. Our reports were posted to the Constitutional Court's website for the public to read.[325] But, once more, the system faltered: the court became busier and busier, its members experienced more and more pressure from their primary task, adjudication, and prison visits became difficult to sustain.

As part of this programme, on 23 April 2015 I visited Cape Town's Pollsmoor prison with my law clerks.[326] Set in lovely winelands, amidst upmarket housing estates, Pollsmoor made a grim contrast. We focused on the awaiting trial and women's sections. We found misery thriving amidst miserable conditions. The extent of overcrowding, unsanitary conditions, sickness, emaciated physical appearance of the detainees, and overall deplorable living conditions were, I said in my subsequent report, 'profoundly disturbing'. Extreme overcrowding of 300% (meaning that three times as many remand prisoners were crammed into every cell than should have been) created appalling conditions. About 65 inmates were cramped into every cell, forced to make do with one toilet and one shower.[327]

The horrendous conditions included unsanitary, health-endangering conditions, medical neglect, unworkable plumbing, lack of artificial light, lack of hot water, lice-infested blankets, no exercise and insufficient food. One inmate's comment was especially chilling: 'We're human beings, but we're treated worse than animals.'

The tough-minded, outspoken Democratic Alliance spokesperson on prisons, Ms Glynnis Breytenbach MP, described comparable conditions at St Albans Maximum Security prison as 'an abomination, a human rights abuse', 'a disgrace', adding that, if the inmates had been her animals, 'I would not have left them there.'[328]

My report (2015 Pollsmoor Report) triggered a public outcry, as well as a constitutional challenge to the conditions. Sonke Gender Justice and Lawyers for Human Rights responded in December 2016. They launched an outspoken campaign[329] and they approached the High Court in Cape Town, charging that the department had failed, in breach of the Bill of Rights, to provide inmates with proper exercise, nutrition, accommodation, ablution facilities and healthcare services. They sought a court-supervised plan (a 'structural interdict') to remedy the failings.

Judge Vincent Saldanha granted the order. He ordered the department to reduce overcrowding within six months to no more than 150% of its approved capacity. He also ordered the department to develop a comprehensive plan to address the problems.[330]

All this affirmed the impact judges' prison visits can have.[331] But, long-term? JICS's Annual Report for 2022/23 rates Pollsmoor Medium A centre as 'good'. Medium B and the women's centre are 'satisfactory'. Only the maximum security prison is declared 'unsatisfactory'. And the report cites all centres in the Pollsmoor cluster for having no educators and no social workers, for the number of deaths, and for Pollsmoor's female and maximum security prisons being amongst the most over-crowded in the Western Cape.

The doubts go deep. Do JICS's outspoken reports, its testimony to Parliament, help gild an irretrievably broken system? We were told, when visiting the Johannesburg High Court in November 2024, to exhort them to more prison visits, that a laudable visit by Deputy Judge President Roland Sutherland and a group of Johannesburg judges to the Johannesburg prison (Sun City) on 6 December 2022, with ensuing reports, intercessions and suggestions, had had no effect or indeed response. Conditions at Sun City remain bleak and the judges' recommendations, without binding force, have had little effect. JICS encouraged these judges to persist – arguing that regular visits, follow-ups and strong, collaborative relationships with prison authorities make a difference. But do they really?

Inspectorates: palliative or perpetuator, or both?

Prisons oversight bodies like JICS find themselves trapped in a paradox. By seeking to improve the lives of incarcerated persons, they help sustain a system whose vices and cruelties may be ineradicable. Do our watchful eyes, our reports and feedback, our complaints, our protestations, do good? How much good? Or do they help preserve an inhumane and brutal system? Does palliating that system help perpetuate it?

Democratic South Africa's wrong turn on sentencing exacerbates this. Minimum sentences, the misconceived and counter-productive 'war on drugs', seem morally indefensible. We speak out about these evils: but do JICS's watchful, beneficent monitoring and reporting help entrench them?[332]

Foucault, whom we introduced in Chapter 2, was particularly scathing about prison 'reform' and 'humanisation'. He scornfully remarked that:

> whether the prisoners get an extra chocolate bar on Christmas or are let out to make their Easter Duty is not the real political issue. What we have to denounce is not so much the 'human' side of life in prison but rather their real social function – that is, to serve as the instrument that creates a criminal milieu that the ruling classes can control.[333]

But there was a problem with Foucault's trenchant tirades. He derided prison reform – witheringly denouncing projects in Europe – yet offered no practical alternatives. He contented himself instead with a radical postulate, that 'there can be no reform of the prison without the search for a new society'.[334] This premise may be true, but what do we do now, for those who suffer intolerable conditions, while we 'search for a new society'?

The question is whether prisons oversight bodies can work within the confines of criminal justice to help build a safer society, one that relies *less* heavily on prisons – a society that may ultimately supplant inspectorates themselves? The debate is familiar to conscientious lawyers and judges under apartheid. Did their participation in apartheid justice do more harm than good? Or did they extend the life of an illegitimate system?

It is not fanciful to invoke the apartheid-complicity example. JICS experiences passionate criticism, even invective, from some inmates and relatives of inmates. They accuse JICS of doing no good. On the other hand, some inmates and their families place too much trust in prisons oversight. They write to JICS in anguish over criminal justice issues that lie far beyond JICS's remit – unfair convictions, unjust sentences, unaffordable bail, the slow-moving cogs of the court system, delays in the parole system and difficulties securing transfers. An inmate's relative wrote to JICS. She said:

> Your organization which was instituted by the late Nelson Mandela whose mandate is solely protecting the dignity of inmates, has clearly lost the plot somewhere along the past 22 years. My view of this as a member of the public is that you have become caretakers of protecting the [salaries] and pension of DCS officials and by doing so also protecting your own livelihood.

She wanted JICS to get her brother transferred. But transfers lie outside JICS's control. JICS has no operational or executive or policymaking power over the Department of Correctional Services. Until the new JICS statute is adopted, JICS has power only to inspect, investigate, report and recommend. All this we explained. When our correspondent's brother was at last transferred, it was to the grim Ebongweni prison at Kokstad, which – understandably – angered her even more: JICS had once again failed. It was, she remarked, 'an embarrassment' and 'a complete waste and burden to taxpayers'.

I keep this letter close, and often quote it, since its scalding assessment reminds us all of how much JICS has to do, and how little it sometimes achieves.

Struggling to navigate the tardy and often dysfunctional parole system, an inmate serving a life sentence turned to JICS. He was entitled to benefit from a 2019 judgment of the Constitutional Court,[335] holding that those whose crimes were committed before 1 October 2004, when the statute imported much harsher parole conditions, were entitled to the parole regime existing at the time when they offended. But the court's judgment was thwarted by bureaucratic delays. The inmate wrote to JICS:

> How long will our cries go unanswered? How long will no one talk about this publicly? How long will rehabilitated offenders remain in prison on whim of a cruel and failing State? How long will valuable taxpayers' monies be wasted on incarcerating rehabilitated offenders? We continue to beg and plead for your intervention or at the very least, activism.

On another occasion, JICS intervened to help an inmate who had spent years in prison for murder but was unable to appeal because his trial record was missing. The applicable principle was beyond any doubt: if a trial record cannot be located or reconstructed, the person convicted is entitled to be acquitted, because their fundamental right to appeal has been denied. The real problem lay with the registrar's office in the Durban High Court, whose conduct suggested either slothfulness or incompetence. JICS assisted the family to obtain pro bono representation until eventually the KZN Society of Advocates assigned a practising advocate to pursue the case.

These complaints and the bureaucratic delays and dysfunction that inmates and their families encounter at all points of the criminal justice system evoke the mythical labour of Sisyphus, who in perpetuity had to roll a huge boulder up a hill, only for it to roll down to the bottom every time he reached the top, so that he had to start all over again.

Because of JICS's limited powers, we try to refer complaints to those with power to act. As often as we can, we step outside our statutory role to act as fellow humans, trying to provide solutions for those in dire straits. But misunderstandings about JICS's powers can lead to frustration, resentment, desperation and anger.

Even during inspections, when inmates report their complaints, the very act of relying on JICS may come at a cost. At our inspection of Polls-moor Medium B in October 2021, JICS encouraged inmates to speak out. Well-spoken and passionate, an inmate raised concerns about access to the hospital, exercise, overcrowding, high prices at the prison shop, and about cell phone and drug smuggling by department personnel. The inmate paid in threats, intimidation and physical assault by a prison official. Lawyers for Human Rights stepped in to arrange protection for him.

The Jali Commission – which reported on shocking abuses in prisons in the early 2000s – doubted JICS's effectiveness:

[T]he staff in the Office of the Inspecting Judge may not be challenging the Department's officials as they ought to do. In particular, the independent visitors [ICCVs] have invariably been seen as an extension of the Department and thus have not been effective in dealing with the treatment of prisoners. The cases that exemplify this are the abuse and torture of prisoners at [Pretoria] C-Max Prison, which apparently were reported to the [ICCVs] without any success. This approach has affected the image of the Office of the Inspecting Judge within the prison population.[336]

Studies by civil society organisations (including Civil Society Reform Initiative and Sonke Gender Justice) and academics have identified impairments to JICS's efficacy.[337] These include inefficiencies within JICS's complaints-handling process, the complex and often ambiguous relationships between ICCVs and officials, and difficulties in gaining the trust of inmates. In addition, JICS's institutional and statutory limitations impair its efficacy. These include lack of consistent and private communications between JICS and inmates, resource constraints, JICS's current inability to issue binding decisions and its lack of enforcement powers, the absence of clear standards for evaluating correctional facilities, and tepid public awareness about JICS.[338]

Other rightful concerns include what some insightful critics fear might become an 'insidious process of bureaucratisation' in JICS's complaints-handling; or that inspections may become a machine-like tick-box exercise, and how ICCVs may become embedded like correctional officials.[339]

JICS's own evaluations have also exposed problems. In 2022, JICS's executive visited all ICCVs in their regions. ICCVs – who do the hands-on, face-to-face, hard work of JICS – revealed many problems. These included ICCVs' worries about job security (they are appointed on contract) and their own safety. In Cape Town, a young woman ICCV was worried that she was part of the very same community with inmates, gangs and correctional officials – who knew where she and her family lived. Speaking poignantly and powerfully, she feared the threat of gang violence and retaliation – or, conversely, pressure and hostility from correctional officials. In circumstances like this, can ICCVs deal boldly enough with complaints? Who will protect them?

These powerful criticisms reveal JICS's sober self-knowledge. They remind us constantly that prisons oversight is tough and may feel unrewarding or, worse, ineffective.

Prisons oversight is no panacea. It cannot guarantee dignified and safe conditions in prisons. It cannot alone 'curb the abuses' it brings to light, nor 'force the spending of necessary resources to fix problems'. And prison oversight bodies should not appropriate the job of the correctional system – they should not become 'a supra-management body ultimately responsible for the clean-up of an agency beyond repair'.[340] Prisons inspectorates cannot enforce criminal justice. What they can do – despite Foucault's sneering observation about the futility of chocolate treats – is try to improve it.

In defence of prisons oversight

We have reckoned daily with the deficiencies of prisons oversight – but our work has also shown us that oversight can have an impact.

1. Protecting elementary human rights

Prisoners' rights are human rights, inalienable, indivisible and interdependent. So obvious, so embedded in our Bill of Rights. Yet impinged upon every day. Prisons oversight can make an impact. The 2015 Pollsmoor Report suggests impact. It prompted litigation challenging grim levels of overcrowding, which obtained a powerfully directed court order. More recently, JICS has been trying to stop solitary confinement and prolonged solitary confinement in super-maximum prisons. In 2021, JICS released scathing reports exposing the practice at Pretoria's C-Max and Kokstad's Ebongweni.[341] The reports led the department to re-transfer 81 inmates. They had been sent to the supermax for minor disciplinary infringements; they were transferred back to their original centres.[342]

Major reforms are still acutely necessary. JICS's struggle continues. In March 2024, a JICS-led seminar at the University of KwaZulu-Natal collated original research that showed the harmful impact of solitary confinement – not only on inmates, but on personnel. The facts are clear. The law is clear. The Constitution is clear. What remains is to summon sufficient institutional will – and public outrage – to end, or at least to significantly ameliorate, the practice.

After inspecting a women's correctional facility and engaging with healthcare staff, we identified troubling gaps in the department's sexual and reproductive healthcare policies. A JICS letter and opinion piece explained how women behind bars face extra hurdles to access abortions.[343] The department responded with a departmental commitment to review the healthcare policy and to address inadequacies.[344] JICS was invited to comment on a draft version of the revised healthcare policies in 2024. We were pleased that the draft requires that termination of pregnancy be performed at state cost, that all inmates who require termination be referred to a designated public health facility and that any inmate requesting termination of pregnancy must be referred to the Maternal and Reproductive Health section regardless of the stage of pregnancy. The draft also requires that any inmate who requests termination shall be counselled before being referred to a designated public health facility. JICS recommended that the procedures be amended to clarify that this counselling must be administered by a qualified healthcare professional and must, in accordance with the Choice on Termination of Pregnancy Act 92 of 1996, be voluntary (non-mandatory) and non-coercive. When we inspected Atteridgeville Gender Responsive Centre in 2024, inmates appeared to have adequate access to abortions.

During the harsh national Covid-19 pandemic lockdown – one of the world's most severe – JICS was initially barred from prisons. The department placed all prisons under lockdown from 15 March 2020. Then, for nine chilling weeks, from 26 March till 31 May 2020, the regulations meant JICS could not enter prisons at all. On JICS's exhortation, the President rectified this by adjusting the regulations.[345] At a time when inmates were cut off from the rest of the world, JICS was able once more to enter prisons and reveal the harsh impact of lockdown there.[346] JICS also engaged with the department on a regular basis to closely monitor the spread of the pandemic within prisons.

In addition to broader issues, JICS tries to help resolve individual complaints. JICS has intervened to ensure that inmates with cancer diagnoses receive treatment.

Although transfers (where inmates request to transfer to another correctional facility) lie outside its mandate, JICS tries to and often succeeds in securing transfers. Thus, inmates who feared for their lives after whistle-blowing, and inmates who were incarcerated far from their loved ones, have been helped.

JICS has intervened at Westville prison, in Durban, to secure improved facilities for LGBTQ+ inmates housed, at their own request, in a separate cellblock. Their separation had benefits, but also disadvantages, which JICS helped ameliorate.

Even though JICS lacks powers over parole, it has helped accelerate parole applications for some inmates. It is also in the advanced stages of arduous negotiations with the National Council for Correctional Services and the Minister of Correctional Services to seek reforms that would improve the sometimes agonising parole process for lifers, which is beset by delays and inconsistencies.

JICS has also started intervening in what it considers to be public interest litigation. In a historic first, JICS secured status as a friend of the court (*amicus curiae*) in a case seeking to secure the right of inmates who were studying to use their laptops in their cells, under specified conditions.[347] Confirming a High Court decision, the Supreme Court of Appeal ordered the department to promulgate a revised policy permitting personal computers in cells for studying – and to consult JICS in doing so.

JICS, while not formally joining the applicant's request to be allowed the use of his computer, pointed out the futility of the department's opposition. This was salient because mobile phones are a prime contraband item within prisons, necessary for communication with families because public telephones are preponderantly dysfunctional, and enabled by smuggling, perpetrated lucratively by many personnel members. JICS proposed an order permitting student inmates their laptops in cells, under strict conditions, while the department figured out a new comprehensive policy. The Supreme Court of Appeal embraced JICS's outline, but the department's further appeal to the Constitutional Court – heard in November 2024 – thwarted its implementation.[348] Judgment is awaited.

2. Early warning signs

Oversight offers windows into systemic patterns and trends. The department responded to JICS's insistent reports on poor, sometimes appalling, prisons infrastructure by reforming its handling of maintenance. Eluding the Department of Public Works and Infrastructure, whose responses at times seem moribund, the Correctional Services Department directed more funds and capacity to local prison management.

In 2021, JICS received complaints about a chickenpox outbreak at Grootvlei Correctional Centre. Concerned about the highly contagious disease, and its potentially deadly consequences, we showed up unannounced. We discovered that the outbreak was spreading because of a lack of access to hot water, clean uniforms and bedding – the lack of resources from the Department of Public Works and Infrastructure and the inability to practise basic hygiene in prisons was to blame. Returning to Johannesburg from Bloemfontein after a sobering visit, we drove over gaping potholes through (what from our car windows seemed) dilapidated towns. These spoke to a larger, more systemic neglect. We refocused on what JICS can do, amidst these conditions, monitoring the outbreak closely.

Another repeated complaint, confirmed by JICS's own inspections, revealed that, countrywide, public telephones in prisons were mostly not working. With cajoling from JICS, some prisons have adopted a new, more reliable model for public telephones, the CallSafe device.[349] Telephones are indispensable for prisoners (at least, those without cell phones smuggled in with the help of corrupt personnel) to stay in touch with loved ones and to contact lawyers and, where necessary, the media.[350]

JICS also discovered that closed circuit television monitoring (CCTV) in many prisons is dysfunctional. Most prisons do not have CCTV or any other electronic security systems at all. Those that do often report that they are non-functional. This undermines the safety and wellbeing of inmates and correctional officials.

How can the lack of necessities like uniforms, bedding, hot water, telephones and CCTVs be explained? And what happens to the public money that goes towards CCTVs and catering contracts? As with the gaping potholes we negotiate when we drive to inspections, corruption and institutional dysfunction have betrayed inmates. The Judicial Commission on State Capture (Zondo Commission) exposed how high-level personnel at the department were involved in corrupt contracts irregularly awarded to Bosasa.[351] Like in other sectors of our society, these corrupt acts have real consequences for human life and wellbeing. An analysis concluded, rightly, that 'a more or less direct line can be drawn between corruption and the human rights abuses that often follow'.[352]

Effectively managing corruption is essential for effective prison oversight. How prisons are *governed* and how prisoners are *treated* are inextricably related.[353] Corruption threatens governance as well as human rights.[354] A misguided amendment – one that JICS mistakenly initiated in the early 2000s – sought to excise JICS's duty to investigate and report on corruption.[355] The statute rightly sustains the Inspecting Judge's duty to report on 'any corrupt or dishonest practices in prisons'.[356]

The newly amended Correctional Services Act expressly affirms the department's obligation to 'immediately' report instances of 'dishonest practices or corrupt activities' to the Inspecting Judge.[357] The JICS bill will further enhance JICS's capacity and role in combating corruption.

The Jali Commission considered corruption in prisons widespread. Corruption and state capture intensified throughout the Zuma years. A belief-defying scandal in 2022 exposed its extent. In June 2022, management of Mangaung Correctional Centre, one of two private prisons, reported that Thabo Bester (who was convicted of rape and murder) had burned to death while alone in his cell. This was reported as a suicide. The prison is nominally run by a consortium, but management and security are handled by G4S, a multinational corporation. G4S's contract with the state ensures that Mangaung is never overcrowded. Hence, maintenance and infrastructure issues are addressed immediately and security is strict. Every inch of the prison is under surveillance. Access and movement are strictly controlled and a carefully determined ratio of guards to inmates is rigorously maintained.

As a result, Mangaung was considered one of the country's most secure prisons, second only perhaps to the supermax prisons in Kokstad and Pretoria. So when JICS investigators received the report that Mr Bester had burned to death in a locked single cell, without drawing the attention of any of the overnight duty officials, their scepticism was immediately activated. The further evolution of the scandal is now a matter of public record.

Sifting through hours of CCTV footage, interviewing dozens of witnesses and analysing medical records, JICS investigators, Ms Dineo Mocumi, later assisted by Mr Oduleng Thakadu, and JICS's head of investigations and inspections, Mr Lennard de Souza, deduced that, far from dying alone in his cell, Mr Bester had made a remarkable escape. Officials must have smuggled a corpse into the prison to fake his death – and by massive collusion managed to elude the prison's supposedly high-tech surveillance and security systems. The fire burned the replacement corpse almost beyond recognition, suggesting that a propellant must have been applied.

JICS communicated its suspicions to G4S, SAPS and the Department of Correctional Services, including the Minister, but months passed and nothing was done. G4S did not appear to take JICS's concerns seriously. Its senior management continued to insist – defying the evidence JICS advanced – that the corpse was Bester's, that he had died by suicide, and that the incident was not an escape.

The department meanwhile appeared to take inordinate time in producing a comprehensive investigation report. And though SAPS agreed with JICS's conclusions, no urgent effort was made to rearrest Bester. It transpired that Bester was living lavishly with a celebrity medical doctor, Nandipha Magudumana, in one of Johannesburg's most luxurious suburbs. JICS noted that Magudumana had frequently visited Bester at Mangaung. In the face of institutional inaction, JICS determined that public exposure was necessary.

GroundUp news[358] unmasked the fraud. After exposure, as the net began to close around him, Bester and Dr Magudumana, his alleged co-conspirator, fled to Tanzania, where they were arrested. They are both currently in prison, standing trial for the escape.

How could Bester have pulled this off? Only with ample heavyweight help and careful high-level co-ordination. JICS and the department's investigations untangled a web of conspiracy and corruption. Even before his escape, Bester was apparently allowed to flout the rules at Mangaung. He was able to run a business and appear in online webinars (supposedly from New York City) while incarcerated. He is alleged to have left the prison for romantic getaways with Dr Magudumana. To facilitate his escape, officials looked away when the corpse, secreted in a wooden cabinet, was smuggled into Mangaung. On the night of his escape, cameras mysteriously stopped recording or were turned away at crucial times. Officials were directed away from Bester's unit by their supervisors. During the investigation, officials gave contradictory and suspicious testimony, while inmates told JICS that prison officials intimidated and threatened them. And G4S top management appeared unaccountably evasive.

Bester's corrupt and collusive escape enthralled and outraged the public. Rightly so. But corruption burdens virtually all South Africa's prisons. Officials have candidly conceded to us that almost all contraband enters via corrupt officials. The thriving trade in cell phones, drugs and weapons – knives and sometimes even firearms – could not exist without official collusion.[359] JICS has heard repeated allegations that, when officials raid cells and confiscate contraband cell phones, the very same cell phones are traded back to other prisoners. Sometimes, those cell phones appear weeks later in other prisons across the country. The seemingly plausible inference is that some officials may be involved in nationwide smuggling.

Corruption flourishes in strictly hierarchical environments, where lack of accountability and transparency means that basic needs are unmet.

Bester's escape is instructive on prisons and JICS's role. Though the outcome creditably displays the skill, commitment and courage of JICS's investigators, failure by G4S and others to respond to JICS's urgent interventions shows JICS's limitations: it is an oversight body with little operational power. What good is JICS's voice when those with power ignore it?

3. Engaging with stakeholders and the public

Oversight bodies can spark debate on how our society deals with crime and punishment. JICS's work challenges that of the Parliamentary Portfolio Committee on Correctional Services, the Minister of Correctional Services and his deputy, as well as the Department of Correctional Services and the National Commissioner. JICS highlights the alarming increase in the number of lifers, the plight of those who cannot afford bail, and dysfunction in the halting and inefficient parole system. JICS has urged Parliament to abolish mandatory minimum sentences and to abandon the calamitously misdirected 'war on drugs'.

In addition, through hosting webinars, conducting TV and radio interviews, developing an X social media account, and publishing opinion pieces designed to provoke debate, JICS engages and seeks to shift public views.[360] Oversight keeps correctional officials vigilant and holds them legally and morally accountable – while offering them a chance to articulate the issues that imperil their own functioning. This shows how the 'culture of a prison changes when outsiders shine a light on its operations and conditions'.[361]

JICS's investigations often uncover abuse, misconduct or negligence on the part of officials. While it can, and does, urge disciplinary or criminal proceedings against those officials, JICS cannot initiate or ensure these itself. JICS has engaged the leadership of the NPA to try to secure prosecutions of at least the most egregious instances.

A number of cases all too vividly demonstrate JICS's regrettable powerlessness. A grievous instance is the killing of an inmate at Boksburg prison, Inmate Y, in October 2018. The department held its own officials liable for the death – yet their sole reproof was final written warnings. So as far as JICS knows, the department still employs all those complicit in the death of Inmate Y. As we write, towards the end of 2024, SAPS is still engaged in what we understand is its investigation. The investigating officer has, however, retired; a new one has taken over. Inmate Y's father continues to press, grievingly, unavailingly, for progress.[362]

JICS's inspections and reports have confronted the deeds of correctional officials and positively engaged them. Some raise problems in their job conditions with JICS. Thus, some officials urge more librarian and social worker posts in correctional facilities as well as better access to working public telephones for inmates. This suggests that independent oversight and input may enable safer and better-functioning prisons – to the benefit of inmates, correctional officials, families, loved ones, taxpayers, and victims and survivors of crime.

4. Encouraging innovation

JICS has urged innovative solutions to longstanding problems. And JICS has helped open doors and create connections for individuals and organisations who want to work in prisons when bureaucratic red tape blocks their energies.

As we mentioned earlier, JICS initiated a book donations drive, which has received the indispensable support and partnership of NICRO. JICS also supports the work of Stellenbosch University's Dr Mary Nel, whose educational partnership with the department seeks to rehumanise learning through the Ubuntu Learning Community at Brandvlei prison.

JICS secured the support of then-incumbent Deputy Minister Phathekile Holomisa for Dr Joel Steingo and the United States Centers for Disease Control (CDC)'s TB HIV Care. This ensured a new co-operative agreement with the US President's Emergency Plan for AIDS Relief (PEPFAR) to establish a best practice model. To make the department a world leader in providing HIV, TB and hepatitis prevention and treatment services.

The aim is ambitious: to make the department a world leader in providing HIV, TB and hepatitis prevention and treatment services – though this may have been thwarted by the new Administration's brutal cut-backs in February 2025 to all aid programs worldwide.

JICS helped Just Detention International South Africa (JDI-SA), an organisation committed to curtailing sexual abuse in prisons, to gain access to transform the department's sexual abuse prevention curriculum into a standard correctional official training.

When private benefactors approached JICS to intervene in prisons, JICS proposed a South African bail fund to assist non-violent indigent inmates who cannot afford bail of R1 000 or less. Right now, JICS is seeking to expedite a bail fund pilot project.

Inside out: prisons oversight in South Africa at 25 years

In his moving book *Just Mercy*, Bryan Stevenson reflects on wise advice he received from his grandmother. She told him 'you have to get close' and that one 'can't understand most of the important things from a distance'.[363] It is a simple and significant lesson – get close to the issues you care about. Stevenson explains how this insight shaped his work and life: 'proximity to the condemned and incarcerated made the question of each person's humanity more urgent and meaningful'.[364] And from working closely with incarcerated people, many on death row in the USA, he learned that each of us 'is more than the worst thing we've ever done'.[365]

The 'power of proximity' lesson resonates deeply with JICS's work. To address human rights abuses and reform our prisons, we have to get close to prisons and the people inside them. This is precisely what prisons oversight seeks to do. Progress requires outsiders to enter prisons and engage first-hand with prisoners and correctional officials.

Prisons oversight in South Africa is just over a quarter-century old. After 25 years, JICS remains bereft of all operational, managerial and executive power. An inmate from Brandvlei explained, helpfully though mortifyingly, that as a watchdog, 'JICS has a bark but no bite.' Indeed. And our prisons are under-resourced and under-capacitated. This hobbles JICS's work every day. Mismanagement of government funds, plus fiscal austerity, deprives prisons of essential funds.

In contrast to the department's billion-rand budget (almost R27 billion for 2024, though in fact it spent closer to R28 billion), JICS has a budget of about R100 million a year. With these resources, it is tasked to oversee 243 prisons, approximately 40 000 personnel (DCS currently employs 37 110 officials, though it has an approved establishment of 42 433 posts), and more than 150 000 inmates. It has only eight inspectors and investigators. JICS cannot afford to permanently hire intrepid ICCVs, who stand closest to the problems we try to address.

Ideally, JICS should flex its muscles through adequate statutory and regulatory powers. More dedicated, talented and well-trained personnel should join. Much can be done to rigorously obtain, evaluate and employ data – statistics, figures, head counts. On these, Lukas Muntingh, director of the Dullah Omar Institute at the University of the Western Cape, has helpfully pointed out that the department once shared detailed, comprehensive statistics with the public. As a public institution, it should do nothing less. Yet, this stopped suddenly in 2011. This thwarts civil society's efforts to advocate for reform. JICS has tried to bridge the resulting chasm by sharing the statistics it has available to it. Though JICS already collaborates with civil society on training for officials, seminars, advocacy and litigation, there is room for more collaboration. And inmates and families should be made aware about what JICS can (and cannot) do.

Some problems may be beyond JICS, or any prisons oversight body, however. Prisons pose particular problems when, as is often the case, their crises stem from systemic failures. Prison reform nevertheless remains an imperative goal, however many doubts and obstructions beset it.

5

Corrections at a Crossroads – Prison Reform in Theory

This book bears first-hand witness to the griefs and injustices of our prisons. In early 2025, as we write this, no one can plausibly dispute that South Africa's approach to crime and punishment has failed. It is not working for us, who want to sleep at night knowing that we and those we love are safe. It is not working for victims and survivors of crime, who do not trust our criminal justice system and justifiably doubt its effectiveness. It is not working for inmates, who are cramped, serving over-long sentences, in overcrowded cells, with no meaningful rehabilitation. It is not working for government, which is responsible for the inordinate expense of incarceration – while accounting for why crime and murder rates remain sky high.

So, where to from here?

There are three possible avenues. First, we build more prisons. Some contend that this will address overcrowding issues and inhumane conditions of incarceration[366] but, as we have tried to explain, more people incarcerated for longer periods of time will not help with violent crime in our country. Plus, it is an expensive and ineffective option. English Prison Commissioner Sir Alexander Paterson noted that 'Wherever prisons are built, the courts will fill them.'[367]

Second, we abolish prisons. We do away with prisons altogether. We acknowledge the failure of the experiment of mass incarceration and increased sentencing and consider other, radical, solutions.

Third, we rethink our approaches to crime and punishment – and substantively reform our prisons.

Most of us are familiar with proposals to build more prisons or reform existing ones. Prison abolition, in contrast, is unfamiliar and difficult to conceive of. We begin our chapter by asking: why is reform so difficult? Despite efforts by prison officials, oversight bodies and civil society, prisons are resistant, even seem immune to, reform. In this chapter, we hope to provoke a much-needed debate on the possibility of prison reform and prison abolition in South Africa. We discuss the alternatives to prisons that abolitionists and reformers propose, the measures we might take to move towards a society without prisons, and how abolitionist ideas can be used to reform our current criminal justice system. Finally, we consider the complexities of abolition – and we affirm that reform is worth pursuing.

Why is reform so difficult?

Reform is more easily demanded than accomplished. A central problem is that we turn our gaze away from prisons. For understandable reasons, we avoid contemplating effective reform. Why?

First, as we acknowledged in Chapter 1, we are haunted by the spectre of an irreformably evil Hannibal Lecter.[368] It is inescapable that some humans are terribly dangerous to others and may have to be locked up in isolation from those vulnerable to their harm.

Second, we all have immediate reasons to be apprehensive about crime. South Africa has one of the highest rates of violent crime in the world. We all dread the violent intrusion on our lives that may damage all that is precious to us. Those of us somewhat protected from crime by where we live, our mobility, our status, even our race, must humble ourselves before the rage and fear that crime plants deep in the hearts of South Africans.

Third, crime management in South Africa is driven by race and class and elite protection. Crime enforcement seems stand-offish about the well connected who perpetrate corruption and who seize state apparatus to loot. By contrast, those convicted of drug use or sale, and sex work, experience harsh criminal laws and a broken prison system. Poverty often means harshness for perpetrators and disregard for victims. Too often, we meet the disjuncture with apathy.

Fourth, if we do too little about crime, people take vengeance themselves. They already do. As corruption and institutional dysfunction have eaten away at our criminal justice institutions, vigilantes have flourished. 'Vigilante justice' is horrific but before we sanctimoniously condemn it, we must acknowledge this: vigilantism is a response to the failure of us, the political elite, to care about those most vulnerable to crime. The poor and the dispossessed seek justice too.

In the early hours of 19 May 2021, in Zandspruit informal settlement, a large group of some 200 people kidnapped nine young men whom they said had been terrorising their community. They awoke them in their homes, undressed them and beat them, then marched them to a field where paraffin-soaked tyres were placed around their necks and set alight. Annah Moyo-Kupeta from the Centre for the Study of Violence and Reconciliation explains how this horrific ritual, 'necklacing them with tyres and setting them alight', evokes 'the apartheid-era style of dealing with impimpis'.[369] Most of them died a horrific death. Their deaths are part of a larger pattern.

Karl Kemp explains the 'new vigilantism': 'Every three months, like clockwork, the number of murders attributable to mob justice creeps up ... out of the just over 27 000 people murdered in South Africa in 2022, roughly 7 per cent perished by mob justice.'[370] In fact, in the three sets of quarterly crime statistics SAPS released for the 2023/24 period, vigilantism and mob justice were the second leading causative factors for murder – outdone only by the broad category of 'Arguments/Misunderstanding/Road Rage/Provocation'.[371] Kemp rightly observes: 'for those who would ask why this is happening, the cynic might perhaps say, *Well, just take a look around.* The evidence is everywhere.'[372]

The anger and fear of a crime-ridden public are well warranted. We ourselves – the academic and intellectual elite, the politicians, the lawyers, the writers, the judges and leaders – bear part of the blame, for we have power to do things that will make our country safer.

Meanwhile, it is true that prisons are resistant to reform. And they do tend to foster abuse. Prisons are closed off and isolated. This is not incidental. As we explained in Chapter 2, the very purpose is to remove punishment from the public eye. Their darkness makes it harder to change them for the better.

Given our fear of crime and 'populist punitiveness', prisoners have almost no social or political clout.[373] Even in vibrant democracies, prisoners are minorities, and their issues are crowded out by the political system, thus making it difficult for prison reform and non-punitive measures to be placed on the political agenda. Academics explain that '[p]enal parsimony and care for offenders are difficult sells at the best of times'.[374]

This is not only a point about democratic political processes but also our shared humanity. When we dehumanise prisoners and frame them as 'the other', we make reform infinitely more difficult. Angela Davis aptly points out that it is too agonising to think that anyone, including ourselves, could become a prisoner. So we think of prisons as disconnected from our own lives and imprisonment 'as a fate reserved for others', for 'evildoers': the prison is 'an abstract site into which undesirables are deposited'.[375]

Even when we learn of human rights violations in prisons, there is generally little outcry, demand for accountability or pressure for change. Many of us approve of harsh treatment of prisoners. Some think that the abuse and violence experienced in prison is part of the punishment. All this impedes improvement.

Prisons are settings of structural violence. Prisons are autocratic, with extreme power imbalances, both between prisoners and officials and between prisoners themselves. The hierarchies are enforced by violence, gang structures, rape and other forms of coercive power. Based on the evidence of prisoners who testified before the Jali Commission, sex in prisons is a 'tradeable commodity'.[376] Power disparities make prisoners particularly vulnerable to abuse. So, too, does the fact that prisoners live entirely dependent lives: to survive, they depend on the decisions of others. So reform within these complex power dynamics becomes increasingly difficult.

But change can be achieved. In fact, it is feasible to create prisons that are not solely punitive and retributive. Prisons based on penal moderation.[377] Prisons that ensure humane treatment and decent conditions while also reforming individuals not to re-offend. Prisons that provide for proportionate forms of punishment.

Nordic prisons present a sharp contrast to those South Africans and Americans know. Nordic countries have paid heed to the sombre truth that many inmates are honed inside to emerge with enhanced criminal skills, and so their prison design and management aim for rehabilitation (to reform behaviour or intentions), normalisation (to ensure that prison life resembles life outside so that individuals can effectively reintegrate into society), and humanisation (treatment and conditions in line with human rights standards).

In Finland, for instance, some inmates serve time in open prisons – meaning prisons with nominal restrictions and hierarchies.[378] Inmates can leave daily for work or education.[379] Their cellblocks resemble dorms. There is a gym. Inmates wear their own clothes. They eat sitting alongside correctional officials. Electronic monitors check family visits. The Finnish prison system is based on 'gentle justice', focusing on harm reduction. This reduces costs and diminishes the prison population.[380] The focus is on rehabilitating inmates and ensuring they become law-abiding citizens.

Norway also features open prisons. Halden and Bastøy, for example, accommodate men who have committed crimes shortly before they are released. Open prisons seek 'dynamic security' – preventing bad intentions as opposed to bad behaviour. A Bastøy official explained: 'Treat people like dirt, and they'll be dirt. Treat them like human beings, and they'll act like human beings.'[381]

Are these solutions idealistic, expensive, perhaps luxurious? Of course. Are they effective? Do they curb crime? The results say: yes. Compared to South Africa's high recidivism rates (approximately 60% to 90%),[382] Norway and Finland have markedly low recidivism rates (around 20% and 30%, respectively).[383] In addition, although the immediate cost is high, their inmates are less likely to re-offend and more likely to find employment and pay taxes. So the long-term benefits of humane forms of incarceration outweigh the costs of punitive imprisonment.[384]

All this is possible without failing to take crime seriously. One example: in 2018, Sweden amended its Criminal Code to introduce the crime of 'negligent rape', criminalising gross negligence in establishing lack of consent with a sexual partner.[385] This suggests that it is possible to take crime seriously while treating imprisoned people humanely.

To be sure, we are not in Scandinavia or Finland. Those countries have strong economies, small, relatively homogeneous populations with (at least until recently) low crime, and excellent welfare benefits. But it would be a mistake to dismiss the Nordic approach as unattainable. Our neighbour to our north, Zambia, established open-air prisons (including farms) coupled with an inmate management unit and alternatives to prisons for juvenile offenders.[386] The aim was to reduce overcrowding and maximise rehabilitation and community-based corrections. This experiment, in our region, may inspire and spur us to do better.

There are key lessons to keep in mind. The Nordic experience suggests that evidence-based reform is possible.[387] Political commitment is essential. But here we should, as in other areas, heed the experts and the evidence they marshal. When we do this, we must acknowledge that the 'war on crime' and mass incarceration have not just brought us nowhere. They have taken us backwards.

Lessons from abolitionists and reformers

Debates about abolition and reform spark contesting views – even among peaceable co-authors. Abolition and reform have much in common, though their end goals are distinct. Foucault denounced reform as an attempt to control the functioning of prisons. '"Reform" [the philosopher's own quotation marks] is virtually contemporary with the prison itself' – and it does not spring from a remorseful sense of failing:

> From the outset, the prison was caught up in a series of accompanying mechanisms, whose purpose was apparently to correct it, but which seem to form part of its very functioning, so closely have they been bound up with its existence throughout its long history.[388]

Prisons have for centuries been a focus for reformers. Since the 1700s, there have been reports, inquiries into prison conditions, debates about forms of punishment and rehabilitation (including solitary confinement), establishment of oversight bodies tasked with 'supervising the functioning of the prisons and for suggesting improvements', advocacy by philanthropic groups, and laws and policies to improve the functioning of prisons and treatment of prisoners.[389]

In South Africa, as we have seen, the Constitution promised dignified conditions of detention: but, as with many other visionary projects of our democracy, we haven't quite managed.

Does reform work? And is it enough? Some answer: no. The prison abolition movement envisages a world without prisons. Though abolitionists generally support reforms to improve the experiences of those currently incarcerated, they envision a society in which prisons are not necessary to keep people safe. They distinguish themselves in this way:

> Reforming the prison entails changing its existing practices to make the system a better one. Abolishing the prison entails dismantling it wholesale. Reformers object to how the prison is administered. Abolitionists object to the prison's very existence.[390]

Prison abolition seems new and radical, but it is not. It, too, has a long history. It can be traced back 'to the historical appearance of the prison as the main form of punishment'.[391] More recently, it has sprung from the Black radical tradition and from how prisons and mass incarceration help enforce white domination in the United States.[392] Abolitionists are of course concerned about inhumane and degrading conditions in prison, but their focus is not on Foucault's 'extra chocolate bar on Christmas'; it is on the social function of prisons. Foucault, as we have noted, claimed that this is 'to serve as the instrument that creates a criminal milieu that the ruling classes can control'.[393] For abolitionists, prisons were not created and do not function to keep us safe. And indeed, it is true that prison populations have little correlation to crime rates.[394]

Rather, prisons are institutions created to enforce control, to maintain power and to reinforce unjust hierarchies; they serve to warehouse those we deem disposable (including at various times poor people, Black people, immigrants, people with mental health issues, vulnerable women and queer people). The demography of prisons, in South Africa and elsewhere, attests to this.

Abolitionists contend that this function is inherent to prisons. It cannot be reformed away. Reform implies prisons are in an unsatisfactory state, but may be repaired or corrected. Instead, abolitionists say, prisons function just as intended. They are sceptical of reform also because reforms may merely strengthen the carceral state, by pumping more money and personnel into the prison system and enabling it to do more harm. They point out that, in America, reforms have often merely enhanced the state's capacity to punish. Thus –

reforms of indeterminate sentencing led to mandatory minimums, the death penalty to life without parole, sexual violence against gender-nonconforming people gave rise to 'gender-responsive' prisons. Instead of pushing to adopt the Finnish model of incarceration – itself a far-fetched enterprise – abolitionists have engaged these contradictions by pursuing reforms that shrink the state's capacity for violence.[395]

Focusing on reform can legitimise prisons and foreclose discussion about alternatives. Angela Davis, in *Are Prisons Obsolete?*, writes that:

As important as some reforms may be – the elimination of sexual abuse and medical neglect in women's prison, for example – frameworks that rely exclusively on reforms help to produce the stultifying idea that nothing lies beyond the prison. Debates about strategies of decarceration, which should be the focal point of our conversations on the prison crisis, tend to be marginalized when reform takes the center stage.[396]

Finally, abolitionists contend that reform is not enough: though it may improve conditions, it cannot remedy the fundamental indignity and inhumanity of locking people up under strict control and surveillance for large parts of their lives. The Statewide Harm Reduction Coalition explains that: 'A cage is a cage is a cage. We want strategies that let people out of cages, not ones that are for building nicer or better cages.'[397] However persuasive or unpersuasive one may find these arguments, abolitionists critically spice a conversation that has been dominated by carceral voices. Abolitionists have helped shift public thinking in the

United States. They have popularised alternatives to the prison system. Grassroots abolitionist organisations have grown, forming connections with other social movements, sparking campaigns and gaining victories. One was the 'first ever reparations package for survivors of racialized law enforcement violence in the US'.[398]

Abolitionists distinguish between reforms that pour more resources into the prison system, lend it legitimacy and expand its reach, and those that 'reduce rather than strengthen the scale and scope of policing, imprisonment, and surveillance'.[399] Improvements that abolitionists do pursue, reformers should also embrace. These include abolishing cash bail, decriminalising drug use, sex work and petty crimes, supporting non-custodial measures and implementing restorative justice. Perhaps most importantly, abolitionists remind us that safer communities are possible only when we find solutions to violence itself by addressing its deep social roots. In working towards these reforms, abolitionists are allies – often leaders – in the fight against over-incarceration.

But if we do abolish prisons, how will we inhibit those who may harm? And punish those who do? What will keep us safe? This may seem an intractable question because, to us, prisons seem 'self-evident'. Foucault notes how, almost since their inception, prisons have seemed irreplaceable. In the first years of the nineteenth century, he writes, people were still aware of the prison's novelty; and yet it seemed 'so bound up and at such a deep level with the very functioning of society' that it supplanted 'all the other punishments that the eighteenth-century reformers had imagined' – there seemed to be no alternative. He dubbed prison 'the detestable solution, which one seems unable to do without':

And, although, in a little over a century, this self-evident character has become transformed, it has not disappeared. We are aware of all the inconveniences of prison and that it is dangerous when it is not useless. And yet one cannot 'see' how to replace it.[400]

131

Abolitionists grapple with how to replace prisons. Rather than calling for overnight closure, they contend that we can work to gradually reduce the role that prisons play in our societies by creating a 'constellation of alternative structures' of safety and justice.[401] Eventually, prisons may in this way become obsolete and cease to exist.

And abolitionists point out that prisons do not exist in isolation. They are supported in their repressive aims by an entire system, of inequality and deprivation, that helps induce criminality. Hence, abolitionist alternatives consist not of a single institutional replacement but a range of alternative strategies and support systems. Abolition means not just closing prisons 'but the presence, instead, of vital systems of support that many communities lack':

> Instead of asking how, in a future without prisons, we will deal with so-called violent people, abolitionists ask how we resolve inequalities and get people the resources they need long before the hypothetical moment when . . . they 'mess up'.[402]

Among the most urgent measures for which abolitionists advocate are the twinned measures of decriminalisation and decarceration. These entail reducing the areas of life into which the carceral system and prisons intrude by trimming use of pre-trial detention, decriminalising petty offences, immigration, sex work, and drug use (along with providing affordable, effective and voluntary drug treatment programmes).[403] They also entail not building new prisons, and opposing expansion of punishment through, for example, hate crime laws and surveillance.[404]

In the United States, abolitionists effectively campaigned against new prisons, with successes in California and other states.[405] While the present temper in America has shifted markedly against decriminalisation, these remain important steps in reducing the role of prisons in public life and the public imagination. In place of prisons (and with financial and other

132

resources they would otherwise devour) abolitionists support a network of strategies to prevent harm.

Some abolitionists urge redistributing wealth and power to combat the harms that arise from abuses of power and inequality.[406] They advocate for free and quality education, free and quality healthcare, including psychological healthcare and voluntary addiction services, social welfare and robust social services to build a society in which people are not pushed into poverty and desperation.[407] In order to combat gender-based violence, some feminist abolitionists seek to counter patriarchal attitudes, through community engagements and public education.[408] They depart from carceral feminism (advocacy of harsher sentences as a way to combat violence against women)[409] and call for free childcare, well-funded shelters, affordable housing, pensions and income grants that allow victims of domestic abuse to escape abusive settings before they become violent or fatal.[410]

These alternatives, abolitionists believe, would be more effective at combating the root causes of harm. They would 'eventually start to crowd out the prison so that it would inhabit increasingly smaller areas of our social and psychic landscape'.[411]

But abolitionists understand that harm will occur, even in a world where needs are more fairly met. To address this, abolitionists support transformative and restorative justice rather than purely punitive systems. They are not alone in this. Many reformers also see the value of moving away from a punitive approach to criminal justice.

Punitive or retributive justice focuses on the individual perpetrator. It defines crime narrowly, and prioritises punishment ('just deserts', or, you must get what you deserve). Since the state and the offender are the primary actors in punitive models, victims have lesser agency and rarely receive reparation.

Transformative justice, by contrast, seeks to understand how we all cause harm and are harmed by others. Hence it addresses *systemic* causes of harm.[412] Under such a system, the needs of the victim and the humanity of the perpetrator are central. The priority is to enquire how to meet immediate justice needs such as ensuring safety, ending harmful behaviour and achieving holistic accountability for each specific situation while also working in the long term to remedy the conditions that allow harm to happen. This approach is specific to each situation. It may include accountability circles, community safety plans such as childcare and walking people home, study groups to allow people to learn about harm and justice together, accessible healing and trauma services, conflict mediation practices, and community interventions.[413]

Restorative justice aims to involve the perpetrator, victim, families and the community collectively to identify and address harms, needs and obligations through accepting responsibility, making restitution, taking measures to prevent a recurrence and promoting reconciliation.[414] It focuses on the needs of the impacted individuals – the victims and survivors – to repair the harm and promote reintegration.[415] Generally, it involves a meeting between the victim of the crime and the perpetrator (it may include community members); the perpetrator typically expresses remorse for the harm caused and agrees to take action to repair the harm. An analysis of studies that compared restorative justice outcomes against conventional criminal justice systems came to a strikingly hopeful conclusion.[416] Restorative justice outperformed imprisonment in reducing repeat offending, reducing victims' post-traumatic stress symptoms, costs and desire for revenge.[417] Both victims and perpetrators reported greater requital.

Many abolitionists and reformers advocate for a combination of transformative and restorative justice programmes. They do so pragmatically and within existing criminal justice systems.

Transformative and restorative justice are not 'soft' options for only petty or non-violent crimes. Proponents urge that restorative justice can be used to reduce mass incarceration – in the form of pre-trial diversion programmes, as an alternative to sentencing or to reduce the sentence imposed.[418] Adriaan Lanni explains that 'the case for restorative justice is not that it promises to radically reduce recidivism, but that it offers a better way to do justice while doing no worse, and likely at least modestly better, than the criminal legal system at reducing recidivism.'[419] There are also pragmatic and moral arguments in favour of restorative justice. Distinguished American legal professor Martha Minow urges that legal officials and institutions should promote forgiveness between individuals, rather than blame:[420] 'To ask how law may forgive is not to deny the fact of wrongdoing. Rather, it is to widen the lens . . . to work for new choices that can be enabled by wiping the slate clean.'[421]

Restorative justice is not starry dreaming. It has been incorporated into South African law and practice. Our TRC is a leading example of restorative justice at work. In the context of everyday crimes, the 2016 White Paper on Corrections affirms that the principles of restorative justice shape the Department of Correctional Services' approach to corrections. Practically, this includes:

> [A]ddressing offences committed and assisting the offender to take accountability for such offence, which may include restoration of relations with victims where appropriate; addressing offences suffered and assisting the victim to reach a stage of forgiveness; addressing anti-social addictions and anti-social habits and thus promote rational thinking, good decision-making and positive behaviour; the promotion of restoration of the offender as a member of the family; the promotion of restoration of communities and community institutions and good governance and enhanced social cohesion.[422]

Currently, the department facilitates victim offender dialogues (VODs) between inmates and those they have harmed. This seeks to encourage the restoration of relations, reintegration and rehabilitation. During the 2022/23 period, the department reported that an impressive 14 844 victims of crime and 4 498 offenders, parolees and probationers participated in VODs and mediation.[423] It is of pivotal importance in rehabilitation and parole,[424] though it may sometimes seem anguishingly ineffective.[425]

Restorative justice plays a more significant role in child justice. There, it is often an alternative to punitive justice.[426] The preamble of the Child Justice Act says that one of its purposes is 'to entrench the notion of restorative justice in the criminal justice system in respect of children who are in conflict with the law'.

When a child is accused of a crime, the statute requires that the matter be diverted away from formal criminal proceedings or that courts consider non-custodial sentences, including community-based sentences, restorative justice sentences, fines or alternatives to fines, or sentences of correctional supervision.[427]

In *S v M*, the Constitutional Court espoused the benefits of restorative justice and non-custodial sentences.[428] The High Court sentenced the mother, who was the primary caregiver of three children, to prison for fraud. The question was whether the court had paid sufficient attention to the best interests of the children. The mother's sentence was one from which she could be placed under correctional supervision after eight months. The Constitutional Court upheld the mother's appeal. It ordered that the mother be released to serve a sentence of correctional supervision, including community service and regular counselling. It also required the mother to repay all those she had defrauded. On correctional supervision, the Court noted that, unlike imprisonment, it keeps open the option of restorative justice:

Central to the notion of restorative justice is the recognition of the community rather than the criminal justice agencies as the prime site of crime control. Thus, our courts have observed that one of

136

its strengths is that it rehabilitates the offender within the community, without the negative impact of prison and destruction of the family. It is geared to punish and rehabilitate the offender within the community leaving his or her work and domestic routines intact, and without the negative influences of prison.[429]

A central component of restorative justice is its capacity to confront (and at least not perpetuate) the stigma and shame associated with criminality.

In *The New Jim Crow*, Michelle Alexander perceptively highlights the close inter-connections between racial subordination and stigma, and between criminalisation and stigma.[430] She explains that the 'stigma of race was once the shame of the slave; then it was the shame of the second-class citizen; today the stigma of race is the shame of the criminal'.[431] She discusses the damaging impact of when shame and stigma attach to criminality and how individuals in conflict with the law are perceived as 'pariahs' and doomed to be in 'social exile'. These markers remain even after release:

> As Dorsey Nunn, an ex-offender and cofounder of All of Us or None, once put it, 'The biggest hurdle you gotta get over when you walk out those prison gates is shame – that shame, that stigma, that label, that thing you wear around your neck saying "I'm a criminal." It's like a yoke around your neck, and it'll drag you down, even kill you if you let it.'[432]

When stigma attaches to criminality, it translates into the collateral consequences of incarceration, where the label of being a criminal can bar one from employment, custody of children and social benefits – but may also bring ostracism and alienation from one's family, loved ones and community.

Can we at least try to challenge this shame and stigma? In *Crime, Shame and Reintegration*, criminologist John Braithwaite insightfully explains the difference between *stigmatised shaming* as opposed to *reintegrative shaming*.[433]

Stigmatised shaming strikes at the individual – at the person's core. They are *a bad person*, and must be treated as an outcast with the indelible label 'criminal'. There is no room or incentive for rehabilitation; rather, further criminal activity and recidivism rates perpetuate when one is branded a criminal. Why try to reform if you will always be seen as a criminal? Why not join a gang where criminal activity flourishes?

By contrast, *reintegrative shaming* focuses on criminal conduct – a bad deed can be committed even by a good person, or at least a person who can take responsibility for their actions, be forgiven and reintegrate into their community as a law-abiding citizen. If you are redeemable after bad behaviour, it is worth reforming and not repeating criminal acts. The key point is that criminal activity should incur some condemnation. When one commits a violent act, they should be judged. But how condemned? And how shamed? The type of shame and how it is communicated matters. According to Braithwaite, when shaming stigmatises, it is counterproductive: it makes crime worse. Yet, when it is reintegrative, it may prevent crime.[434] 'Societies that degrade and humiliate criminals,' Braithwaite says, 'have higher crime rates.'[435]

Restorative justice carves out an avenue for forgiveness and reintegration into communities. At least some evidence supports the positive impact of reintegrative shaming and shame acknowledgement through restorative justice programmes.[436]

South Africans have grappled with stigma – the stigma of racial subordination and exclusion under apartheid, the stigma of HIV and AIDS, the stigma of queerness. They know not just the external labels that stigma applies but its injurious inner effects, when external condemnation finds an internal voice, one that endorses what is learned, wrongly, from outside.[437] Our national experience of stigma may help us to understand its dangers, its damaging effects, when we try to find a way of reducing our crime levels.

Criminologist Casper Lötter rightly notes that, along with socio-economic inequality, and politicised exploitation of crime and imperatives to retain prisons, a stigmatised shaming culture plays a role in our high recidivism rate and low rehabilitation rate.[438] A fundamental reform is to ensure that programmes focus on restorative justice and that these cater for reintegrative shaming while acknowledging the humanity of those who have committed criminal acts.

This accords with our constitutional vision of dignified approaches to punishment. And it also has practical value, in reducing our high recidivism rate. And it calls on us – as a society – to reconsider how we judge, ostracise, shame and stigmatise those who have been in conflict with the law.

From punishment to progress?

Abolitionists' and reformers' debates about prisons find their mark in our country. We rely on long sentences and confinement to prisons to solve our overwhelming crime problem, and yet we are no safer. This itself shows us that something is gravely amiss. In the United States, abolitionism and decarceration and curtailment of over-long sentences are publicly debated. As we've mentioned before, in the United Kingdom, Prisons Minister James Timpson has articulated a commitment to rehabilitation and reform.[439] By contrast, we South Africans seem loth to challenge the existence, effectiveness or fairness of our prisons. We prefer not to talk about how ineffectual our long sentences are, and how damaging our prisons.

As we've said, we turn our gaze away. We are angry and scared. We find it difficult to contemplate reform, let alone abolition. Violent crime is rampant, and we have lost trust in our criminal justice system. Our human urge for retribution is stronger than ever. We are so scared of drowning we are not able to learn to swim.

It is true that, because we have not had these debates here, abolitionist theories may seem far removed from us. Can these ideas resonate with a deeply unequal society ravaged by violent crime? Or are they hopelessly misplaced?

We understand all too well why many dismiss abolition. During our prison inspections, we have met those who have done unspeakably terrible things. We have worked to ensure access to healthcare for prisoners who have been convicted of child pornography and to challenge solitary confinement for people who have been convicted of murder, or who run criminal gangs from their cells.

We do this not because we ignore what some have done, but because we recognise a common humanity – and because we recognise, too, the inhumanity of what we, their jailers, are doing now. It is our own humanity, the humanity of our society, that is at stake when our prisons fail. Overwhelmingly, the prison officials we meet agree that sentences are over-long; that prisons are over-used and under-equipped; that we rely, futilely, on incarceration to solve societal problems.

Our experience in prisons has shown us that some harm others in terrible ways, but they have also left us in no doubt that we need radical change. Through our questions and doubts, we see how our dire predicament with crime and prisons demands new ideas. Whether convinced by abolition or reform, or neither, we know their proponents can enrich our national debate with critiques and reforms that challenge traditional wisdom. Whether working towards an abolitionist vision or merely trying to achieve more dignified, humane prisons, effective reforms are urgently imperative.

6

From Cells to Solutions – Practicable Prison Reforms

Now we get practical. To give effect to our constitutional promise of humane and dignified treatment, there are measures that can reasonably be implemented both inside and outside prisons. They aim to keep us all safer, to decrease the numbers we lock up and significantly to improve conditions for those inside.

In this chapter, we show how practicable steps to improve our prisons are possible. They can be implemented simultaneously, or one after another. These steps do not seek to abolish the prison system. They address a two-sided problem. Our prison system is *over-inclusive* (severely over-crowded with huge numbers of remand detainees awaiting trial, and with inmates serving over-long sentences); yet also *under-inclusive* (because too often the most dangerous and 'deserving' criminals escape prosecution and prison, or are mistakenly paroled).

Can we ensure that those who commit violent and other dreadful acts are removed from society while being given a chance to rehabilitate in less overcrowded prisons? Yes, this is feasible. Our national debate on crime and prisons is stuck in a dangerous donga – to the detriment of us all. Policymakers, politicians, lawyers, judges, legislatures, researchers and the public can search for fresh ideas, fresh practical plans to deal with crime, while also improving our overstuffed, rancid prisons.

1. Improve policing, starting with crime intelligence

Violent crime has been rising since the Zuma presidency eviscerated crime intelligence in 2011. Long mandatory sentences have done nothing to stop this rise. What does? It is the *certainty* of detection, arrest, arraignment, trial and prison. It is the *certainty* of getting caught. This means that effective policing, based on effective crime intelligence,[440] must be our first step – not longer and harsher sentences.

Yet the yearning for harsher sentences is understandable. It springs from the legitimate concern that, when awful crimes occur, the criminal justice system does not do enough to hold offenders accountable and to prevent recurrence. And the public's angry perception that not enough offenders are arrested, charged, convicted, and sentenced to prison is correct.

Our news headlines trumpet crimes across towns, municipalities, cities and provinces, rural and urban areas. Copper cable theft, pillaging of whole rail lines, massive criminal accumulation and sale of scrap metal, cash in transit heists, a crisis in starkly rising political assassinations, syndicates controlling artisanal miners, cross-border car thefts, kidnapping for ransom, bombing of ATMs, 'mafias' extorting payoffs from construction companies, extortion rackets for 'protection' at commercial venues, decimation of rhino populations, illicit tobacco trade so huge that it has almost supplanted taxpaying manufacturers and suppliers, 'mafias' sabotaging sewerage plants and water supply systems so their equipment can be lucratively rented, and cross-border traffickers.

Caryn Dolley has written extensively on the links between organised crime, extortion syndicates, gangs, collusion, transnational drug cartels and trafficking networks.[441] She explains how the 'subtle' and 'sophisticated' web of organised crime extends to the state – how police and crime intelligence units play a role.[442] While we may not always see the connections, organised crime is all around us and flourishes from the townships to the leafy suburbs of prominent neighbourhoods. Two analysts have recently stated that crime in South Africa is not just the province of individual perpetrators – organised crime has 'taken on an almost industrial character'.[443]

Criminal syndicates' operations sap service delivery and enervate national infrastructure, impoverishing us all. Extortion syndicates undermine state legitimacy in 'demanding a local "tax" [that] is in essence a quasi-political act'.[444]

The Zondo Commission clearly depicted systemic patterns of corruption, state capture and organised crime.[445] The Global Initiative against Transnational Organized Crime (GI-TOC) explains how organised crime, along with corruption within the political elite, and the weakening of state institutions, created a 'self-sustaining, self-protecting and self-expanding criminal economy'.[446]

This has spawned well-organised criminal markets, which the GI-TOC insightfully divides into three areas: (i) *Selling the illicit* (drugs, firearms, human trafficking and smuggling, and wildlife, fishing and environmental crimes); (ii) *Dealing in violence* (including extortion, kidnapping for ransom, organised robbery and organised violence); and (iii) *Preying on critical services* (a 'predatory and parasitic relationship with the fabric of the South African state and the mechanisms of everyday life', including critical water and power infrastructure, illegal mining, mass public transport, cyber-crime, economic and financial crime and health sector crime).[447] The GI-TOC found that organised crime in South Africa has become 'highly connected', 'entrepreneurial' and 'violent'.[448]

The violent insurrection of July 2021, in the wake of Zuma's imprisonment for the crime of contempt of court, resulted in more than 350 deaths. The riots and looting cost the economy R50 billion. Almost two million jobs were lost. There were racially motivated crimes – in Phoenix, near Durban, 36 people were killed by armed community members.[449]

The insurrection gave us 'the three bloodiest days in South Africa's democratic history'.[450] Instead of being held accountable, some of the instigators now represent Zuma's uMkhonto weSizwe Party (MKP) in

Parliament. The mayhem they caused was the product of catastrophic police and crime intelligence failings (or collusions).

An expert panel found in November 2021 that the police expected 'some planned protests', but did not anticipate 'the speed, scale and manner in which the protests would manifest'.[451] The panel scathingly exposed the failings: insufficient capacity meant that simultaneous outbreaks in distant areas could not be contained; large crowds descending on shopping malls and warehouses to loot were unfamiliar to police, leading to an inept response that didn't adapt as the protests spread:

> It is unclear why [the National Police Commissioner] did not realise that the modus operandi of the looters was not what the police had initially expected. It is more worrisome that the looters continued to use the same modus operandi for the next seven days or so, without the police substantially changing their plans.[452]

This glimpse of disabling ineptitude gives an inkling of why the police fail to protect the public from robbery, hijacking and rape.

Trouble was brewing long before 2021. The link between firearms and murder is starkly revealing. After 2000, and particularly from 2006 to 2011, South Africa's murder rate declined.[453] In 2011/2012, SAPS reported 15 609 murders.[454] This was no miracle. The decrease stemmed from a reduction in firearm-related murders: this, in turn, resulted partly from well-implemented laws regulating firearms (specifically the Firearms Control Act of 2000).

But the murder rate began to climb after 2011, when the Zuma presidency's deliberate disablement of law enforcement agencies took hold. Today murders are almost 76% higher than then (in 2023/2024 SAPS reported 27 590 murders). Some of the increase is because police fail to enforce gun legislation – or, worse, because police themselves supply firearms to criminals and gangs.[455] Zuma's purge of the police, and his seemingly deliberate corrupt and incompetent top appointments, enabled mafias and vigilantes to resist enforcement.

Solving cases of murder to enable a suspect's arrest has dramatically deteriorated since 2011/2012. Lizette Lancaster of the Institute for Security Studies found that 'the police's ability to solve murders has declined by 38% since 2011/12, with the result that in 2019/20, detectives were only able to solve 19 out of every 100 murders'.[456]

Why? Here is at least one piece of the puzzle. SAPS has, over the years, lost nearly 9 000 detectives (from 26 000 in 2016/2017 to 17 600 today – a loss of 8 400).[457]

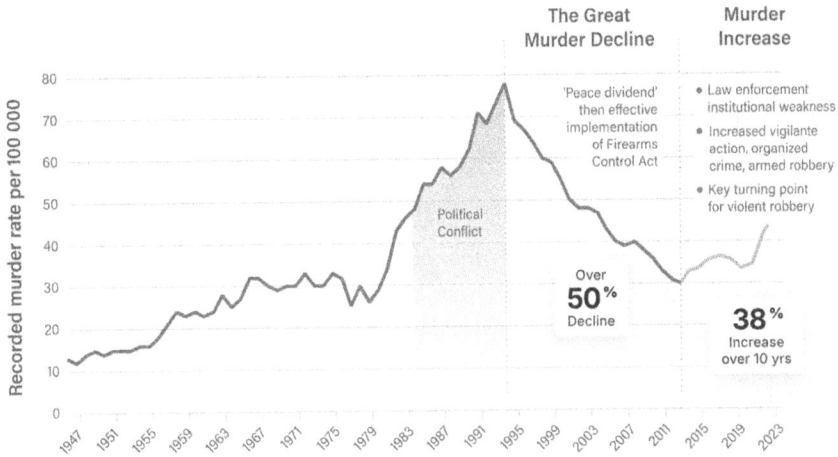

Figure 8: South Africa's murder rate per 100 000 (1947–2022)[458]

The insightful writer Jonny Steinberg draws two lessons. First, when bureaucracies fail, many die. Second, despite this, *we can put things right*. Policing 'with a modicum of competence' is, he writes, 'well within SA's grasp'.[459] From widespread insurrection to daily murders, deployment of adept, competent, well-resourced and non-corrupt police and crime intelligence can help keep people safe.

145

Gareth Newham, who heads the Justice and Violence Prevention Programme at the Institute for Security Studies, explains that we need to invest resources and improve the capabilities of our police as well as our crime intelligence. Along with high-density, visible public safety policing, police can reduce organised crime by targeting those 'individuals and networks that commit the most harm'. This requires well-resourced crime intelligence. It also requires willingness to arrest highly placed and prominent figures profiting from (and enabling) the criminal gangsters. This would help ensure that police resources are correctly focused, and that investigations are targeted to convict 'the most harmful offenders'.[460]

Crime intelligence has suffered eviscerating corruption and criminal capture – but it has also languished in a regulatory vacuum.[461] This enabled politicians not only to use its resources for their own enrichment, but to fight factional battles. The result was a collapse of accurate, efficient and effective intelligence work.[462] With committed leadership and equipped with the necessary expertise, skills, independence and integrity, a well-functioning service can help keep us safe.

2. Effectively curb gender-based violence and femicide

Gender-based violence and femicide (GBVF) are deeply violent crimes that target women and girls across South Africa. Many see the criminal justice system as *the* primary tool to deal with these heinous forms of violence. The predominant current feminist approach, 'carceral feminism', seems to be advocacy for longer, harsher sentences for perpetrators.[463] With numerous calls to ensure tougher sentencing, the South African government falls back on this approach.[464] Has the carceral-centric approach made women and girls safer? We need to demand more.

Make no mistake: those who commit these awful crimes must be stopped and punished, but do longer sentences actually curb GBVF? The evidence is shaky. Despite South Africa's many attempts to enforce harsher sentences against perpetrators of GBVF, our conviction rates are dismal (for intimate partner femicide, they have actually decreased from 29,4% in 1999 to 19,5% in 2020/2021 – while for non-intimate partner femicide, they have decreased from 25,9% in 1999 to 13,2% in 2020/2021).[465] As we have shown, South Africa still has one of the highest femicide rates in the world.

This is in part because of dysfunctional policing and prosecution (there is limited deterrence when perpetrators know they are unlikely to be arrested and punished), but it is also due to inherent characteristics of GBVF. These are crimes that, for many understandable reasons, victims and survivors are hesitant to report, crimes that often take place in private and within intimate or familial relationships, and for which little hard evidence is generally available, making them difficult to prove beyond reasonable doubt.[466]

GBVF victims and survivors often cite degrading treatment from police, prosecutors, magistrates and judges. Tepid conviction rates undermine trust in the effectiveness of the state to keep victims and survivors safe.[467] And the criminal justice system punishes some victims and survivors when they defend themselves against GBVF using violence.[468]

In the rare instances where a perpetrator is convicted, often after trial proceedings that are traumatic for the victim, does prison help? Our prisons only enforce hierarchy, toxic gender stereotypes and masculine power dynamics. Sexual violence, especially in prison, is a tool of power and coercion.[469] Can prisons rehabilitate rapists when rape is part of prison culture? Worse, when those imprisoned for petty offences are exposed to sexual violence, what do they take back to their communities? While we share the urge to lock up perpetrators of GBVF for longer and longer periods, the facts invite us to pause.

So, what does help confront GBVF? A myriad of factors. These range from regulating alcohol sales and firearms[470] to ensuring that there are enough well-resourced shelters, social workers and psychologists to support victims and survivors, empowering women with more choices by providing them with education and employment opportunities, and challenging deeply embedded social and cultural gender norms. And if government is earnest about punishing GBVF through the criminal justice system, then forensic data systems must be developed and court backlogs tackled.

At present, shelters for victims and survivors of GBVF are chronically underfunded, even while provincial departments of Social Development return hundreds of millions of rands of unspent funding to National Treasury.[471] In contrast, the Department of Correctional Services spent almost R28 billion in 2023/24. Let us be clear: we do not contend that perpetrators should escape imprisonment, but we question the practical utility of longer and longer sentences to solve GBVF. We favour an approach that prioritises the safety, wellbeing and protection of victims and survivors, while also insisting on punishment of perpetrators.

Focusing solely on long sentences stops us from opening the aperture and looking at other effective strategies – remedies that are victim-centric and based on social justice. Our dilemmas are not novel. Feminists elsewhere also grapple with the problematic dynamics between mass incarceration and GBVF.[472] We need to demand *more* from our government, and from ourselves, to deal with the causes and consequences of GBVF.

3. Reduce prison overcrowding

The next vital step is tackling the critical weakness in our prisons – chronic, disabling overcrowding. Overcrowding oppresses two groups of inmates. The remand population – detainees innocent until proven guilty in a court of law – typically comprises around 30% of the total prison population, but is now inching up toward 40%. And, of course, sentenced inmates, the numbers of whom have burgeoned because of sentence inflation since democracy. What can be done?

3.1 Reduce the remand detainee population

Foremost, the evils of cash bail. Many remandees are imprisoned for months and even years simply because they cannot afford to pay their bail – this after a court-conducted risk assessment that found in their favour, that they qualified for bail. The purpose of bail is to ensure an accused attends their trial. At the end, their money is returned. Bail has a pragmatic objective. It is not designed to punish. In a country as unequal as ours, cash bail operates grossly unequally. Freedom depends on social position and money power.

In 2019, a mid-winter inspection of the Johannesburg Correctional Centre in Diepkloof (the infamous Sun City) showed graphically what 80% overcrowding means – nearly twice as many bodies as planned were crammed into the cells.[473] The majority of these were remandees. The co-ordinator of the remand detention centre alerted us gravely to the number of remandees who were inside solely because they could not afford small bail amounts.[474] He gave us a long list of names. Against each were the charges and the amount of bail the court had granted. The list included many petty crimes – and small bail amounts of R200-R300:[475] small for us, for most readers, but not 'small' at all for resource-deprived fellow South Africans, many thousands of whom join long queues every month simply to receive the Social Relief of Distress grant (SRD) of R370 per month.

And the cost? The co-ordinator explained that it costs the government R330 every day to keep a remandee behind bars – a staggering R10 000 every month.[476] This is not unique to the Johannesburg remand centre. Across the country, we meet remand detainees who have been awaiting trial for months and sometimes years. Most are imprisoned because of trial delays, but some simply because they cannot afford to pay bail. Recently, in 2024, to answer a question posed by the Parliamentary Portfolio Committee on Correctional Services, JICS asked the National Commissioner for the costs of detaining remand detainees. His office calculated that it now costs the state approximately R12 125 per month to accommodate every remandee (amounting to over R400 each per day).[477]

Applying these numbers, JICS calculated that the department may spend approximately R64 868 750 a month just on remandees awaiting trial for longer than two years together with remandees unable to afford bail of R1 000 and less. The cost is staggering and imposes a massive burden on our overcrowded and under-resourced detention centres.

The predicament is almost as old as our democracy. Nearly twenty-five years ago, Judge Hannes Fagan, then Inspecting Judge, spoke out powerfully about the crisis of unaffordable bail. He decried it as a gross injustice, leading to overcrowding. He lamented two instances: a 'person accused of stealing three mangoes' who could not afford their bail of 'R500'; and 'a person accused of crossing railway lines' who could not afford their bail of 'R1000'.[478]

All these years later, the problem still obtrudes. It is a radical breach of human rights (violating protections of class, social origin and race) while also a misbegotten institutional burden: we keep thousands of poor people in prison simply because they are poor.[479] JICS has rightly called them 'prisoners of poverty', and their plight, also rightly, a crisis. Reliable reports from JICS's on-the-ground staff and its regional centres indicate that between 2000-3000 remand detainees are in prison because they cannot afford bail of R1 000 or less.[480]

There are two statutory means of redemption that could help solve the crisis. Yet, too often, they are overlooked. Section 63A of the Criminal Procedure Act (CPA) empowers the head of a correctional centre, if 'satisfied that the prison population of a particular prison is reaching such proportions that it constitutes a material and imminent threat to the human dignity, physical health or safety of an accused', to apply to court to either release that accused on warning, in lieu of bail, or to amend the bail conditions. The provision recognises that overpopulation poses a threat and that lack of money unnecessarily protracts imprisonment.

In addition, section 49G of the Correctional Services Act provides that the maximum incarceration of a remand detainee may not exceed two years from the initial date of imprisonment without this being brought to the attention of the court for further consideration.

The department does try to invoke these provisions. Success can mean reduction of bail, placement under correctional supervision, warning, withdrawal of cases and placement of children in secure care facilities. The department's 2023/24 Annual Report records that it submitted a total of 19 391 referrals to court under section 63A – but only 5 091 (26,25%) were successful. It also referred 9 667 applications to court under section 49G – but its success rate was tiny, only 2,83%.[481]

Why do most of these applications fail? Our surmise is that at least a contributory cause is that too few judicial officers know what our prisons are like and understand the urgent need to decongest them.

Another reason the provisions are under-utilised is that many remandees don't know about them. And the statutory mechanisms are clunky. They require bold decision-making, but lots of paperwork. Officials may be reluctant to invoke them for fear of bungling – what if they back a remand detainee who later fails to show up for trial or, worse, every official's nightmare, commits another offence? The section 63A provision in addition requires owning up to how dismal conditions for remandees are. This could expose the Department of Correctional Services to litigation.

These inhibitions may be real – but freeing poor people and freeing up departmental resources are both imperative. Everyone should be made aware of the provisions. And rigorous processes – which may include a departmental advisory body – should encourage officials to track and advocate for those remandees who may benefit.

On the other hand, the department has also made productive use of a SAPS protocol that allows for temporary release of remand detainees for further investigation. To expedite cases, the department surrendered 487 remandees to SAPS.[482]

We have witnessed the injustices – and often the indignities – of freedom in exchange for cash. While inspecting Kgosi Mampuru II Women's Centre, we witnessed a woman's release on cash bail. Across the counter in the administration area, she explained to us that she had been in a bar fight. She'd smashed a man's face with a glass bottle, claiming self-defence, since her child was in her arms. She was charged with assault with intent to commit grievous bodily harm (GBH). On appearing in court, she was granted bail of over R1 000.

After she spent a few days in detention, her husband arrived. Until then, she had no idea whether her children were okay and if her employer knew why she had not arrived for work. A credit card was swiped, after which an official handed over her belongings and clothes. She undressed and changed in front of all. As she left, officials reminded her of her court date. She breathed a deep audible sigh. It was far from a dignified experience. In our system, freedom almost always has a price.

A cash bail system is not only unjust, but also archaic. Unlike South Africa, some countries have completely abandoned cash bail.[483] Others partially use cash bail but invoke it only in exceptional cases. They rely on non-monetary bail conditions. These include periodically reporting to a local police station, handing in passports, curfews, electronic monitoring, and other conditions (for example, not tampering with evidence or contacting witnesses).

Electronic monitoring of accused persons and of those granted parole would help. It was introduced with great fanfare some years ago, but senior JICS staffers suggest it may have flopped embarrassingly because of inefficiency and corruption. Right now, the Council for Scientific and

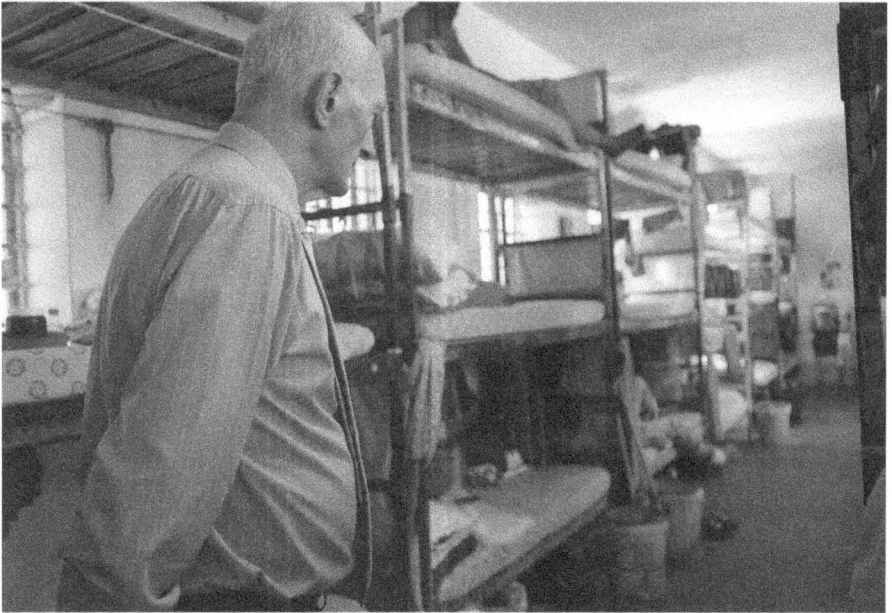

Top: Administrative building, Durban
Bottom: Communal cells, Durban

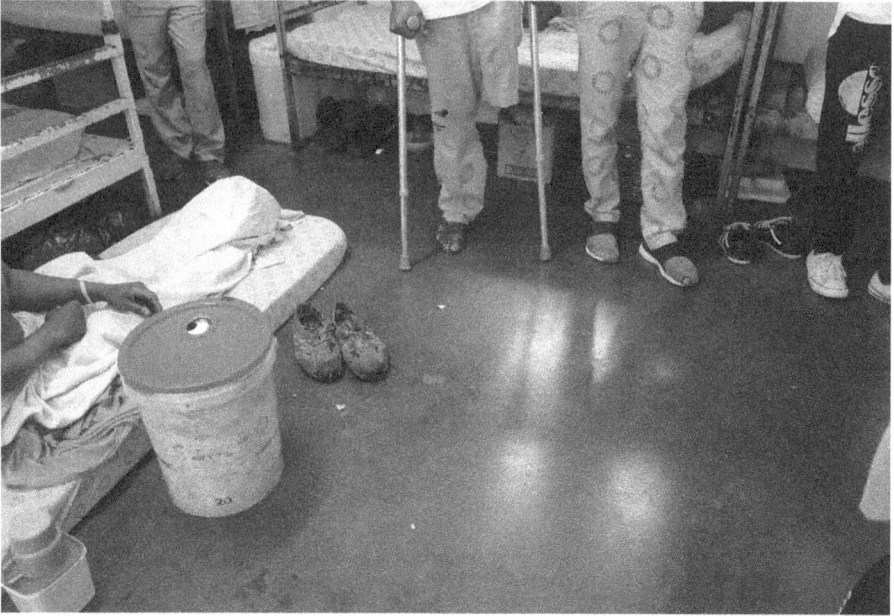

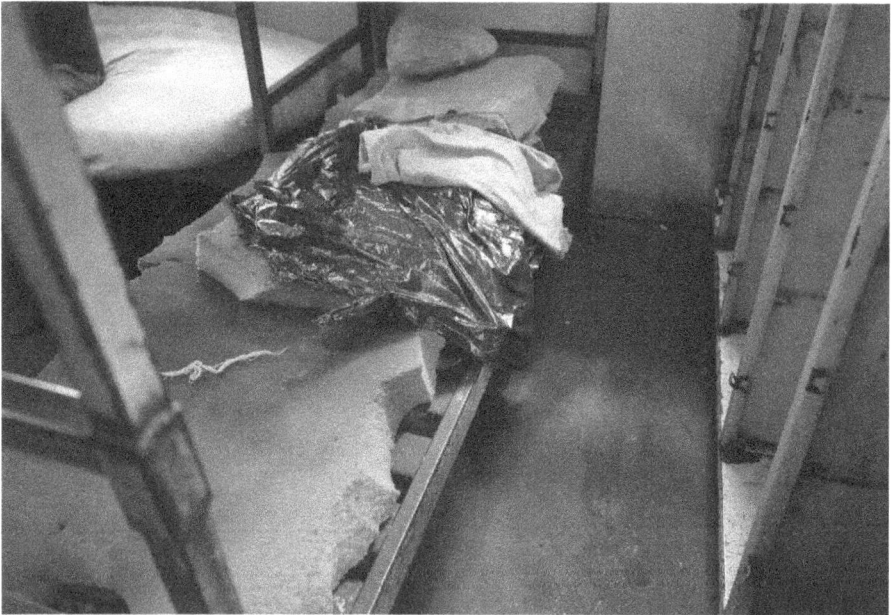

Top: Communal cell, Durban
Bottom: Communal cell, Maphumolo

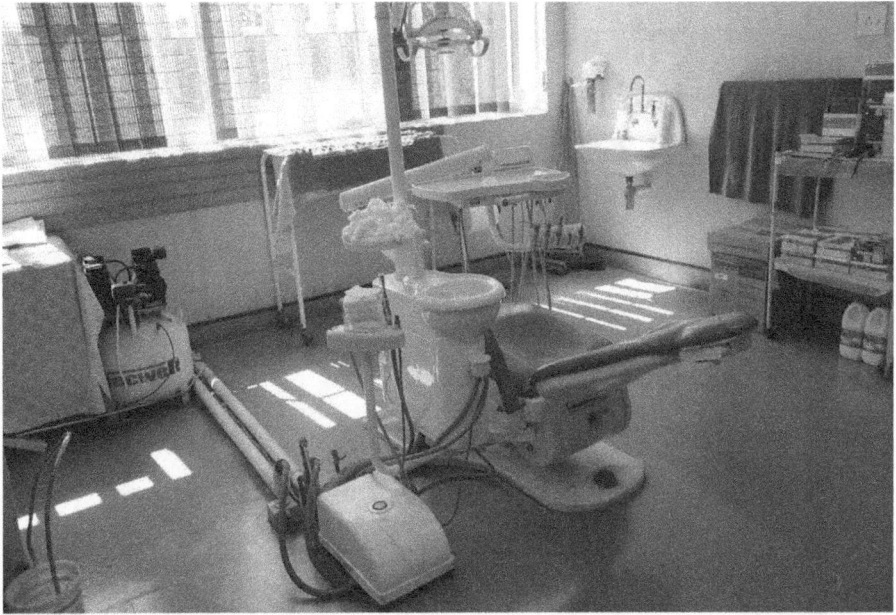

Top: Dental clinic, Durban
Bottom: Tuck shop, Durban

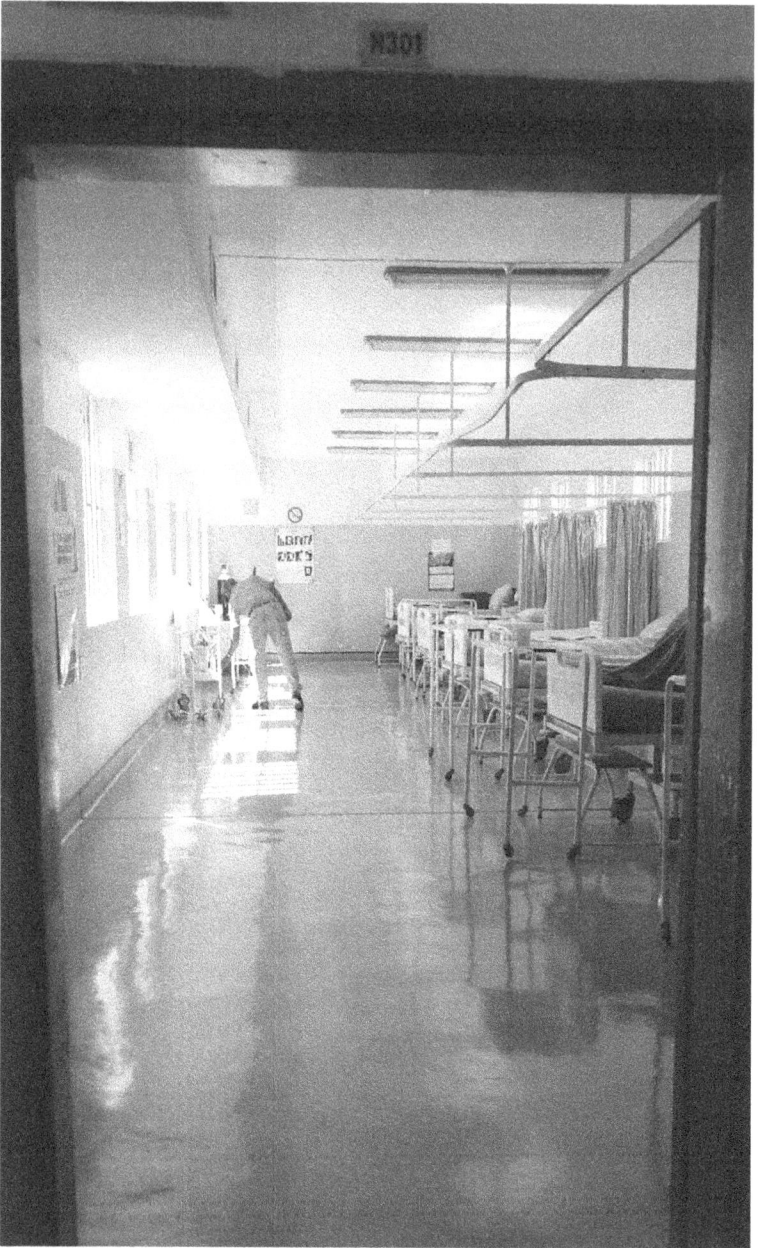

Hospital wing, Durban

Top: Vegetable garden, Newcastle
Bottom: Classroom, Pietermaritzburg

Top: Communal cells, Pietermaritzburg
Bottom: Kitchen, Pietermaritzburg

Communical cells, Elliotdale

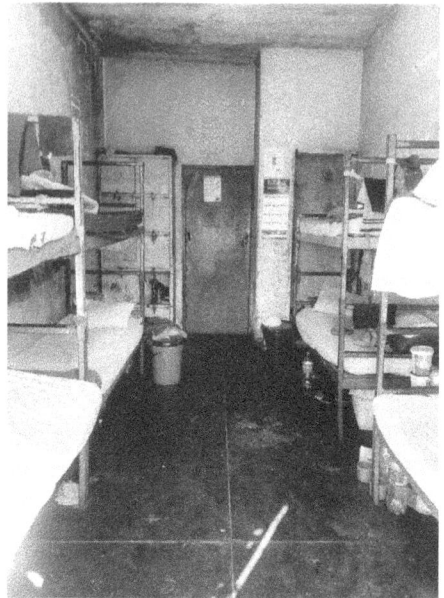

Top left: Imates play chess in the courtyard, Elliotdale
Top right and bottom: Communal cells, Elliotdale

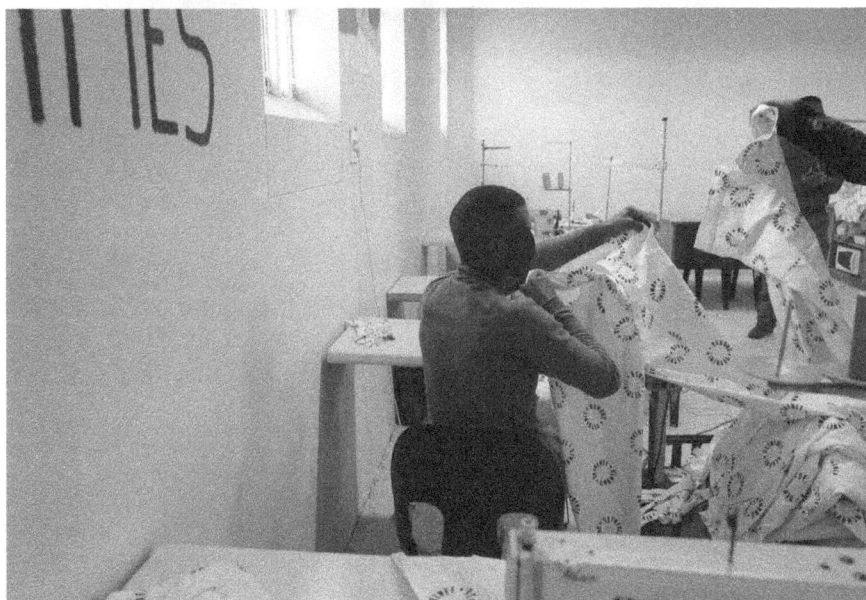

Top: Sohela Surajpal, Acting Head Mr Mbini and correctional centre officials during a JICS inspection and handover of donated books, Elliotdale

Bottom: Inmates sewing, Port Elizabeth

Single cells, Pretoria

Top: Rebecca Gore with colleagues from JICS and
the National Preventive Mechanism, Durban

Bottom: Vegetable garden, Vryheid

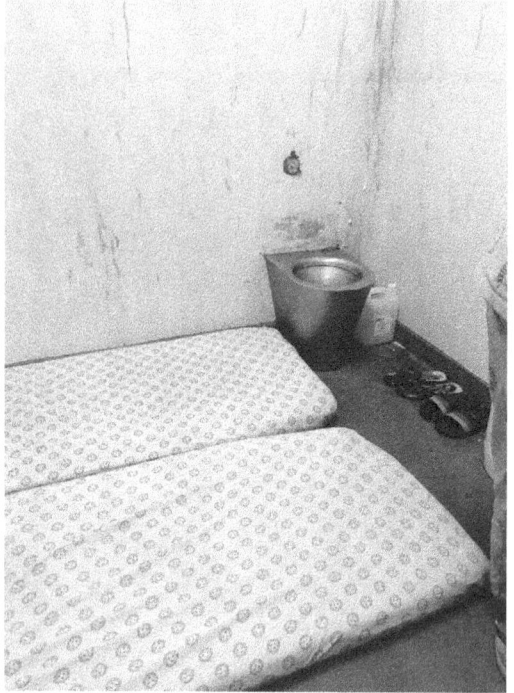

Right:
Youth cell, Vryheid

Bathroom, Vryheid

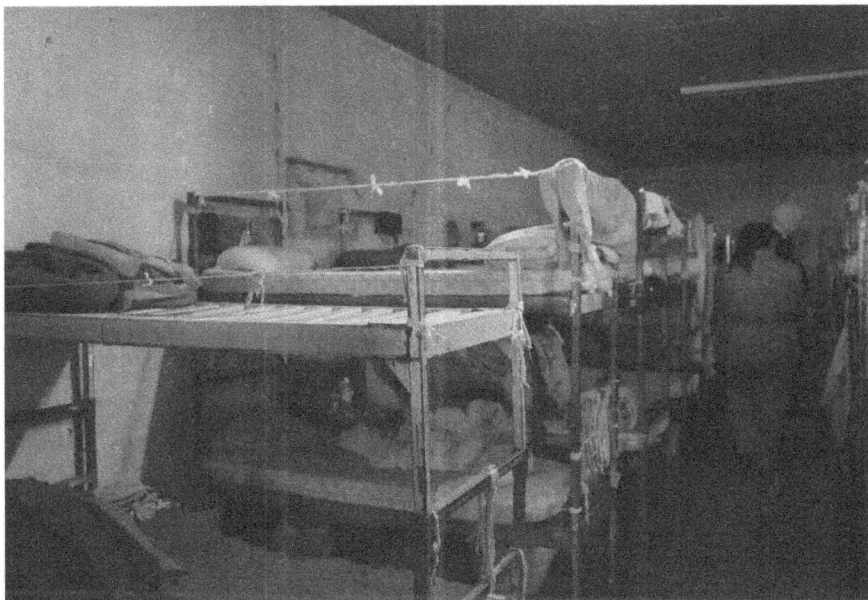

Top: Communal cells, Port Elizabeth
Bottom: Single cell, Port Elizabeth

Top: Communal cell, Port Elizabeth
Bottom: Single cell, Port Elizabeth

Bathroom, KwaDukuza

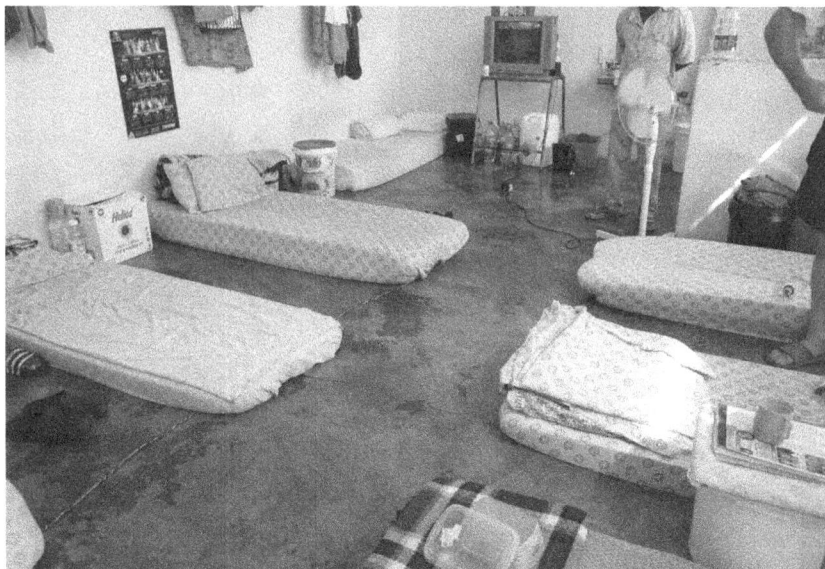

Top: Communal cell, KwaDukuza
Bottom: Prison fence, KwaDukuza

Industrial Research (CSIR), under a contract from the department, says it is developing a programme for custom electronic bracelets.[484]

In the 1990s, the Department of Justice partnered with a non-profit, the Vera Institute of Justice, to introduce a Pre-Trial Services project.[485] This project attempted to provide magistrates with independently verified information about defendants (like their criminal history and financial means) in order to help magistrates make fairer bail decisions, prevent the granting of bail to dangerous criminals and avoid setting unaffordable bail. A pilot project was launched in three of the country's busiest magistrates' courts with some success. Average bail amounts set by magistrates *did* decrease, though even decreased amounts remained unaffordable for many remand detianees, but there was an increase in magistrates denying bail and little overall effect on the size of the awaiting trial population. Regrettably, the long-term effects of the programme could not be studied because when Vera handed the project over to the state, funding evaporated.

All of this tells us that a complete or partial overhaul of our cash bail system (to non-monetary conditions) is by no means a radical step.

For now, however, we are stuck with cash bail. One way to alleviate its unjust effects is through a bail fund.[486] The notion of a bail fund is unfamiliar in South Africa.[487] In the USA, communities, families and political movements have pooled resources to ensure that those who cannot afford bail remain free pending trial.[488] In the 1920s, the American Civil Liberties Union (ACLU) organised the first large-scale, national bail fund for suspected communists and political dissidents.[489]

Inspired by bail fund initiatives in the US, some private investors, activists and religious leaders are working with JICS to encourage social impact investors to contribute to a fund that will support remandees granted bail but who cannot pay. The proposed fund aims to target those accused of non-violent offences and who are at low risk of re-offending. The fund will encourage conditions to incentivise showing up for trial.

Support will include text message reminders and transport. Ideally, instead of being exposed to gangs, violence, drugs and sexual abuse in pre-trial detention, remandees may access pre-trial services, including rehabilitation programmes, education and employment openings.

The fund will aim to decouple justice and freedom from socio-economic status, reduce overcrowding, nudge remand detainees in directions that will reduce recidivism and possibly help generate useful data on remand detainees and their interactions with the criminal justice system.

Dr Jean Redpath, an academic with expertise in criminal justice, drew our attention to the Justice Administered Fund, which manages monies paid to courts, including monies paid for bail, as a possible funding source for a bail fund.[490] Some of these monies (about R115 million of the R207 million paid for bail in 2022/2023) are never collected, and the fund generates a massive amount of interest each year.[491]After covering bank charges, in that period the fund was left with an excess of about R19 million of interest.[492] This could be used to cover bail amounts and the administrative costs of a bail fund. Director of Accountability Now Paul Hoffman SC has pointed out that there are billions in unclaimed pension and provident funds that could be administered similarly to the COVID Solidarity Fund, so as to minimise corruption. These ideas suggest that the resources for a bail fund may be at hand. Great suffering could be alleviated with creative reallocation.

But a bail fund, no matter how well funded and administered, is only a partial solution. It should be coupled with deeper reforms – to the bail system entirely, and to adequately provision critically needed services.

As we write in early 2025, the South African Law Reform Commission is reviewing the criminal justice system, including the bail system. The Commission recommends a raft of legislative amendments to address unaffordable bail and prolonged pre-trial detention. These include amendments allowing accused persons to pledge property as security for bail in place of cash, prohibiting pre-trial detention for certain offences, recognising poverty as grounds for release on warning while awaiting trial, and including presumptive limits for the maximum amount of time an accused may be held in custody without conviction, depending on the offence. The Commission also recommends non-legislative reforms, like reducing the number of arbitrary arrests and establishing a task team to investigate and fast track cases. Many of the Commission's proposed reforms relate to improving court capacity by deploying experienced magistrates and judges to busy jurisdictions, establishing courts to deal exclusively with non-trial matters like bail applications and pleas, instituting Saturday courts to combat case backlogs, and expanding court capacity by appointing acting magistrates, additional interpreters, clerks, prosecutors and Legal Aid defence lawyers. These deeper reforms have the potential to transform pre-trial detention in South Africa.

3.2 Reduce the number of inmates serving long sentences

As we have explained, long sentences don't on their own help to reduce crime. The main outcome of the mandatory minimum sentences Parliament enacted in 1998 is that prisons are overflowing with inmates serving long sentences, while most perpetrators are unpunished.

A large proportion – about 12%, or one-eighth of the entire prison population – are lifers, that is, serving life sentences. This while murders and other crimes have continued to skyrocket. A stark fact: in 1996, some 518 people were serving life sentences in South Africa. The figure in 2024 is 18 795[493] – a 36-fold increase.

Much of this is futile, counter-productive and unjust. Sentencing reform is urgently necessary. We propose three steps – each in close conjunction with improved crime intelligence and police and prosecution.

First, restore flexibility in sentencing. Abolish mandatory minimum sentences. We explain that the sentencing guidelines and sentencing council the Law Reform Commission recommended decades ago would create just precepts without imposing rigidity. Second, explore non-custodial sentences wherever appropriate. Third, fix the creaky and unjust parole system for lifers.

Flexibility: The mandatory sentencing regime supposedly avoids sentencing disparities and guards against leniency.[494] In Chapter 2 we recorded that Parliament introduced mandatory sentencing as a temporary measure. As public concern over crime mounted, this measure became permanent. Not only has our misdirected sentencing regime meant that the number of sentenced inmates serving long sentences has burgeoned – while failing to curb crime – but it is doubtful whether it ensures consistency.[495] A fundamental principle in sentencing is that the public *interest* counts, not only public *opinion*. It is not in the public interest to have overcrowded prisons clogged with inmates serving over-long sentences, while the criminal justice system fails to apprehend the great majority of perpetrators.

There are other options. The South African Law Reform Commission offered them to government.[496] After extensive consultations and expert opinions, it set out alternatives to blunt minimum sentencing. It considered other jurisdictions and sentencing schemes: these included sentencing guidelines that would presumptively apply,[497] voluntary sentencing guidelines, and legislative guidelines to determine the choice and length of punishment and sentencing principles. Instead of political rhetoric driving sentences, the report suggested developing sentencing principles that would be clearly articulated in legislation – together with establishing an independent sentencing council that would research and consult to establish sentencing guidelines for particular categories or sub-categories of offences.[498] The council would comprise an authoritative mix of judges and magistrates, prosecutors and prisons personnel, plus an expert outsider.[499]

The sentencing council proposal chimes with an observation by retired US federal judge Nancy Gertner that sentencing is a 'system' of various role players – lawmakers, lawyers (prosecutors, defence lawyers, legal aid), prison administrators, criminologists, other academic experts and the public.[500] A sentencing council would ensure these role players have a say in the sentencing scheme. To make sentences either discretionary (entirely up to each judicial officer) or over-rigid (constrained by tight mandatory minimums) offers false alternatives. It is time for us to find a midway.

Alternatives to prison: The Law Reform Commission report also suggested focusing on non-custodial sentences and community penalties instead of imprisonment. This points to our second step, which is to consider innovative and effective sentences that do not require imprisonment.

Shortly before democracy, in the late 1980s, Parliament established correctional supervision as a sentencing option. This permits individuals to serve a 'community-based form of punishment' through, for example, community service.[501] This created a helpful distinction between two kinds of offenders: 'those who ought to be removed from society by means of imprisonment, and those who, although deserving of punishment, should not be so removed'.[502] The courts welcomed correctional supervision, while the Constitutional Court warmly endorsed its primary focus on rehabilitation. It described correctional supervision as 'a milestone in the process of "humanising" the criminal justice system' because it 'brought along with it the possibility of several imaginative sentencing measures including, but not limited to, house arrest, monitoring, community service and placement in employment'.[503]

Sadly, the post-apartheid 'crime wave' nearly obliterated this. Instead, our new democracy, following the Clinton administration in the US, and the Blair government in the UK, sought salvation in 'tough-on-crime' approaches. Correctional supervision was shadowed by fears that it was too soft. And judges rightly feared that the Department of Correctional Services was not properly monitoring correctional supervision.[504]

Fears that those under correctional supervision are destined to re-offend may be overstated, however. JICS's experience has been mostly positive as the department reports low levels of re-offending. Recently, the department has renewed its support for correctional supervision and called it 'the best opportunity for reforming' the criminal justice system 'in ways that will promote public safety, efficiency and fairness'.[505] The department asserts a '99% level of compliance' with their conditions during 2022/23 by those on correctional supervision.[506] So, correctional supervision seems a viable option, especially for first-time offenders or individuals unlikely to repeat-offend. It still holds individuals accountable but reduces imprisonment and the collateral consequences of imprisonment. Despite this, bar limited instances,[507] correctional supervision is under-utilised. Reconsideration and revitalisation are overdue.

Fix parole for lifers: Mandatory minimum sentences require life imprisonment for an extensive list of crimes.[508] As we've shown, this has led to a vast ballooning of inmates serving life sentences. The numbers are staggering: in 1996, 518 people in South Africa were serving life sentences. In 2024, there were 18 795.[509]

This is out of line, demonstrably so. South Africa has one of the highest lifer populations in the world. In their authoritative *Life Imprisonment: A Global Human Rights Analysis*, Dirk van Zyl Smit and Catherine Appleton show that, between 2000 and 2014, South Africa's lifer population grew by 818% – the highest expansion recorded anywhere.[510] The accelerated increase in the number of lifers profoundly aggravates overcrowding; and of course severely hits the public purse.[511]

The minimum non-parole period for lifers adds more complexity and Parliament has pushed it upwards. Before 1987, a lifer's non-parole period was 10–15 years. It was then increased to 20 years. But from

1 October 2004, lifers have to serve at least 25 years before they can apply for parole.

Annual index rate of growth of life-sentenced prisoners around the world, 2000-2014

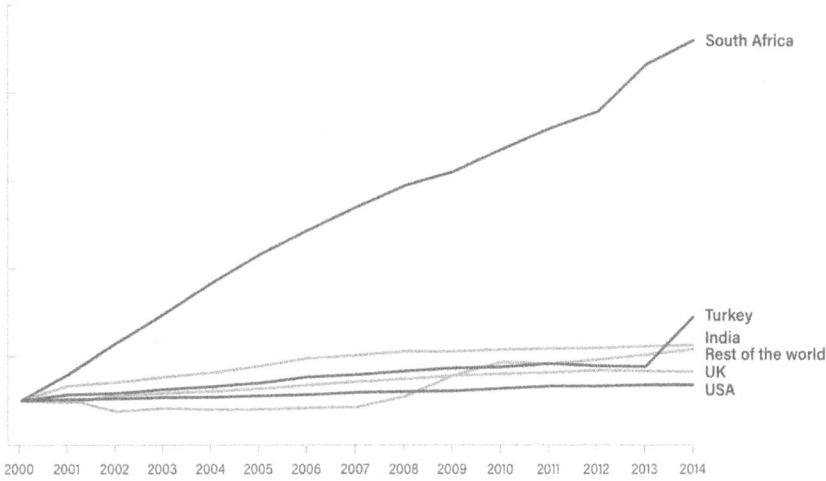

Figure 9: Growth of life-sentenced prisoners around the world (2000–2014)

In May 2019, the Constitutional Court gave a slender straw to those lifers who had committed crimes before 1 October 2004.[512] Parliament brought the longer non-parole period into effect from the date on which sentence was imposed. If you were sentenced before 1 October 2004, you benefited from the more lenient parole regime; if the day after, you suffered the much harsher regime. Thus two offenders who committed misdeeds on the same day, where one was sentenced on 30 September and the other on 1 October, would serve vastly different sentences. The court struck this down as arbitrary and irrational – the date of the offence had to be the touchstone.

Lifers bear the brunt of the most punitive aspects of our prison system, yet research shows lifers may not be more of a risk than other inmates.

Van Zyl Smit and Appleton suggest lifers should face no additional burdens, restrictions and hardships for the mere reason that they are serving
a life sentence. They propose principles that promote individualisation,
normalisation and progression. And they underscore how important it is
to create a pathway to possible release.[513]

In South Africa, lifers are often transferred to Pretoria C-Max and even
to the Ebongweni supermax, in Kokstad, where security and other harsh
measures (including bleak single cells and severely truncated exercise)
trump rehabilitation.

Parole is the lifeblood not just of our prison system, but of every carceral system. Deputy Chief Justice Dikgang Moseneke would recount to
colleagues in the Constitutional Court how, the moment the key turns in
the lock, getting out becomes every inmate's first and constant aspiration,
even obsession.

No inmate has a *right* to parole. This includes lifers. What they have,
after serving their non-parole period, is a right to be *considered* for parole.
Another way to frame the importance of the possibility of parole has been
articulated by the European Court of Human Rights. That court called the
possibility of parole 'the right to hope'.[514] In the light of the prohibition
of torture and inhuman or degrading treatment or punishment, the court
held that inmates serving life sentences should not be deprived of the
hope of being granted release.

Judge Power-Forde observed that:

[H]ope is an important and constitutive aspect of the human person.
Those who commit the most abhorrent and egregious of acts and
who inflict untold suffering upon others, nevertheless retain their
fundamental humanity and carry within themselves the capacity to
change. Long and deserved though their prison sentences may be,
they retain the right to hope that, someday, they may have atoned
for the wrongs which they have committed. They ought not to be

deprived entirely of such hope. To deny them the experience of hope would be to deny a fundamental aspect of their humanity and, to do that, would be degrading.[515]

Some go further, arguing that once an inmate satisfies the prerequisites for parole, they have a legitimate expectation to be released on parole, not merely a right to be considered for release. According to this view, parole should be denied only if the decision-maker has good reason to do so. We endorse this as the better view, while noting that the currently accepted position is a right only for consideration – a right to hope – rather than a legitimate expectation of release.

JICS receives very large numbers of complaints about our parole system. It is not only over-clogged, inefficient and slow – it also yields inconsistent decisions. So the system is doubly dysfunctional. First, too many inmates unsuitable for parole are released without sufficient monitoring and incentives for reintegration. Second, the opposite: too few who deserve release are granted it. An efficient and rigorous process would upturn these anomalies, keeping bad-risk inmates inside, but releasing more good-prospect inmates.

The parole process for lifers remains in particular crisis. JICS receives scores of anguished complaints – not only from lifers themselves, but from their families, and indeed from correctional officials, who are disturbed by delays and anomalies, and who must manage the consequences. In 2021, 'concerned lifers' at Witbank Correctional Centre wrote to JICS, threatening a hunger strike. They said this was their only remaining option.

A 51-year-old inmate who has been in Zonderwater for 31 years approached JICS. He claimed that, despite positive recommendations and a clean record, the minister had not placed him on parole. His lawyers said, justly, it seemed to us, that this was a 'travesty of justice'. As in other cases, the only suggestion we could make was a court challenge.

As we write, another case in which JICS sought to help received national prominence.

Dr Liza Grobler, an experienced criminologist, took up the case of Inmate Z. He was denied parole because he refuses to confess to a crime he insists he did not commit. Dr Grobler exposed starkly the deficiencies of the entire system. It is 'purely an administrative function designed to adhere to policies, legislative requirements and meeting targets' – while it should be 'a behavioural function conducted by professionals'. She rightly concluded that the system was 'deeply flawed and too often arbitrary': 'Parole boards, generally, do not have requisite behavioural professionals such as psychologists, psychiatrists, criminologists or social workers serving on them.'

Dr Grobler decries the absence of suitable experts on the National Council for Correctional Services (NCCS), and 'the often shockingly poor quality of assessments and concomitant referrals for treatment'.[516] Meanwhile, somewhat bizarrely – or, at the very least, anomalously – Inmate Z's two co-accused, who confessed to the murder, while now exonerating him, have been released on parole. Thirty-one years later, he remains imprisoned.

Why is the parole process for lifers so ineffective? The statute gives *only the minister* the power to make the ultimate decision on lifers' parole – this after consideration and decision by the Correctional Supervision and Parole Board (CSPB) through the NCCS.[517] This has led to what appeared to JICS to be a massive backlog on the minister's desk: no fewer than 4 494 lifers are eligible *now* – but over the preceding year, only 36 were granted parole.

Can the minister possibly have capacity to consider each individual parole application? It is (or should be) a laborious task: so much is at stake. If each application were considered for only ten minutes, the backlog would take over 400 days to eliminate, provided the minister works exclusively on lifers' parole for seven hours, every day, seven days a week. Is this practicable? Of course not. We must offer hope to parole-thwarted lifers; without it, the system faces perilous dysfunction.[518]

As we were writing during 2024, two disturbing examples of neglect or inefficiency in the ministry were brought to our attention. Two inmates sentenced to life were, according to JICS's records, submitted for consideration in 2019 and 2020 respectively. The NCCS considered their applications, and approved their release on parole. The NCCS thereupon submitted its recommendations, in 2021 and 2022, for the minister to approve. But nothing happened. JICS repeatedly expressed grave concern to the ministry about delays and backlogs in the management of lifer parole. This was met with assertions that there was no backlog. The two waiting, anxious inmates would not have thought so. Their cases were eventually prioritised for consideration by the new minister.

After the formation of a government of national unity (GNU) in the wake of the 2024 election, Correctional Services was separated into a stand-alone ministry – a welcome and long overdue systemic change. In fact, the new Minister for Correctional Services, Dr Pieter Groenewald, says he has eradicated the backlog – though in doing so he seems to have rejected more than 90% of the parole applications, each one of which the NCCS had systematically considered and approved for parole before they reached his desk.[519]

But even with extraordinary focus and diligence, and more generous parole approvals, the system needs urgent fixing. Soon, the lifers sentenced under the stricter minimum sentences and parole provisions that Parliament imposed in 2004 will become eligible for consideration[520] – placing the minister under enormous pressure.

JICS and the NCCS have recommended major reforms. The bodies jointly proposed that the council should give a final decision on lifer parole, subject only to a veto by the minister, to be exercised within a stipulated period. Obviously, not all lifers must be granted parole. And some political oversight at the end of the process accords with other modern democratic systems. But applications should be rigorously considered, *and promptly.*

The outcome, as well as reasons, should be communicated clearly and expeditiously. Life imprisonment should be employed not near-indiscriminately, as now, with a bloated list of crimes, but more cautiously and proportionally. And without shutting the door permanently on freedom, hope and reform.

3.3 Decriminalise to reduce those imprisoned in the first place

Many people have been arrested, detained, accused or convicted of conduct that should *not be crimes* at all – they should not feel the criminal law's big brutal stick nor be in prison. The outcome: many people who are branded as criminals unnecessarily choke up our prisons and face the collateral injuries of mass incarceration.

The United Nations' 8 March Principles create a principled framework for decriminalisation. Resulting from a five-year process of international consultation comprising UNAIDS, the Office of the High Commissioner for Human Rights (OHCHR) and the International Committee of Jurists (ICJ), they urge a human rights-based approach to crimes associated with sex, drug use, HIV, sexual and reproductive health, homelessness and poverty. The expressive function of the criminal law is to tell us who is worthy of protection – and who should be condemned and ostracised. But over-reach has drastic consequence for people's lives, especially on groups vulnerable to discrimination and stigma.

In addition, criminal proscriptions may reinforce structural inequalities; they may codify discrimination, invest them with the law's power, and foster stigma. All this may wreak terrible harm:

> Criminal law may thus impel hostility, exclusion, inequality, discrimination and marginalization of individuals and groups, sometimes to the point of violence. As a result, human rights, democratic values and social inclusiveness all suffer.[521]

164

When newly democratic South Africa embarked on its misbegotten 'war on crime', it embraced this punitive approach to stigmatised and 'moralised' conduct.[522] But in signal cases, this was especially damaging. Particularly with drug use and sex work, 'warring on crime' is both ineffective and counter-productive. Using drugs, and possessing them for personal use, raises fraught questions. Here, apartheid-era crimes, as we explained earlier, are largely still in force.

Using dagga and other drugs, and possessing them for private purposes, should not be crimes. We say this fully aware of the sometimes disastrous consequences drug use and addiction have for the users, their loved ones and communities. But, like using alcohol – another dangerous, addictive substance – drug use is an urgent *public health* issue. It should be regulated and countered with counselling, rehabilitation and other public health interventions, with support that is evidence based, and with harm-reduction services.

The blunt fact is that the 'war on drugs' has been a catastrophic failure. It was a failure from the start. Like Prohibition in America, which empowered gangsters and criminal networks, and corrupted public administration, drug crimes have had a calamitous impact on people's lives and wellbeing – and on governments. And the illicit drug market has flourished, to the extravagant benefit of druglords and drug armies, and, in our own Cape Flats neighbourhoods, the benefit of often violent gangsters.

There is also a class dimension: affluent cocaine users, inside gated communities, are seldom, if ever, targeted. Nor are the kingpins, who profit from prices vastly elevated by prohibition. Their profits are ample enough to buy allies in law enforcement. Supply remains ample.[523] Who suffers? Disproportionately, economically marginalised Black and Coloured people. Women using drugs, too, are subjected to gendered discrimination and exclusion.

By a sad irony, prisons are key sites for drugs. Anyone walking through a prison in South Africa almost invariably encounters the rich permeating whiff of cannabis. Two decades ago, the Jali Commission acknowledged the widespread smuggling of drugs, by correctional officials and inmates, through corrupt gang networks.[524] In the two decades since then, this has only become worse.

The views we propound here are no longer outré. They have shifted from periphery to mainstream acceptance. The UN High Commissioner for Human Rights, Volker Türk, states that criminalisation 'has neither diminished drug use nor deterred drug-related crime' and 'instead, more and more lives [are] ruined, not just by the use of drugs in itself, but also by the fallout of counterproductive policies'.[525] An extensive report outlines the disastrous effects of the war on drugs, which was effectively a 'war on people'.[526] These include human rights violations, 'a culture of corruption within law enforcement bodies' and discrimination against poor and marginalised groups.[527]

The report plainly sets out how disproportionate criminalisation of drugs has ballooned prison populations.[528] It calls for alternatives, to address overcrowding and over-incarceration.[529] The commissioner recommends coupling decriminalisation with a human rights- and health-based approach (including harm-reduction services) and regulatory systems to ensure legal access to controlled substances so as to avoid illegal drug trafficking markets.[530]

There have been promising signals in our country. In 2018, the Constitutional Court at last struck down criminal sanctions for privately possessing and using small amounts of cannabis (dagga).[531] The National Drug Master Plan 2019–2024 concedes that, historically, most nations' strategies for addressing substance use disorder centred on a punitive 'war on drugs'. This, the plan says, has had 'almost no effect on the levels of the use or supply of drugs and has resulted in collateral harms'. It calls for 'a major shift in mentality' – namely recognising that South Africa must shift from a criminal to an evidence-based public health approach.[532] It opts for 'social justice' and 'social protection' over 'conviction' and 'punishment'.[533]

Former President Kgalema Motlanthe has added his considerable authority to the call for South Africa and other states to decriminalise drugs and drug use.[534]

Shortly before the May 2024 elections, President Ramaphosa appended his signature to the Cannabis for Private Purposes Act 7 of 2024, which entirely removed cannabis from the Drugs and Drug Trafficking Act. This steps in the right direction, though possession of specified amounts of drugs and dealing remain criminalised. The statute is only a beginning.

These developments mean that decriminalisation of drugs is not a radical step, but a prudent necessity, implemented with sound public health and other regulatory measures.

Portugal blazed a trail in 2001. While drug-dealing and trafficking remain crimes under the Criminal Code, public and private use and possession of drugs were decriminalised. Instead of making criminals of drug users, Portugal established the Commissions for the Dissuasion of Drug Addiction and promoted public health interventions and harm-reduction campaigns (including a needle exchange programme). Drug use and possession bear administrative sanctions (fines akin to traffic tickets and agreeing to treatment). Users are referred to state-funded rehabilitation centres. Results have largely been promising. By 2017, heroin users had decreased from 100 000 to 25 000. Overdose deaths had fallen by more than 85%.[535] Portugal's drug death rate is now the lowest in Europe.[536]

Yet decriminalisation holds no magic – some blame it for recent crime waves in Portugal.[537] Supporters counter by blaming defunding of public rehabilitation centres.[538] But the debate warns us against unrealistic expectations. Decriminalisation does not bring a drug-free paradise. Dedicated resources are key, as are interventions – to save lives, heal lives, and safeguard communities – which must be based on evidence of what works.

Contrast America's 'war on drugs' – there, as many Americans have died of drug overdoses as were killed in the Vietnam, Afghanistan and Iraq wars, in total.[539] At least in the case of marijuana, there is growing bipartisan support for an end to the 'war on drugs'.[540]

In the US, Oregon's decriminalisation of drug use (including meth, heroin and cocaine) from 2020 has had adverse effects – including an increase in overdose deaths.[541] Measure 110 was repealed after more than three years.[542] Some blame leadership failures, lack of police training and lack of access to treatment providers, as well as other unforeseen factors, including the Covid-19 pandemic and the proliferation of fentanyl (an enormously addictive, highly dangerous drug).[543] Others suggest the lack of incentives, urging that nudges and administrative consequences for drug use and treatment in Oregon (the carrot-and-stick approach) should have been used more.[544] Others claim the initiative failed because the proponents misunderstood the nature of addiction and Oregon's already progressive approach to drug possession.[545]

In Canada, the province of British Columbia recently developed a decriminalisation pilot programme to treat drug addiction as a 'health issue' by providing an exemption for the use of hard drugs (meth, cocaine and heroin) in public for personal use.[546] Amidst the opioid crisis and fentanyl crisis, this has been unsuccessful in reducing addiction and over-doses, however.[547]

Still, the Portuguese model is a promising starting point for reform. It has shown considerably better results than criminalisation. Key are administrative penalties and nudging users to treatment at state-funded reha-bilitation programmes and harm-reduction services. And we should not allow genuine complexities to induce despair about lifting the blunt destructive force of crime and prisons from drug use in South Africa.

Of course we do not advocate disorder and lawlessness. We are not blind to drug use in schools, parks, hospitals, transport services and other public spaces. We do not paper over the tragic consequences for families and communities of drug overdosing.

But we need to start somewhere. We must de-link drugs from violence, gangs, overdoses and other social ills – all of which crimes and imprisonment foster.

Our starting point should be the staggeringly high cost, in money and lives, that criminalisation inflicts.[548] From there, we can learn from cautionary tales in other jurisdictions. And we must aim to secure enough public funding, support and treatment services – especially opioid substitution therapy (OST) – to persuade users away from drugs.

We should not conceive this funding as additional, but as substituting for the hugely expensive, futile and counter-productive cost of the 'war on drugs'. In sum, decriminalisation is the first step and should be coupled with evidence-based forms of regulation.

Community-based harm reduction in South Africa already has a positive impact. One University of Pretoria programme[549] has enabled people dependent on drugs to access medication-assisted treatment, needle and syringe services, screening and treatment for psychiatric issues, psychosocial services, trauma counselling, vocational training, and sport and recreational activities. Shaun Shelly, a dedicated researcher on drug use at the University of Pretoria's Department of Family Medicine and, since 2024, executive director of Harm Reduction International, challenges our thinking about drugs:

> Unless we stop demonising drugs, criminalising or pathologising the people that use them and abandon the goal of a drug-free society, we will continue to be distracted from the real problems that cause many of our youth to find solutions in the dependent use of drugs.[550]

Harm-reduction and treatment services must be expanded outside prisons and should be made available *inside* prisons. Instead of further punishing inmates for their use of drugs once inside (by penalising them or transferring them to max or super-max centres), prisons are key sites to treat and prevent.[551]

Thus, in Kenya, a collaborative intervention by the United Nations Office on Drugs and Crime, the Kenyan Prison Service and Mombasa County Health Authorities supports medically assisted therapy (MAT) services for inmates.[552] A clinic at Shimo La Tewa Prison, inside the compound of a maximum security prison, treats inmates affected by opioid use disorders. Morocco, Mauritius and the Seychelles also offer opioid substitution therapy in prisons.[553] Why can't we? The Department of Correctional Services successfully tests and treats those with HIV and AIDS. It successfully delivered Covid-19 vaccinations behind bars. Nothing stops us from doing this, beneficially, with drug use too.

Sex work – where adults consent to sex on terms of payment to one of them – somehow remains contentious. Within feminism and gender studies, debates continue about the social harms of sex work. Advocates of decriminalisation contend that these harms spring from the context in which it operates, and not from sex work itself. Evidence from public health and criminology bears this out.[554] This is inarguable: making sex work a crime in a country beset by gender-based violence, public health problems, police brutality, unemployment and inequality inflicts a hideous cost on women and transgender people and indeed all sex workers.[555] The Sex Worker Advocacy Taskforce (SWEAT) rightly says that 'criminalisation kills'.[556] Criminal penalties condemn sex workers to unsafe, unregulated working conditions, with no worker protections, no access to justice, and little access to healthcare or other support.[557]

In 2019, Human Rights Watch interviewed sex workers across South Africa. Its study found that criminalising sex work heightens workers' vulnerability because they are forced to work in or go to dark, dangerous places. This was because criminals, 'including sadists, thieves, and rapists, pretending to be clients, knew [sex workers] had bad relations with the police'. Sex workers recalled police laughing at them when they tried to report rape. Some were told that, as sex workers, they could not be raped. Why would one then report rape or abuse? Almost three-quarters of the 46 sex workers interviewed had experienced multiple arrests, sometimes two or three a month.[558]

The SA Medical Research Council and the Perinatal HIV Research Unit at the Chris Hani Baragwanath Hospital surveyed over 3 000 sex workers countrywide. It found they experienced 'extremely high' levels of physical violence. Nearly three-quarters of those interviewed had been assaulted, and more than half raped – one in seven by a policeman.[559]

Once arrested, sex workers are detained in often filthy police cells, without adequate food, water, toilets or blankets. They are often deprived of access to phones as well as medical treatment (a significant concern for those taking antiretroviral medications), and their property is confiscated and sometimes not returned. Sex workers have described their arrests and detention as humiliating and degrading. Though frequently arrested, they are seldom convicted; and little is known about their experiences in prisons.[560] All this reinforces the arbitrary cruelty of criminalising sex work. Where convictions do occur, they preclude employment in the formal sector.[561]

Criminal laws and the violent policing of gender roles and sexual morality have punished and stigmatised, but never stopped, sex work. Criminalisation is a 'symbolic' proscription – an ineffectual prohibition that cruelly marginalises.

Some claim that ending the crime licenses exploitation and increased sex trafficking. They propose instead the 'Nordic model' or 'end demand approach'. This approach eliminates criminal sanction for sex workers – and offers them support services and exit pathways – while criminalising the users instead. These are the 'johns', who seek sex from sex workers, as well as the third parties who trade in and profit off sex work (the workers' 'pimps' or controllers or agents, as well as residential sex work locations, including managers, brothel keepers, receptionists, maids, drivers, landlords, hotels that rent rooms to sex workers and anyone else who is seen as facilitating sex work).[562] In other words, having paid sex with a sex worker is still a crime, only the crime is committed by the service-user and all their enablers. There is no evidence that this model reduces trafficking, however,[563] and, further, it depicts the sex worker as victim – another stigma.

Criminalisation *in any form* harms and degrades and stigmatises sex workers and their clients. It exudes contempt for who they are and what they do, including the monetisation of sexual services. The Nordic model springs from constrictive moralism.[564] It conveys distaste for and disapproval of what sex workers do, that is, providing sexual services for reward. In this, the model is fundamentally offensive. What is more, it condemns sex work to secrecy, without transparency or regulation. As a result, the model 'intensifies the surveillance and harassment of sex workers' and triggers other brutal harms.[565] Sex workers and human rights organisations contest the Nordic model as deeply offensive, and urge that 'sex work is work' and not inherently exploitative.[566]

In contrast, non-moralistic and human rights-based approaches aim to decriminalise *all* aspects of sex work. They seek to eradicate harmful stigma, to respect agency and dignity on the part of sex workers and their clients, and to replace criminal sanctions with personal protections within socially beneficial regulation.

The worldwide movement for full decriminalisation of voluntary adult sex work is gaining pace.[567] On 30 November 2022, before the GNU, the South African cabinet at last approved publication for public comment of a draft statute to abolish criminal penalties for sex work.[568] The bill rightly scraps the crime of buying and selling adult sexual services. It signalled hope at last for activists who, over many long years, have campaigned for safety and labour protections without stigma.

However, the draft statute focused on decriminalisation without making provision for regulation. This elicited opposition from state law advisors.[569] The result was yet more delay, while terrible harms continue to be inflicted on sex workers.[570] Former Minister of Justice and Correctional Services Ronald Lamola and Deputy Minister John Jeffrey supported the bill; we wait to see how the new incumbents in the GNU will act.

Meanwhile, SWEAT in May 2024 launched a constitutional challenge to sex work crimes.[571] The application identifies a trend: the impugned laws yield no ascertainable prosecutions and no convictions at all.[572] Instead, they are used to arrest and detain and harass and exploit sex workers – but no formal charges, sentences and prison ever ensue.

Criminalisation in this way inflicts stigma, risk and punishment but without deterrence or rehabilitation: it is a vector for abuse and exploitation, a remnant of apartheid-era legislation, which criminalised sex across the colour bar and same-sex relationships,[573] and it remains a blemish on our justice system.

Associated with these considerations, the Regional Campaign to Decriminalise Petty Offences in Africa challenges laws that disproportionally impact the poor and marginalised. Louise Edwards from the African Policing Civilian Oversight Forum explains that:

> Criminalisation has the effect of entrenching discrimination and social exclusion, and is a significant contributor to detention overcrowding, which impacts on myriad human rights, including to health, fair trials, freedom from arbitrary arrest, and ill-treatment.[574]

The campaign has made considerable strides, prompting the African Commission on Human and Peoples' Rights in October 2018 to adopt Principles on the Decriminalisation of Petty Offences in Africa.[575] These acknowledge how petty offences can lead to discrimination and arbitrary arrests and detention. In December 2020, the African Court on Human and Peoples' Rights handed down an advisory opinion on vagrancy laws, which criminalise homelessness, poverty or unemployment. The court found that these laws are incompatible with the African Charter as well as the Children's Rights Charter and the Women's Protocol.

The Pan African Lawyers Union submitted to the court that 'vagrancy laws do not punish specific acts of individuals but a status that individuals involuntarily entered into', by either targeting or having a 'disproportionate impact on poor and vulnerable persons'.[576] Recently, the Economic Community of Western African States (ECOWAS) Court of Justice found that Sierra Leone's vague loitering laws violated various rights, including equality and non-discrimination, and that they disproportionately impacted impoverished and marginalised people.[577]

Chikondi Chijozi, from the Southern African Litigation Centre, explained that the judgment 'builds on the calls for decriminalisation of poverty in Africa' and that '[m]any vulnerable communities including sex workers are disproportionately targeted under such vague laws'.[578]

Drug reliance, sex work and petty offences related to poverty are issues that cry out for evidence-based public health and social justice engagement. The criminal justice system should not punish, stigmatise or ostracise in these ways, nor clog up prisons with the supposed transgressors.

4. Improve existing conditions

4.1 Scrap solitary confinement

Solitary confinement glaringly violates prisoners' rights. It is unlawful and unconstitutional. It transgresses international standards. JICS has fought against it, but departmental practice has proved stubbornly resistant. This shows how difficult it is to eradicate abusive practices.

'Solitary' (as it is called) consists of the confinement of prisoners for 22 hours or more per day without meaningful human contact. Under international law, solitary confinement may amount to torture, or cruel, inhuman or degrading treatment or punishment when used as punishment during pre-trial detention, when indefinitely prolonged (more than 15 days), or when used on women, LGBTQ+ persons, juveniles or persons with mental disabilities.[579]

As we illustrated in earlier chapters, in South Africa, solitary confinement has a haunting history. The apartheid government used it to punish and control inmates and to break down opponents. Many were subjected to long periods in solitary. These they described to the TRC as psychologically damaging: 'the worst kind of torture that can be inflicted on a human being'.[580] Nelson Mandela described his three days in solitary as 'the most forbidding aspect of prison life'.[581] Calling for abolition, Zahrah Narkedien said she would 'never recover' from the long-term effects of her seven months in isolation:

I was damaged. A part of my soul was eaten away as if by maggots, horrible as it sounds, and I will never get it back again.[582]

Given this dark history,[583] our democracy should have banished solitary confinement. It has not. The 2008 Correctional Services Amendment Act excised solitary confinement, providing instead for a softer form known as 'segregation'. Yet the Jali Commission presciently perceived that, in practice, segregation 'is ultimately nothing more than solitary detention'.[584]

But, at least in theory, segregation is subject to strict preconditions and safeguards that are designed to avoid the most abusive aspects of solitary.[585] First, segregation may be imposed only for specific reasons. The statute permits segregation: at an inmate's own request; to penalise through restriction of amenities; if prescribed by a medical practitioner on medical grounds; when an inmate displays violence or is threatened with violence; if an inmate has been recaptured after escape and there is reasonable suspicion that they will again attempt to escape; and if requested by the police and the head of centre considers that it is in the interests of the administration of justice. Second, segregation may not exceed seven days, unless the head of centre believes it is necessary to extend it, and a medical practitioner or psychologist certifies it and the National Commissioner grants permission. Even then, this extension may not exceed 30 days. Finally, an inmate subjected to segregation may appeal to the Inspecting Judge. So, post-2008, solitary confinement – particularly prolonged solitary confinement – is unlawful.

That is according to the law books, but what happens in reality? Does segregation occur only in a few isolated instances? Or is it being enforced in a more structured way – sometimes under the guise of security? And in a way that is de facto solitary confinement?

A previous Inspecting Judge, Justice van der Westhuizen, reported on the Ebongweni supermax in December 2019.[586] In 2021, JICS conducted three unannounced inspections: at Ebongweni, Pretoria/Kgosi Mampuru II C-Max and Mangaung Public Private Partnership Correctional Centre in Bloemfontein.[587]

These inspections and reports revealed that, albeit not explicitly sanctioned in policies, prolonged solitary confinement continues as a matter of fact at South Africa's super-maximum security prisons Ebongweni and Kgosi Mampuru II C-Max. These two centres were specifically designed for solitary and they practise it. Mangaung has no single cells, except in its separate segregation unit, Broadway. Inmates spend months and even years in solitary. This is not new – the Jali Commission two decades ago called these centres 'institutions of solitary confinement'.[588] As we discussed in Chapter 3, inmates are detained in single cells with minimal to no meaningful human contact or stimulation.

Our JICS reports were shared with the erstwhile minister, deputy minister and acting national commissioner. We sent them to the Parliamentary Portfolio Committee on Justice and Correctional Services. We released an opinion piece and, when we elicited no response, uploaded the main report to a public platform.[589] We anticipated a public uproar, but there was little response.

What does that reveal about our society? Does it suggest that violent

176

and oppressive practices are normalised in our lives and our news headlines?

Solitary confinement is heinous. The extreme isolation and minimal stimulation is unnatural and traumatic. Solitary detention can cause adverse health effects after only a few days. The UN Special Rapporteur on torture and other cruel, inhuman or degrading treatment or punishment has found its effects may include 'psychotic disturbances', anxiety, depression, anger, cognitive disturbances, perceptual distortions, paranoia and psychosis and self-harm.[590] These may be new symptoms or severe aggravation of existing mental wellness conditions.

Symptoms are not confined to the period in solitary. Studies have found that cognitive damage persists even after release.[591] After lengthy periods of solitary people may experience long-lasting personality changes, social withdrawal, social anxiety, sleep disturbances, phobias, emotional dependence, confusion, and impaired memory and concentration.[592]

Solitary affects not only those subjected to it but also the mental health of correctional officials.[593] Also affected are the indirect victims – families (especially children), loved ones and communities of the inmates in solitary, who have less contact with the outside world, meaning fewer phone calls and less access to visitors (and contact visits).

JICS in partnership with the University of KwaZulu-Natal conducted an exploratory study in 2023 at Ebongweni. It found evidence of heightened mental wellness issues amongst not only inmates but also correctional officials.[594] Given the clear evidence that solitary confinement harms, why is it so difficult to eradicate?

There are reasons to isolate some dangerous and high-risk inmates. Ebongweni and C-Max, in particular, were designed to accommodate the most violent, the most dangerous, the most disruptive inmates or those at high risk of escaping (including gang leaders, prisoners who have escaped before, prisoners sentenced for acts of terrorism, those who have killed law enforcement officers, and feared internationally connected offenders).

Security reasons may thus require periods of incarceration under stricter security measures. However, prolonged solitary confinement is *over-used* and *lacks safeguards*.[595]

JICS identified administrative wormholes in transfers and admission systems, such as sudden, overnight, mass transfers of inmates to these centres for reasons difficult to establish. Is it because those sent are serving life sentences? Or for disciplinary reasons – possessing cell phones or drugs? Or for warder-on-inmate payback? Such infractions are common, but why are they considered sufficient to condemn some, but not others, to C-Max or Ebongweni?

Some inmates are transferred between the two supermaxes (multiplying their time spent in solitary). During an inspection, we identified two inmates under 30 years old. Compared to the many hardened criminals around them, they looked considerably younger and starkly out of place. Their gaunt faces were stricken. They had committed violent crimes, yet their records did not suggest they might still be dangerous or at risk of escape. They seemed to have been part of a mass transfer after a stabbing at another prison. The major motivation? Punishment, we thought. Collective punishment.

The Africa Criminal Justice Reform at the Dullah Omar Institute makes a telling observation: prison violence did not decrease after the supermax prisons were established.[596] There are fewer escapes – but this is the result of better departmental management rather than because of supermaxes. In fact, the Jali Commission found that the high number of escapes twenty years ago resulted from officials' collusion, negligence and corruption rather than deficient prison design.[597]

Those detained at Ebongweni and C-Max must at some point return to other prisons and – one day – to broader society. Solitary confinement undermines rehabilitation and reintegration.[598] Sharon Shalev, an expert on solitary confinement, explains that, '[u]nable to regain the necessary social skills for leading a "normal" life, some may continue to live in

178

relative social isolation after their release'. In this way, solitary confinement operates against one of the main purposes of prison, 'which is to rehabilitate offenders and facilitate their reintegration into society'.[599]

Humans are inherently social. Renowned American surgeon and public health authority Atul Gawande notes a paradox: starving people of companionship does not rehabilitate offenders – it leaves them less fit for social interaction.[600] Isolation runs counter to everything imprisoning an offender seeks to achieve. From a philosophical perspective, Kimberley Brownlee explains how solitary confinement is a form of *social contribution injustice*. Instead of inmates being considered human beings and social contributors, solitary confinement cuts social ties, deprives inmates of minimal human contact and treats them as 'social nonentities'.[601] Not only does it lead to long-lasting health issues, but also social consequences (the inability to reintegrate socially into society and lead a social life).[602] Brownlee warns that solitary confinement 'threatens, stretches, and breaks social bonds'.[603] And severing social connections is linked to re-offending tendencies (lack of accommodation, employment, family, loved ones and support).

What these experts say resonates with our experience. A mother of an Ebongweni inmate poignantly asked, how can we expect people 'to be reformed when they are treated worse than animals' or 'to fit back into society after they are released from a life of torment'. We could give her no answer.

In addition, the architecture of Ebongweni and C-Max was designed for single-cell accommodation, with few communal spaces for meaningful human interaction. Changing entails reconstruction, at cost and effort. But none of this justifies solitary confinement.

There is little public appetite for reform – less even for reform benefiting the most dangerous. JICS's efforts against solitary have not yet resulted in the complete overhaul we seek,[604] yet have brought some amelioration – the request of the new head of Ebongweni for JICS to deliver books for inmates, which we mentioned in Chapter 3, is a flickering light-point.

Measures should be put in place to guard against solitary confinement. Strict security and single-cell accommodation can be enforced without solitary confinement – so long as inmates are not deprived of meaningful human contact for 22 or more hours a day. Relatively minor operational adjustments could afford inmates at Ebongweni and C-Max adequate human contact and stimulation, even in single cells.

Thus JICS has recommended permitting meaningful human contact, stimulation and access to rehabilitation by: increasing access to education and rehabilitation programmes; increasing exercise time and improving exercise facilities; allowing meals to be eaten outside cells, at least for lower-risk inmates; increasing the number of telephone calls, non-contact visits and, where appropriate, contact visits; increasing access to books by amplifying the selection and the number allowed to be borrowed at once, and by more regular library visits; and allowing and facilitating access to television, radio, clocks, calendars, and natural light.

Adopted with due prudence, these measures would safeguard both security and human rights. But even these minor reforms have found pushback. The department maintains that security and operational reasons require conditions to remain, despite how harsh and oppressive they are.

4.2 Improve access to healthcare in prisons

Prisons constitute intense vectors for the spread of infectious viruses and diseases.[605] And the myth that prisons and their inmates are insulated from the rest of society is folly. Prison healthcare impacts public healthcare – not indirectly: directly. What happens in prisons unavoidably spills over into communities. The prison healthcare system needs urgent attention.

In overcrowded prisons with insufficient protection from the cold, sometimes dire sanitary conditions, inadequate diet, sexual assault and unprotected sex (even when consensual), prisoners are especially vulnerable. HIV/AIDS, tuberculosis and mental illness are common. Some years, the department records suicide as the leading cause of unnatural death in prisons (though the JICS Annual Report for 2023/24 states the leading cause of unnatural deaths as 'unknown other').

In addition, many inmates have special healthcare needs, like the elderly, pregnant women, and prisoners with disabilities.[606] Beyond the UN Mandela Rules 'equivalence of care' standard, the notion that those in prison have a right to a standard of healthcare equivalent to that available to the general public, prison conditions entail a heightened duty of care for the state.[607]

In some aspects, spurred by public interest litigation,[608] the department's work is impressive.[609] During inspections, distribution of antiretroviral drugs (ARVs), treatment of TB and provision of special healthcare diets are almost always first-rate. And the department handled the risks the Covid-19 pandemic imposed particularly well. We feared a catastrophic wave of disease and death in prisons, as happened elsewhere in the world. That never eventuated.

In other ways, however, healthcare services behind bars fall short. JICS has reported that inmates do not have regular access to nurses and doctors. This reflects a bigger crisis in public healthcare – while some hospitals desperately need more healthcare professionals, many trained and eager doctors cannot find jobs.[610] The prison setting has inherent problems; as people flow in and out of prisons, adherence to medication and continuity of care are ongoing challenges.

Small, rural prisons do not always have full-time medical professionals on duty nor the capacity to treat serious illnesses or injuries. The healthcare resources here may be a single nurse and single examination room, with no trained professional to step in when the nurse is on leave, goes home for the day or is otherwise occupied. Some small prisons do not even have a dedicated nurse. Sessional doctors visit only occasionally.

Specialists like dentists and psychologists even less often. This shortage is a result of the difficulty the department faces recruiting healthcare professionals. It is also due to the formula the department uses to allocate professionals to prisons. For instance, the department's accepted ratio for nurses is 1 nurse for every 240 inmates. As a result, centres with fewer than 240 inmates may not be allocated a dedicated nurse.

Even large, urban prisons suffer from a lack of skilled professionals. They also struggle with infrastructure and equipment. When we visited Durban Medium B (which houses 3 280 inmates) we found a large hospital in relatively good condition. Facilities included a pharmacy, palliative care unit, optometrist and dentist's office. The hospital handled a staggering workload. It provided 1 032 inmates (a 31% prevalence of HIV) with ARVs. In addition, 32 prisoners were being treated for TB. And 122 were diagnosed with and receiving treatment for mental wellness issues. Among the most common manifestations were depression, schizophrenia, and drug-induced psychosis.

One cell housed 63 inmates with mental wellness challenges. Designed for about 20 inmates, the cell was – like most in the prison – grossly overcrowded, dirty, with little light or fresh air. The atmosphere was uniquely tense and disturbing. The mental distress and vulnerability of its occupants were palpable. Officials warned us that there had been violent incidents among the cell's prisoners. It seemed to us that the bleak, dangerous conditions of detention could only heighten mental distress and frustrate any efforts at treatment.

In the face of serious healthcare issues facing inmates, the prison's hospital was chronically under-staffed. Prisoners performed vital tasks to keep things running. The hospital's location within the prison structure was vulnerable to flooding, water damage and mildew. We saw the obvious signs, and smells. The dentist, who visited twice a week, told us that some lights, including overhead lights for dental care, had stopped working a year before and had not been repaired.

Clinics in prisons are cramped, with limited privacy for consultations. Endemic staff shortages mean that officials are not always available to escort inmates to outside healthcare facilities. Health check-ups and screenings on admission are not always conducted and medical files are not always updated. Remote prisons especially may struggle to obtain medications. These may not always be dispensed on time and some may have expired.

State patients with statutorily declared mental wellness problems remains a painful issue. The department lacks the capacity to care for the high number of declared state patients. They should be in psychiatric hospitals, but are accommodated in prisons. The courts have formally pronounced these prisoners to be lacking in criminal capacity or unable to stand trial. They suffer pronounced mental illness or intellectual disability. The Health Care Act stipulates that they must be transferred to healthcare or psychiatric facilities.[611] Only when these lack capacity may they be temporarily accommodated in prisons until bedspace becomes available at specialised facilities. As of 31 February 2025, JICS recorded 292 declared state patients in prison. Many wait indefinitely for transfer to a psychiatric hospital – months and sometimes even years.

State patients are a particularly vulnerable group. Prisons are not appropriate environments for them. In overcrowded, under-capacitated prison settings, the mental-health challenges they face may make them either victims or perpetrators of violence and conflict. In addition, their unique needs impose unfair responsibility on personnel, who are not equipped to provide the specialised care they need.

Correcting requires urgently capacitating prisons with the resources needed to care for the vulnerable people under their charge, including skilled human resources, equipment and medication. And mental healthcare facilities countrywide will need to be expanded and resourced to ensure that state patients can be transferred immediately to healthcare facilities rather than being accommodated in prisons. This is not easy in a country that struggles to provide adequate healthcare to the general public. In fact, some inmates receive better care in prison than they would outside – not because healthcare in prison is exemplary, but because of its dire state elsewhere.[612]

Improving healthcare in prisons will also require addressing the causes of poor inmate health by decongesting prisons, improving nutrition, hygiene and sanitation, combating violence, and promoting safe sex by ensuring that condoms are readily available, and expanding the American-funded TB HIV Care programme, which has started providing prophylactic ARV drugs (pre-exposure) for men having sex with men in prisons. As we were finishing this book, newly elected US President Donald Trump suspended virtually all foreign aid. Though a temporary exception had been mooted for life-saving ARVs, fear and uncertainty surround the future of this vital programme. Re-establishing US funding or securing sustainable alternatives is imperative.

Overall, prison healthcare suffers from a lack of independence. Renowned medical ethicist Professor Solomon Benatar explains that, under apartheid, medical care for prisoners was provided through district surgeons managed by the Department of Health. When the security police arrested Steve Biko in 1977, district surgeons failed to offer him proper treatment because they succumbed to pressure from the security police (as we recounted in Chapter 2). In 1995, the Department of Health began to dismantle the district surgeon services – after which the Department of Correctional Services began appointing nurses and medical staff to deliver healthcare in prisons. Benatar doubted that rights to healthcare in prisons are remotely met:

> The retrogressive step of diverting some responsibilities for healthcare away from the Department of Health towards the Department of Correctional Services made it possible to dilute the loyalty of some health professionals to their patients by ranking allegiance

to prison authorities higher than professional responsibility to patients.[613]

Benatar saw greater reluctance on the part of health professionals to work in prisons resulting.

By contrast, prisoners in England and Wales benefited when prison healthcare services were transferred into the national health service (NHS).

In the trial action Llewellyn Smith and others brought, Judge Ellem Francis underscores the worry that lack of independence may engender disturbing complicity.[614] In that case, officials assaulted inmates to extract information about illicit cell phones and other infractions. The beatings were so severe and caused such serious physical and psychological injuries that the High Court concluded that they amounted to torture and the minister was held liable.

It was found that the department's nurses and a doctor had failed to record the full extent of the injuries the personnel inflicted. Judge Francis found they downplayed the severity of the injuries and failed to treat them properly. In the case of one prisoner, electric shocks inflicted neurological damage and spinal degeneration. Where independent doctors would have ordered hospitalisation or specialists, prison healthcare officials offered only mild painkillers and rubbing ointment. And, despite serious injuries, nurses confirmed that the inmates were fit for segregation. The judge deplored this. The nurses, especially, 'had failed to examine and adequately record and treat the plaintiffs' injuries and this was an attempt to conceal the true nature and the extent of the plaintiffs' assault at the hands of the [Department's] officials'.[615]

Healthcare professionals in prisons should be independent of the Department of Correctional Services. This accords with near-universal recommendations – including by the TRC,[616] the UN's Mandela Rules,[617] the World Health Organization, the UNODC,[618] and the Association for the Prevention of Torture.[619] Prisons healthcare professionals should be

185

shifted to the Department of Health, and proper channels of authority and oversight established. And healthcare professionals should be provided specific training for the prison environment. That they should be accessible, proactive and willing to speak out should go without saying.

Benatar reminds us that Biko's death occurred 'without adequate medical care in prison' and it 'provides an opportunity to remember past failings and reconsider the lessons these hold for our society'.[620] Whether it be access to ARVs, TB prevention and treatment, assault wounds, or cancer treatment, inmates should not be further punished by the by-products and limits of the prison setting.

4.3 Improve treatment and conditions for women inmates

Prisons mostly house men – they are designed for this. They cater to male needs and their reactions to violence and imprisonment. All prisoners experience the hardship deprivation of liberty inflicts – yet women, as well as LGBTQ+ people, may experience unique vulnerabilities, and have basic needs overlooked.

Since 2000, the number of women and girls imprisoned worldwide has increased by more than half.[621] In the past two decades in Africa, there has been a 42% increase in women imprisoned.[622] The causes are many, including the disproportionate harshness on women of punitive drug policies.[623] South Africa stands out in contrast. While our general prison population has skyrocketed, democratic reforms have ensured that the proportion of women has remained largely stable. After 2000, South Africa's female prison population steadily declined, remaining between 2% to 2,6% of the total, though recent years have seen a slight increase (inching toward 3%).[624]

Given our miserable overall trend, it is to be welcomed that the numbers of women in prison have declined overall since 2000. Yet there is still much reason to be troubled about which women we imprison, why we imprison them and the conditions in which we imprison them. They are a microcosm of some of the most marginalised in our society. It seems the gender inequalities that permeate our society are accentuated in the prison setting.

Many women in prison are from poor, under-educated, and Black and Coloured communities. There are distinct gendered pathways to crime. These include experiences of and responses to gender-based violence.[625] A study found that experiences of rape or domestic violence are three times higher among women in prison than among other women.[626] Many women imprisoned for violent crimes have themselves experienced violence and physical, sexual and psychological abuse, which may directly or indirectly affect crimes they commit.[627] For instance, some women kill their abusive partners after experiencing cycles of abuse,[628] while others are pulled into the criminal world by abusive partners involved in gangs, trafficking and drugs.[629]

Many women are in prison for addiction-related offences or offences committed as a result of mental health issues.[630] Women are also imprisoned for economic crimes and their responses to pressures of caretaking and motherhood (especially single motherhood). Psychology expert Bianca Parry's interviews with 17 incarcerated women found a relationship between motherhood and criminality. Parry explains that contrary to the benign social perception of motherhood, the burden of primary caregiving may contribute towards women's conflict with the law. Incarcerating them then inflicts a devastating impact on their children, which Parry calls 'the motherhood penalty'.[631]

While we note the gender-pathways to crime, which often call for non-prison alternatives, we acknowledge the unique circumstances and agency of each woman in conflict with the law.[632]

International and domestic standards guarantee all incarcerated persons a full range of rights. These make special provision for women. The Correctional Services Act specifies that women must be incarcerated separately, with special provisions for pregnant women, and allows for female inmates to be accommodated with their child for a specified period. In its Annual Report 2023/2024 JICS reported 66 infants imprisoned with their mothers in specialised mother and baby units during that reporting period.[633]

Incarcerated women experience hardships common to all in prison – but on top of those are unique gender-specific challenges. Many assume that female correctional centres are not as violent and dysfunctional as men's. Some even think them 'luxurious' by comparison. Wrong. Like most correctional centres, they are grossly overcrowded. And violent.

Women lack rehabilitation, vocational training and education programmes. And often the programmes that are on offer tend to reinforce gender stereotypes by focusing on domestic skills.[634] They need hygiene and sanitary products – 'carceral period poverty' is an ongoing issue.[635] After complaints that women at Kgosi Mampuru II did not receive adequate sanitary pads, JICS facilitated large donations of sanitary products from the public. In 2023/2024 alone, JICS received 118 urgent complaints concerning access to feminine hygiene products.[636]

Women require appropriate healthcare, especially reproductive, pregnancy and abortion-related healthcare, as well as menopausal treatment. Mental health is a concern. One nurse spoke of high levels of depression in their facility, and told us that women request medication because 'they want to be numb'.

Many lose contact with their children. They yearn for contact with their families. Some are incarcerated far away from their families, while others do not want their children to see them in prison. Women awaiting trial, who make up a significant portion of women in prison in South Africa,[637] tend to experience even greater deprivation.

Women in prison also experience violence, inhumane treatment, invasive strip searches, verbal abuse from officials and sexual violence – often reproducing the abusive conditions in wider society.[638] Sexual violence amongst women is not taken seriously. At Westville prison near Durban,

188

we had complaints of rape. Male officials are restricted from entering the centre and from accessing the keys, but they can work at the entrances and administration. They allegedly raped two women who were cleaning the entrance and visitors' area. This is a sober reminder that even a prison entrance hall may not be safe for women.

During an inspection of a female juvenile centre, we identified a young female remand detainee who said she was pregnant, and looked pregnant – but without medical confirmation. She was housed in an overcrowded and undernourished cell. The head of centre assured JICS she would be taken for medical examination.

One case still haunts us. In November 2022, JICS learned of a woman incarcerated in Johannesburg who had been diagnosed with cervical cancer. She was receiving no treatment. Her health had so deteriorated that she was in immense pain. And her cellmates shunned her, thinking her dirty or unhygienic. JICS intervened. Dr Duvern Ramiah, head of Oncology at Charlotte Maxeke Academic Hospital, responded instantly. For the first time, she received treatment.[639]

But these piecemeal interventions do little to address systemic abuse and deprivation. The UN Rules for the Treatment of Women Prisoners and Non-custodial Measures for Women Offenders (the Bangkok Rules) provide guidelines. They spell out the need for gender-specific and -sensitive mental, physical and reproductive healthcare; for safety and security; for contact with family members; for staff training; for care for pregnant women and mothers with children; and for prisoner rehabilitation and reintegration. The rules require states to consider women's caretaking responsibilities when determining admission to prisons and where they are detained:

> The accommodation of women prisoners shall have facilities and materials required to meet women's specific hygiene needs, including sanitary towels provided free of charge and a regular supply

189

of water to be made available for the personal care of children and women, in particular women involved in cooking and those who are pregnant, breastfeeding or menstruating.[640]

Perhaps most innovatively, the rules urge states to develop and implement gender-specific diversionary measures and non-custodial pre-trial and sentencing alternatives. These must consider caretaking responsibilities and any history of victimisation. The rules also require states to address the most common causes that bring women into the criminal justice system. These interventions, along with reforms, including decriminalising sex work and drug use, take place outside prisons but may limit the harm women suffer in the justice system. The rules should be implemented within South Africa.

Women are outliers in a system designed for men. Their particular needs are too often overlooked and under-served. In December 2022, the department launched the Atteridgeville Gender Responsive Centre, to cater to incarcerated women's unique needs. Based on the prescripts of the Bangkok Rules, it is 'the first of its kind' in South Africa and Africa[641] and accommodates almost 500 inmates. Some of these women have committed violent or serious offences, others have not. Many are awaiting trial (192 when we last visited in November 2024). And a significant number are non-nationals who have been arrested for immigration offences.

Our inspection of Atteridgeville in November 2024 was unannounced. The centre functioned in many ways like a normal prison, with many of the same challenges we encounter everywhere. But there were key differences. Atteridgeville was quieter, cleaner and with more empathetic management. Inmates basically had no complaints. Violence and assaults seemed rare. Crucially, the centre was not overcrowded. The communal cells we visited were well taken care of, with new bedding, decent natural light and ventilation, and absent the usual smells and dirt of male prisons.

There were a few notable distinctions. Many rehabilitation programmes were on offer – church services, the opportunity to work in the garden or on the farm, a fully functioning salon where inmates received training and work experience, a well-stocked library, a functional UNISA hub for tertiary education, and a school, where we saw inmates writing the November exams. We spoke to a social worker who told us that during the December holiday season, her primary focus would be encouraging bonding between incarcerated mothers and their children, by facilitating visits from those children in the care of the Department of Social Development. Earlier in the year, under the theme 'women in conflict with the law', the centre showcased art, drama, poetry and speeches by the women in prison. They spoke out about their lived experiences, how they ended up in prison and their current treatment.

But challenges were still apparent: dysfunctional telephones, maintenance troubles that left three of the centre's 24 cells out of order. The health centre was under-staffed, despite its well-stocked pharmacy and consulting rooms, with four nurses responsible for almost 500 inmates and three infants. Another serious concern: juvenile inmates and, distressingly, even a child. That child was fourteen years old, awaiting trial after being arrested for engaging in sex work. We understood that she remained in prison because she had run away from home and appeared to have a troubled home life. She was detained in the hospital ward, with adults, because there was no special children's unit. Though the centre sought to minimise the risk by accommodating younger inmates in the hospital ward, or with elderly and ill inmates, it seemed clear that under these circumstances the young inmates were not receiving specialised or appropriate care.

Our overall impression, however, was positive. It was evident that the centre's management sought to cater to women's needs, including reproductive health, ensuring sufficient uniforms, and facilitating good relationships with family.

Atteridgeville shows that with enough political will and resources, it is possible to run a well-functioning prison committed to the needs of the inmates and their rehabilitation. Still, to fully comply with the Bangkok Rules, more work must be done. And even though the centre was well run, it was still a bleak environment. As we left, JICS's head of inspections and investigations, and one of it most senior staffers, Lennard de Souza, quietly noted the atmosphere of profound despondency and depression that weighted the whole centre.

4.4 Improve treatment and conditions for LGBTQ+ inmates

LGBTQ+ prisoners face distinct challenges. The UN Special Rapporteur on torture has reported that 'a strict hierarchy' usually prevails in detention facilities – 'and those at the bottom of this hierarchy, such as children, the elderly, persons with disabilities and diseases, gays, lesbians, bisexuals and trangender persons, suffer double or triple discrimination'.[642]

Many in detention engage in same-sex intimacy, without identifying as gay, lesbian or bisexual. But self-identified (or visibly) LGBTQ+ inmates are a distinct and vulnerable minority, at risk of stigma. They are especially vulnerable to mistreatment, violence and sexual assault – at the hands of both officials and other prisoners. They are often disrespected for being, or being seen to be, queer.

Transgender persons are denied gender-appropriate clothing, hygiene products and healthcare. While actual reports of sexual assault in South Africa are low, meaning we have few reliable statistics, in the USA transgender prisoners are reported to be about ten times more likely to suffer sexual assault. And 40% of transgender persons in state and federal prisons reported sexual assault in the previous year.[643]

The Yogyakarta Principles, a set of principles on the application of international human rights law in relation to sexual orientation and gender identity, outline some of the ways states can protect LGBTQ+ persons in detention. These include: adopting and implementing policies to combat violence, discrimination and other harm, including on placement, body or other searches, gender expression, gender-affirming treatment and medical care, and 'protective' solitary confinement; adopting policies on placement and treatment that reflect the needs and rights of persons of all sexual orientations, gender identities, gender expressions and sex characteristics, and ensuring that persons are able to participate in decisions regarding the facilities in which they are placed; and providing for effective oversight of detention facilities, to address specific vulnerabilities of LGBTQ+ people.[644]

In two cases in South Africa, courts have ordered the department to remedy painful challenges LGBTQ+ inmates face. Ms Jade September was a transgender woman in Helderstroom, a maximum security prison for males some 120 km from Cape Town. Under the Alteration of Sex Description and Sex Status Act,[645] a transgender person who alters their sex is treated and detained in terms of their altered sex. But changing one's legal sex description is a demanding process. Medical intervention and validation are required. Though intending to seek medical treatment, Ms September had not yet done so. As a result, she was treated as male because of her birth registration, as reflected on her arrest warrant. She was not allowed to wear feminine clothing or underwear, use make-up, or wear her hair in ways that female inmates ordinarily would. Her request to be referred to by female pronouns was ignored.

She took the department to court,[646] contending that her treatment amounted to unfair discrimination and harassment. She asked the court to order that she be allowed to express her gender identity in prison. The department argued that because she had not legally altered her sex description, it was correct to treat her as male: there was no unfair discrimination. Curiously, the department contended that they refused to allow her to express her gender identity for her own safety – hence the discrimination was fair.

Judge Chantel Fortuin in the Equality Court in Cape Town would have none of this. She found that being treated as male had caused Ms September severe mental suffering. This resulted in feelings of fear, anguish, inferiority and humiliation, which violated her constitutional right not to be subjected to cruel, inhumane or degrading treatment. Additionally, until she could undergo medical treatment, presenting and expressing herself as a woman were the only ways she could express her gender identity. Denying her this infringed upon her human dignity and free expression.

Finally, Judge Fortuin held that the prison's neutral application of rules applicable to all was discriminatory since it made no provision for transgender inmates. She agreed with the department that allowing Ms September to express her gender identity in a communal cell would put her at risk of sexual assault, but found that a less restrictive measure – detention in a single cell – could protect her.

The court ordered amendments to the department's policies (replacing 'underpants' and 'panties' with 'gender appropriate underwear') and ordered prison management to take reasonable steps to give effect to Ms September's rights – either accommodating her in a single cell in a male or female prison, but in either case allowing her to express her gender identity (returning her make-up, allowing her to wear her hair long and in feminine styles, addressing her as a woman and with female pronouns).

As we write, Lawyers for Human Rights, building on these precedents, has initiated proceedings to secure protection for a transgender inmate at Johannesburg Medium B.[647] Despite the precedent Ms September's case established, the applicant has not been allowed to express her gender by wearing her hair as she wishes, wearing make-up or using feminine pronouns. Additional relief sought is an order that the Correctional Services Act is constitutionally invalid in so far as it permits denial of gender-affirming healthcare.

In another matter,[648] Mr Tumelo Mapodile, a man self-identifying as gay, was detained in a communal cell at 'Sun City' (Johannesburg) with inmates who considered him a woman and humiliated and harassed him. He sought prison management's intervention. A medical professional provided a letter recommending he be accommodated alone or with other LGBTQ+ inmates. All unavailing. He turned to the High Court. The department contended that accommodating him in a single cell or in a communal cell with other LGBTQ+ inmates would be difficult because of overcrowding. Accommodation could be made available in a cell with two LGBTQ+ inmates, but he would have to sleep on the floor since that cell had no more beds. The applicant accepted this because he slept on the floor anyway in his overcrowded communal cell.

Judge MM Mabasele in the High Court noted that the prison regulations provide for separation of specific categories of prisoners to safeguard their dignity and privacy – including men from women, youth offenders, and inmates suffering from mental or chronic illness or on grounds of health. He found that LGBTQ+ inmates are similarly positioned and therefore entitled to the same protection. He ordered the department to accommodate the applicant in a single cell or in a cell with other LGBTQ+ inmates.

In many of the prisons we visit, LGBTQ+ inmates request and are granted single cells. Though this provides more safety, it also means that they serve their sentences in isolation, which imposes its own burdens.

Durban Correctional Centre, has allowed self-identifying LGBTQ+ inmates to request transfer to a unit reserved exclusively for them, managed by an official who himself identifies as gay. This enables separation without isolation. Given overcrowding, this may not always be possible. But even Westville's solution is imperfect. Inmates complained to us that, for their safety, they were often excluded from activities and facilities (like family or sports days). And while other sections enjoyed pool tables, they did not.

We inferred that officials were grappling with balancing safety and inclusion. They warmly embraced JICS's offer to facilitate donated pool tables and board games, which by private generosity were delivered not long after and installed in the LGBTQ+ section.

Prisons are inescapably repressive. But within these confines, the risks LGBTQ+ people face can be effectively reduced. The safe and supportive environment officials created at Westville has made a beneficial difference to the lives of LGBTQ+ inmates.

This was on joyous display at an affirming Pride celebration the LGBTQ+ inmates specially organised in November 2023 to thank JICS for its intervention. We travelled by road to join the celebration as guests of honour. The social worker team at Westville, led by Ms Ruth Joubert, helped realise a memorable and unusually touching event.

The way forward

That prisons need to be humanised does not mean 'that there are no humans in need of imprisonment'.[649] Put differently, that some dangerous people need to be imprisoned is not inconsistent with our journey towards improving and reforming our approaches to crime and punishment.

The star guiding our standard of punishment should not be retribution and vengeance. These have done us no good. Rather, not extinguishing *hope* can be a meaningful standard for punishment.[650] Kimberley Brownlee notes that one standard 'an overall system of punishment must meet to be legitimate and morally justifiable' is that of a 'reasonable person retaining hope both in the present and for [their] future after punishment'.[651]

Another way to understand this is by considering the opposite – a system without hope is one where there are high rates of recidivism, violence, self-harm and suicides. This is too often the case in our prisons now. How do we begin the hard work of developing a standard of accountability for harmful conduct based on hope? Throughout this chapter, we have shown how prison reform is possible and worth pursuing.

7

How to Start on Hope, Discovery and Remediation

Just as societies in the past came to be shocked by public executions, by stoning and whipping, will future generations judge our current approaches to crime and punishment with appalled shock? Will future generations look back with horror and moral censure because of our over-reliance on mass incarceration in overcrowded prisons? As we reach the end of our book, we invite you, the reader, to join us in grappling with these perplexing questions.

Our legacy of violence

South Africa's legacy of inequality, injustice and deprivation spills into our lives today, in the violence we inflict on each other. We struggle to understand its causes. And our response to it is too often crude, ineffectual and damaging. We have tried to persuade you that mass incarceration and lengthy sentences are poorly suited to address both the causes and their symptoms.

Apartheid's discriminations were built on violence – violence by the state, through a brutal criminal justice system; and structural violence in crude theories and grotesque enactment of racial supremacism, subordination and deprivation – in landownership, employment, education, healthcare and economic justice.

The legacy remains. Today, South Africa is one of the world's most violent societies. Murder, violence against women, violence against children, and vigilantism are widespread.

What to do? Caution is necessary. Some may commit crimes regardless of social context. Trying to understand how violence occurs is not to excuse it.[652] And no single factor sufficiently explains South Africa's violence.[653] Yet insightful frameworks may help us understand the particular manifestations of our violence.

Writing in 2004, Bill Dixon, a Nottingham-based criminologist with insights about post-apartheid South Africa, suggests explanations.[654] The *control theory* posits that the 'institutional violence' of apartheid, combined with anti-apartheid movements' strategy of violent ungovernability, entrenched a deep-rooted culture of violence. The *strain theory* suggests that the cavernous gap between high hopes and unmet expectations South Africa's democracy inflicted on most of its people manifests in violence. The *opportunity theory* notes how organised crime and gang control may prosper when widespread poverty mixes as it does in South Africa with wealth, sophisticated infrastructure, and access to firearms. Finally, *the structural theory* invites us to ask how inequality, lack of education and employment, under-development, gender inequality and other social ills account for crime and violence.

These postulates are interrelated, not separate; and none is complete. But they may help us understand. Violence does not dissipate overnight. Though the advent of democracy, at least in theory, curtailed the state's power to invoke violence, Marikana and other contemporary horrors show its omnipresence.

The factors impelling South Africa's violent crime, both legacy (institutionalised violence, dispossession, social dislocation, migrant labour, fractured families, urbanisation) and current (toxic masculinity, alcoholism, poverty, unmet socio-economic needs, newly violent governance), converge.[655]

And lack of trust or confidence in the criminal justice system, unable to serve victims and survivors, despite reform, enables more violence.[656] Persisting violence may contribute to a 'collective cumulative trauma' since many people have experienced violence at home or in their communities, or have themselves perpetrated violence. The overall impact is a pervasive sense that violence is inevitable.[657]

There is no all-embracing answer. But the urgent insight of this book is that prisons and lengthy sentences offer no solutions. Worse, they distract us from the painful task of trying to understand why our society is so violent, and how to change it.

The reforms to criminal justice that we have proposed demand broader sustenance – improved access to education, employment opportunities, quality healthcare, supportive social services, and basic elements of good governance. After a dangerously heady transition from apartheid, thirty years of democracy have imposed a new sobriety about the urgency for practical interventions.

Not all of us can do everything. But we have power, individually and together, to address errors of policy and practice that urgently invite beneficial reform. Among these, prisons and sentencing policy prominently claim our practical intervention.

We can do better

It is true that some challenges seem so overwhelming they tempt us to inaction, despair and cynicism. Yet our recent history urges us to more engaged, more hopeful, responses. The epidemic of AIDS – a virally borne calamity of disease and death that confronted our new democracy in the 1990s – was rightly understood as a catastrophe, one compounded by deeply etched patterns of racial, sexual and moralistic stigma. The stigma led to a further catastrophe – presidential denialism, under Thabo Mbeki, that inflicted inexpressible suffering and death on millions of families and households.

Yet, spectacularly, even with AIDS, engagement and action prevailed: practically directed, evidentially backed, principled action. The Treatment Action Campaign, led by Zackie Achmat, successfully challenged the strangling grip international pharmaceutical companies exerted on ARV drug prices.

It then, perforce, had to confront President Mbeki and his government. Aided by Bill of Rights protections and entitlements, and committed judges willing to enforce them, activists secured victories against both monopolistic pricing and government misdirection.

Today, through citizen action, constitutional protections and government systems, South Africa has the largest publicly provided ARV programme anywhere in the world. Nearly seven million people – including one of the authors of this book – owe their lives to a simple, and now inexpensive, daily regimen of combined medications.

What seemed unimaginable and overwhelming just two decades ago, has been accomplished.

We can do the same with crime and violence. Not overnight. Not with any magical solutions. But with our practically directed, evidentially armoured, interventions. With only enough energy and determination, no more, we can begin to reform our prisons and the factors that overcrowd and corrupt them. And through that modest beginning, that limited commitment, we start to embark on a more hopeful journey to address the fear and anger and deprivation that beset all our lives.

About the Authors

EDWIN CAMERON

President Mandela appointed Edwin Cameron a judge in 1994. After retiring with 25 years' service as a judge, he was elected Chancellor of Stellenbosch University, and President Ramaphosa appointed him Inspecting Judge of prisons.

A human rights lawyer under apartheid, Cameron helped secure the historic inclusion of sexual orientation in South Africa's Constitution.

Cameron was an outspoken critic of then-President Mbeki's AIDS-denialist policies. He has written two memoirs, Witness to AIDS (2005), and Justice: A Personal Account (2014). He was the first, and remains the only, official holding public office in Africa to state publicly that he is living with HIV/AIDS.

President Ramaphosa awarded him South Africa's highest civilian honour, the Order of the Baobab (Gold). In 2023, President Masisi appointed him as a non-resident member of the Court of Appeal of Botswana.

REBECCA GORE

Rebecca Gore worked as a law clerk and legal researcher at the Judicial Inspectorate for Correctional Services under Inspecting Judge Edwin Cameron. She clerked at the Constitutional Court of South Africa in the Chambers of Justices Cameron, Mhlantla, and Majiedt. Rebecca has worked for a variety of international human rights institutions in South Africa and abroad. She is currently a pupil advocate at the Cape Bar.

Rebecca holds a Bachelor of Social Science in Politics, Philosophy, and Economics (PPE), a postgraduate Honours degree, and an LLB from the University of Cape Town, where she is a research associate at the Centre for Law and Society. She holds a Master of Laws (LLM) from Harvard Law School, where she was awarded the Henigson Human Rights Fellowship.

SOHELA SURAJPAL

Sohela Surajpal works for the Judicial Inspectorate for Correctional Services as law clerk and legal researcher to Inspecting Judge Edwin Cameron.

Before this, she did advocacy work on the rights of sexual and gender minorities in Africa at the University of Pretoria's Centre for Human Rights and clerked for Justice Mbuyiseli Madlanga at the Constitutional Court.

Sohela has a Master of Laws in Democracy and Human Rights in Africa from the University of Pretoria. Her interest in prisons began when she wrote her LLM mini-dissertation on Prison Abolition as a Decolonial and Human Rights imperative in Africa.

Judicial decisions

Vinter and Others v the United Kingdom Application nos. 66069/09, 130/10 and 3896/10 (2013)
Whittaker v Roos and Bateman; Morant v Roos and Bateman 1912 AD 92

Endnotes

FOREWORD

1   Angela Y Davis, *Are Prisons Obsolete?* (New York: Seven Stories Press, 2003), 15. Davis notes that 'the prison is present in our lives and, at the same time, it is absent from our lives'.

CHAPTER 1

2   See Hartmut Lang, 'The Population Development of the Rehoboth Basters', *Anthropos* 93 (1998): 381–391.
3   Act 41 of 1971.
4   'Die middel waarvan daar die meeste misbruik in die wêreld gemaak word'. See Hansard, 5 May 1971, column 5997. The authors are grateful to Connie Mulder's son, Dr Pieter Mulder, for sharing these sources.
5   See Hazel Crampton, *Dagga: A Short History* (Johannesburg: Jacana Media, 2015).
6   Tembisa Waetjen, 'Apartheid's 1971 Drug Law: Between Cannabis and Control in South Africa', *The Social History of Alcohol and Drugs* 36, no. 2 (2022): 164–200. Waetjen helpfully explains at 197 that: 'It is evident that the 1971 drug law augmented the NP government's notorious carceral powers, including political control over anti-apartheid activism. In rural areas where dagga was cultivated, dagga raids and herbicidal spraying by military aircraft were concrete demonstrations of the state's capacity to use force. Drug control became a tool aligned to the apartheid state's racist and anti-insurgent agendas.'
7   *S v Vermaas, S v Du Plessis* [1995] ZACC 5; 1995 (3) SA 292; 1995 (7) BCLR 851 (CC) (8 June 1995).
8   See Hugh Lewin, *Bandiet Out of Jail: Seven Years in a South African Prison* (Johannesburg: Umuzi, 2000).

9   *Goldberg v Minister of Prisons* 1979 (1) SA 14 (A). See also *Rossouw v Sachs* 1964 (2) SA 551 (A).

10   John D Battersby, 'Hanging Now the Routine at Pretoria Prison', *New York Times*, 1 December 1988, available at https://www.nytimes.com/1988/12/01/world/ hangings-now-the-routine-at-pretoria-prison.html, accessed on 5 December 2024.

11   See Prakash Diar, *The Sharpeville Six: The South African Trial that Shocked the World* (Toronto: McLelland & Stewart,1990).

12   A *New Yorker* profile claimed also, without offering evidence, that anti-apartheid activist and poet Breyten Breytenbach's trial judge had conversed with Prime Minister John Vorster, who some speculated had 'personally dictated the sentence'. See Lawrence Weschler, 'An Afrikaner Dante', *The New Yorker*, 8 November 1993, 92, available at https://www.archive.stevenson.info/docs/Breytenbach_New_Yorker_ Article.pdf [https://perma.cc/9XV9-XF2X], accessed on 14 August 2024.

13   See Thomas Grant, *The Mandela Brief: Sydney Kentridge and the Trials of Apartheid* (London: John Murray, 2022).

CHAPTER 2

14   Norval Morris and David J Rothman, eds. *The Oxford History of the Prison: The Practice of Punishment in Western Society* (Oxford: Oxford University Press, 1998): vii.

15   Edward M Peters, 'Prison before the prison: The ancient and medieval worlds', in *The Oxford History of the Prison: The Practice of Punishment in Western Society*, eds. Norval Morris and David J Rothman (Oxford: Oxford University Press, 1998): 3–23.

16   Peters, 'Prison before the prison', 3. See also Randall McGowen, 'The well-ordered prison' in *The Oxford History of the Prison: The Practice of Punishment in Western Society* , eds. Norval Morris and David J Rothman (Oxford: Oxford University Press, 1998): 80. McGowen notes that: 'Only a small minority were actually imprisoned as punishment, usually for such minor offences as vagrancy. In theory two types of institutions existed, the jail and the house of correction. The former contained felons and debtors, as well as those held for trial, whereas the latter received petty offenders sentenced for short terms.'

17   McGowen, 'The well-ordered prison', 80; and Andrew G Coyle, 'Prisons', in *Encyclopaedia Britannica*, available at https://www.britannica.com/topic/prison [https://perma.cc/EQQ3-CT8L], accessed on 20 October 2023.

18   Florence Bernault, 'The politics of enclosure in colonial and post-colonial Africa', in *A History of Prison and Confinement in Africa* (Social History of Africa Series), ed. Florence Bernault (Heinemann, 2003): 1.

19   Bernault, 'The politics of enclosure in colonial and post-colonial Africa', 1.

20   Michel Foucault, *Discipline and Punish: Birth of the Prison*, trans. Alan Sheridan (New York: Pantheon Books, 1977): 7–8.

21 Though public spectacles of torture and execution left the public domain, as Foucault notes at 15, neither torture nor execution were completely erased from the criminal justice system. These 'haunted our penal system for a long time and still [haunt] it today'.

22 Foucault, *Discipline and Punish*, 9.

23 McGowen, 'The well-ordered prison', 85–97. See further Davis, *Are Prisons Obsolete?*, 43–44: 'It may be important at this point in our examination to acknowledge the radical shift in the social perception of the individual that appeared in the ideas of that era. With the rise of the bourgeoisie, the individual came to be regarded as a bearer of formal rights and liberties [...] Before the acceptance of the sanctity of individual rights, imprisonment could not have been understood as punishment. If the individual was not perceived as possessing inalienable rights and liberties, then the alienation of those rights and liberties by removal from society to a space tyrannically governed by the state would not have made sense. Banishment beyond the geographical limits of the town may have made sense, but not the alteration of the individual's legal status through imposition of a prison sentence. Moreover, the prison sentence, which is always computed in terms of time, is related to abstract quantification, evoking the rise of science and what is often referred to as the Age of Reason. We should keep in mind that this was precisely the historical period when the value of [labour] began to be calculated in terms of time and therefore compensated in another quantifiable way, by money.'

24 Davis, *Are Prisons Obsolete?*, 40–41, referring to Foucault, *Discipline and Punish*.

25 Davis, *Are Prisons Obsolete?*, 41.

26 Davis, *Are Prisons Obsolete?*, 48.

27 Davis, *Are Prisons Obsolete?*, 47. See also Peter Scharff Smith, 'The Effects of Solitary Confinement on Prison Inmates: A Brief History and Review of the Literature', *Crime and Justice: A Review of Research* 34 (2006): 441–458, at 456–457. Cherry Hill was an example of the 'Pennsylvania model'. In contrast, Auburn Penitentiary in New York permitted offenders to work together in a strict regime of total silence (the 'Auburn model'). Smith explains that in the USA 'the Auburn model became the more popular, whereas the Europeans favored the Pennsylvania system and therefore solitary confinement. Between 1830 and 1870, several hundred European jails and prisons were constructed (or modernized) on the basis of a system of social isolation.'

28 Michel Foucault, *The Punitive Society: Lectures at the Collège de France, 1972–1973* (London: Picador, 2018): 109–111.

29 Foucault, *Discipline and Punish*, 61. He explains at 63: '[T]he people never felt closer to those who paid the penalty than in those rituals intended to show the horror of the crime and the invincibility of power; never did the people feel more threatened, like them, by a legal violence exercised without moderation or restraint. The solidarity of a whole section of the population with those we would call petty

offenders – vagrants, false beggars, the indigent poor, pick-pockets, receivers and dealers in stolen goods – was constantly expressed: resistance to police searches, the pursuit of informers, attacks on the watch or inspectors provide abundant evidence of this. And it was the breaking up of this solidarity that was becoming the aim of penal and police repression.'

30 Michel Foucault, 'Alternatives to the Prison – Dissemination or Decline of Social Control?', *Theory, Culture & Society* 26, no. 6 (2009):15.

31 The Thirteenth Amendment: 'Section 1. Neither slavery nor involuntary servitude, *except as a punishment for crime* whereof the party shall have been duly convicted, shall exist within the United States, or any place subject to their jurisdiction. Section 2. Congress shall have power to enforce this article by appropriate legislation.'

32 See Ruth Delaney, et al, 'American History, Race, and Prison', available at https://www.vera.org/reimagining-prison-web-report/american-history-race-and-prison%20 [https://perma.cc/Z9YT-SALN], accessed on 22 November 2024.

33 Black Codes refer to 'a series of laws passed throughout the South in the wake of emancipation. Although often professing to respect the equality and civil rights of the newly emancipated, in reality most of the Black Codes were specifically designed to curtail the economic, political, and social freedom of African Americans.' See the National Constitution Center, available at https://constitutioncenter.org/the-constitution/historic-document-library/detail/mississippi-south-carolina-black-codes-1865 [https://perma.cc/QGY4-JS6G], accessed on 22 November 2024.

34 See Michelle Alexander, *The New Jim Crow: Mass Incarceration in the Age of Colorblindness* (New York: The New Press, 2010). The author's thesis has generated criticism, none of which detracts from the observation we quote here.

35 Bryan Stevenson, 'Slavery Gave America a Fear of Black People and a Taste for Violent Punishment. Both Still Define our Criminal-Justice System', *New York Times*, 14 August 2019, available at https://www.nytimes.com/interactive/2019/08/14/magazine/prison-industrial-complex-slavery-racism.html [https://perma.cc/XL9F-YCKN], accessed on 10 February 2021.

36 Alex Lichtenstein, *Twice the Work of Free Labor: The Political Economy of Convict Labor in the New South* (New York: Verso, 1996): 13.

37 Davis, *Are Prisons Obsolete?*, 15.

38 Jeremy Sarkin, 'Prisons in Africa: An evaluation from a human rights perspective', *Sur – International Journal on Human Rights* 9 (2009): 2. Florence Bernault, in 'The politics of enclosure in colonial and post-colonial Africa', at 2, explains further that '[p]enal incarceration was unknown to sub-Saharan societies prior to the European conquest, when colonial regimes built prisons on a massive scale for deterring political opposition and enforcing African labor'.

39 Sarkin, 'Prisons in Africa', 2.

40 Bernault, 'The politics of enclosure in colonial and post-colonial Africa', at 8, explains that, for the most part, they did so without regard to race.

41 Dirk van Zyl Smit, 'Public Policy and the Punishment of Crime in a Divided
    Society: A Historical Perspective on the South African Penal System', *Crime and
    Social Justice* 21/22 (1988): 148. See also Dirk van Zyl Smit, *South African Prison
    Law and Practice* (Butterworths, 1992).
42 Shanta Singh, 'The historical development of prisons in South Africa: a penological
    perspective', *New Contree* 50 (2005): 18.
43 Bernault, 'The politics of enclosure in colonial and post-colonial Africa', 3.
44 Bernault, 'The politics of enclosure in colonial and post-colonial Africa', 3.
45 Van Zyl Smit, 'Public Policy and the Punishment of Crime in a Divided Society',
    149.
46 Bernault, 'The politics of enclosure in colonial and post-colonial Africa', 8.
47 Van Zyl Smit, 'Public Policy and the Punishment of Crime in a Divided Society',
    149.
48 See Robben Island Museum, 'Imprisonment 1730–1879', available at https://www.
    robben-island.org.za/imprisonment-1730-1879/#:~:text=The%20black%20men%20
    imprisoned%20for,1869%20(right) [https://perma.cc/Y8Y3-6SAQ], accessed on
    7 November 2023).
49 Van Zyl Smit, 'Public Policy and the Punishment of Crime in a Divided Society', 149.
50 Van Zyl Smit, 'Public Policy and the Punishnent of Crime in a Divided Society',
    150–151 and Bernault, 'The politics of enclosure in colonial and post-colonial
    Africa', 8.
51 Bernault, 'The politics of enclosure in colonial and post-colonial Africa', 8.
52 Bernault, 'The politics of enclosure in colonial and post-colonial Africa', 8–9.
53 Van Zyl Smit, 'Public Policy and the Punishment of Crime in a Divided Society', 155.
54 Van Zyl Smit, 'Public Policy and the Punishment of Crime in a Divided Society', 155.
55 Van Zyl Smit explains how the role of the state as the provider of unskilled black
    labour for the mines through the penal system 'had become manifest'.
56 Van Zyl Smit, 'Public Policy and the Punishment of Crime in a Divided Society', 155.
57 Van Zyl Smit, 'Public Policy and the Punishment of Crime in a Divided Society', 157.
58 Report of the Committee on Convicts and Gaols G2-88 (2nd report) (1888) in
    Annexures to Votes and Proceedings of the House of Assembly Cape of Good Hope.
    As quoted in Van Zyl Smit, 'Public Policy and the Punishment of Crime in a
    Divided Society'.
59 Bernault, 'The politics of enclosure in colonial and post-colonial Africa', 9.
60 Pass laws were widely introduced in the 1870s. Van Zyl Smit, 'Public Policy and the
    Punishment of Crime in a Divided Society', notes at 156: 'Failure to produce a pass
    meant that they were sentenced to imprisonment and thus forced labor. There is
    evidence that by 1888 a significant proportion of the prison population had been
    created in this way.'
61 Eirwen Elizabeth Oswald, 'Writing in hostile spaces: A critical examination of
    South African prison literature' (PhD diss., University of Johannesburg, 2005), 3.

62 For instance, courts held that prisoners had the right to approach courts when treated unfairly. Judges also ruled it unlawful to subject those awaiting trial to solitary confinement. Remissions for good behaviour were adopted. See Singh, 'The Historical Development of Prisons in South Africa', 21–22, 25.

63 Truth and Reconciliation Commission Report Volume 4 Chapter 7, 'Institutional Hearings: Prisons' (hereafter TRC Prisons Report), 199, para 3.

64 Singh, 'The Historical Development of Prisons in South Africa', 23. Noting that 'The impetus for its appointment had come from the Penal Reform Committee of the South African Institute of Race Relations (SAIRR).'

65 Lansdowne Commission on Prison and Penal Reform Report (1947).

66 Amanda Dissel and Jody Kollapen, 'Racism and Discrimination in the South African Penal System', Report for Penal Reform International and the Centre for the Study of Violence and Reconciliation (2022): 25.

67 Section 23(1)(b) of the Prisons Act 8 of 1959 stipulated that: 'In every prison— as far as possible, white and non-white prisoners shall be detained in separate parts thereof and in such manner as to prevent white and non-white prisoners from being within view of each other.' Section 23(1)(c) stated that: 'wherever practicable, non-white prisoners of different races shall be separated.'

68 Singh, 'The Historical Development of Prisons in South Africa', 23.

69 Dissel and Kollapen, 'Racism and Discrimination in the South African Penal System', 27.

70 Dirk van Zyl Smit, 'Contextualising criminology in contemporary South Africa', in *Towards Justice? Crime and State Control in South Africa*, eds. Desirée Hansson and Dirk van Zyl Smit (Oxford: Oxford University Press,1990): 2, referencing newspaper editorials.

71 Van Zyl Smit, 'Contextualising criminology in contemporary South Africa', 2.

72 Sonia Bunting, 'The prisons of apartheid', *Africa South in Exile* 4, no. 4 (1960), ed. Ronald M Segal, 47.

73 Bunting, 'The prisons of apartheid', 48. In the late 1950s, 'there were altogether 286,372 convicted prisoners serving sentences in our jails, of whom 147,212 or 51. 4 per cent were petty offenders serving sentences of one month or less, many of them with the option of a fine which they couldn't afford to pay. In the words of the United Party's Dr. D. T. Smit during the debate on the Justice Vote in Parliament last year: "Many of these people should never have seen the inside of a jail. This is how many young Natives are linked with criminal gangs and become hardened criminals."'

74 TRC Prisons Report, 200, para 8. Made more vicious under the misnamed Natives (Abolition of Passes and Co-ordination of Documents) Act of 1952, available at https://www.sahistory.org.za/article/pass-laws-south-africa-1800-1994 [https://perma.cc/J2AD-YW85], accessed on 25 November 2024.

75 Bunting, 'The prisons of apartheid', 48.

76 TRC Prisons Report, 202, para 16.
77 TRC Prisons Report, 203, para 17.
78 TRC Prisons Report, 203, paras 17–18.
79 See Testimony of Benjamin Pogrund at the Truth and Reconciliation Commission at justice.gov.za/trc/special/prison/pogrund.htm [https://perma.cc/92FZ-K64R], accessed on 14 August 2024.
80 *Komani NO v Bantu Affairs Administration Board, Peninsula Area* 1980 (4) SA 449 (A).
81 *Oos-Randse Administrasieraad v Rikhoto* 1983 (3) SA 595 (A).
82 The enforcement of migration laws against cross-border job-seekers from Africa, also often impoverished and hungry-looking, is poignantly reminiscent of the enforcement of the pass laws.
83 TRC Prisons Report, 199, para 1.
84 TRC Prisons Report, 204, para 22.
85 South African History Online, 'End Conscription Campaign (ECC)', available at https://www.sahistory.org.za/article/end-conscription-campaign-ecc [https://perma.cc/TLP7-FD2N], accessed on 20 November 2023.
86 South African History Online, 'David Bruce', available at https://www.sahistory.org.za/people/david-bruce [https://perma.cc/2U2V-ZRDW], accessed on 20 November 2023.
87 South African History Online, 'End Conscription Campaign'.
88 TRC Prisons Report, 206, paras 27–30.
89 *Sonke Gender Justice NPC*, para 26, relying on the statements by Paula McBride and Henry Makgothi.
90 TRC Prisons Report, 211, para 43.
91 TRC Report Volume 4 Chapter 5, 'Institutional Hearing: The Health Sector', 112. See further 'Health Care in Custody', in *An Ambulance of the Wrong Colour: Health Professionals, Human Rights and Ethics in South Africa* , eds. Laurel Baldwin-Ragaven, Leslie London and Jeanelle de Gruchy (Cape Town: University of Cape Town Press, 1999).
92 TRC Report Volume 3 Chapter 2, 'Regional Profile: Eastern Cape', 66–67. The TRC found that: 'In view of the fact that Biko died in the custody of law enforcement officials, the probabilities are that he died as a result of injuries sustained during detention.'
93 TRC Prisons Report, 220–221.
94 TRC Prisons Report, 202, para 14.
95 TRC Prisons Report, 201, para 12.
96 TRC Prisons Report, 201, para 14.
97 TRC Prisons Report, 208–209, paras 35–36.
98 There were exceptions. A handful of judges interpreted statutes and regulations in light of Roman-Dutch common law principles related to individual wellbeing,

dignity and freedom. Some human rights lawyers urged fair judges not to resign and to continue to make decisions that mitigated punitive laws and sentences to alleviate the harshness of apartheid laws. See further John Dugard, 'Should Judges Resign – A Reply to Professor Wacks', *South African Law Journal* 101, no. 2 (1984): 286.

99 *Rossouw v Sachs* 1964 (2) SA 551 (A), 565.
100 *Whittaker v Roos and Bateman; Morant v Roos and Bateman* 1912 AD 92, 122–123.
101 *Rossouw v Sachs*, 564.
102 TRC Prisons Report, 213, para 47.
103 TRC Prisons Report, 213, para 46.
104 TRC Prisons Report, 213, para 49. The TRC noted that: 'Over the period of the Commission's mandate, over 2 500 people were hanged in South Africa.'
105 TRC Prisons Report, 213, para 47.
106 TRC Prisons Report, 214, para 50.
107 See Edwin Cameron et al, 'Who is "everyone" in s 35(2)?', 47.4.1, in 'Chapter 47 Rights of incarcerated and detained persons', in *South African Constitutional Law*, edited by Jason Brickhill, Adila Hassim, Michael Bishop, and Tembeka Ngcukaitobi (Cape Town: Juta, 2023).
108 Frank Snyckers and Jolandi le Roux, 'Criminal procedure: rights of arrested, detained and accused persons', in *Constitutional Law of South Africa* 2nd edition, eds. Stuart Woolman and Michael Bishop (Cape Town: Juta, 2013): 50–51.
109 See Cameron et al, 'Constitutionalising the *residuum* principle', at 47.5.3, in 'Chapter 47 Rights of incarcerated and detained persons', in *South African Constitutional Law*. Recently, the Constitutional Court in *Sonke Gender Justice NPC* stated at para 30 and fn 69 that: '[Prisoners] may not be subjected to any illegal treatment, or infringement of their liberty not warranted by, or necessary for, the purposes of correctional centre discipline and administration. Incarceration per se is not a justification for the limitation of inmates' rights, and they continue to enjoy all rights save those which it is absolutely necessary to curtail in order to implement the sentence or order of a court (the *residuum* principle).'
110 Section 13 of the Constitution of the Republic of South Africa, 1996.
111 Sections 37(1)(b) and 40 of the Correctional Services Act provide that sentenced offenders can be compelled to perform labour related to 'any development programme or which generally is designed to foster habits of industry'. However, despite the safeguards in place, this arrangement leaves room for exploitation. Some DCS officials have drawn our attention to the fact that the remuneration received by inmates is pitifully, unfairly low. The 'gratuity', as the act calls it, is determined by the National Commissioner and should be regularly increased. During a prison visit in 2024, we were told that inmates who worked every day doing hard manual labour on the prison farm earned no more than R150 a month. This was not enough to buy goods from the prison tuck-shop or to save for release. And it was especially low for

those inmates who did not receive regular visits, gifts or money from their families. Despite this, our experience has been that work positions are rare and highly valued amongst inmates. For perspectives on prison labour in South Africa see further Dirk van Zyl Smit, in *Prison Labour: Salvation or Slavery? International Perspectives*, edited by Dirk van Zyl Smit and Frieder Dünkel (Ashgate Pub Ltd, 1999, reissued 2018): 222–237.

112 White Paper on the Policy of the Department of Correctional Services in the New South Africa (1994); White Paper on Corrections in South Africa, 7, available at https://dullahomarinstitute.org.za/acjr/resource-centre/White%20Paper%20on%20 Corrections%20in%20South%20Africa.pdf [https://perma.cc/M4FJ-32MD], accessed on 26 November 2024.

113 White Paper on Corrections in South Africa, 14.

114 White Paper on Corrections in South Africa, 49. 'Restorative justice, as opposed to retributive justice, requires synergy across the integrated justice system as to the purpose of sentencing an individual, the purpose of incarceration, and the role of correction.' In the first of her Reith Lectures, delivered on 26 November 2024, Dr Gwen Adshead, a forensic psychiatrist working in United Kingdom prisons, strongly endorsed restorative justice, audio available at https://www.bbc.co.uk/ sounds/play/m0025cmg [https://perma.cc/JMF4-AVDZ].

115 White Paper on Corrections in South Africa, 38.

116 Singh, 'The Historical Development of Prisons in South Africa', 31–32. We note that some of these reforms predated the 1990s.

117 Section 1 of the Correctional Services Act.

118 Section 2 of the Correctional Services Act.

119 Correctional Services Regulations GN R914 in GG 26626 of 20 July 2004.

120 In terms of section 134(2) of the Correctional Services Act, the National Commissioner is empowered to issue orders that are consistent with the act and its regulations. These orders 'must be obeyed by all correctional officials and other persons to whom such orders apply'. Section 134(2) lists the areas which those orders may cover. The standing orders provide detailed requirements regarding issues such as lighting, air supply and floor space in cells, required regular inspections of cells, dealing with contagious and other diseases, and overcrowding.

121 See right to accommodation at section 7 of the Correctional Services Act, right to reading material at section 18, right to nutrition at section 8, and the right to access healthcare at section 12.

122 Section 85(2) of the Correctional Services Act provides: 'The object of the Judicial Inspectorate for Correctional Services is to facilitate the inspection of correctional centres in order that the Inspecting Judge may report on the treatment of inmates in correctional centres and on conditions in correctional centres.' The mandate of JICS 'was introduced to contribute to the *holistic transformation* of correctional services so as to promote rehabilitation within a humane and safe correctional system'.

Roundtable discussion on oversight over the prison system, *Civil Society Prison Reform Initiative*, 2009, available at https://acjr.org.za/resource-centre/ Roundtable%20discussion%20on%20oversight%20over%20the%20prison%20 system.pdf [https://perma.cc/97LE-Q5C4], accessed on 8 January 2023.
123 *S v Makwanyane* [1995] ZACC 3; 1995 (6) BCLR 665; 1995 (3) SA 391 (6 June 1995), para 88.
124 TRC 'Special Hearings – Prisons', 21 July 1997, available at https://www.justice. gov.za/trc/special/prison/masondo.htm [https://perma.cc/P5VK-CMJY], accessed on 26 February 2021.

CHAPTER 3

125 JICS has been working laboriously for some years with the Bertha Centre at the University of Cape Town to set up a bail fund that would on strict conditions offer bail for selected offenders whom the courts have granted bail but who cannot afford it. It is hoped that a pilot project will get off the ground in 2025.
126 Institute for Economics and Peace, 'Global Peace Index: Measuring Peace in a Complex World', 2024, available at https://www.economicsandpeace.org/wp-content/uploads/2024/06/GPI-2024-web.pdf [https://perma.cc/LBL9-P9WC], accessed on 14 March 2025.
127 Marvin Charles, Jeff Wicks and William Brederode, 'SA's murder rate rises to two-decade high – and cops are powerless', *News24*, 16 November 2023, available at https://www.news24.com/news24/southafrica/news/sas-murder-rate-rises-to-two-decade-high-and-cops-are-powerless-20231116, accessed on 27 May 2024.
128 Naeemah Abrahams et al, 'Research Brief: 20 years of femicide research in South Africa', South African Medical Research Council, September 2024, available at https://www.samrc.ac.za/policy-briefs/20-years-femicide-research-south-africa [perma.cc/2S6B-466B], accessed on 26 November 2024. See World Population Review, Femicide Rates by Country 2024, available at https://worldpopulationreview.com/country-rankings/femicide-rates-by-country [https://perma.cc/P6J9-82MS], accessed on 20 May 2024.
129 UNICEF, 'Time to protect children from violence and save lives now', 20 February 2024, available at https://www.unicef.org/southafrica/press-releases/time-protect-children-violence-and-save-lives-now, accessed on 15 May 2024.
130 Edwin Cameron, 'Imprisoning the nation: Minimum sentences in South Africa', University of the Western Cape Dean's Distinguished Lecture (2017): 5, available at https://www.groundup.org.za/media/uploads/documents/UWCImprisoningThe%20 Nation19October2017.pdf [https://perma.cc/PL6G-B6T5], accessed on 26 November 2024.
131 Anine Kriegler and Mark Shaw, 'Facts show South Africa has not become more violent since democracy', *The Conversation*, 21 July 2016, available at https://

theconversation.com/facts-show-south-africa-has-not-become-more-violent-since-democracy-62444 [https://perma.cc/46WY-S9PC], accessed on 26 November 2024.

132 Jonny Steinberg, 'Prison Overcrowding and the Constitutional Right to Adequate Accommodation in South Africa', paper commissioned by the Centre for the Study of Violence and Reconciliation, January 2005, citing figures from the Institute of Security Studies 'Criminal Justice Monitor', available at www.csvr.org.za/docs/correctional/prisoncovercrowding.pdf [https://perma.cc/B5U5-YSPE], accessed on 26 November 2024.

133 Dirk van Zyl Smit, 'Swimming against the tides: controlling the size of the prison population in the new South Africa', in *Justice Gained? Crime and Crime Control in South Africa's Transition*, eds. Bill Dixon and Elrena van der Spuy (Cape Town: University of Cape Town Press, 2004): 231. At 233 he explains the disjunct between public perceptions and the actual crime rates: '[U]ntil the late 1990s, there was no significant increase in the number of cases that the criminal justice system was being called upon to process and there was indeed a decline in the number of offenders recorded as being found guilty of crime.'

134 Marecia Damons and Nathan Geffen, 'How bad is South Africa's murder rate', *GroundUp*, 2 June 2023, available at https://groundup.org.za/article/how-bad-murder-in-south-africa/ [https://perma.cc/YV95-A7EW], accessed on 3 December 2024.

135 SAPS Annual Report 2011/2012 15 609, 20, available at https://www.gov.za/sites/default/files/gcis_document/201409/sapsanrep11-12.pdf [https://perma.cc/MC4L-UHYH], accessed on 3 December 2024.

136 Kriegler and Shaw, 'Facts show South Africa has not become more violent since democracy'.

137 Edwin Cameron, 'The Crisis of Criminal Justice in South Africa', *South African Law Journal* 137, part 4 (2020): 32 at 35. Based on the National Victims of Crime Surveys in 1998 and 2003, the fear of crime amongst South Africans more than doubled from 25% in 1998 to 58% in 2003.

138 Kriegler and Shaw, 'Facts show South Africa has not become more violent since democracy'.

139 TRC Report Volume 2 Chapter 7, 'Political Violence in the Era of Negotiations and Transition, 1990–1994', 583, para 2 (hereinafter TRC Report Volume 2).

140 TRC Report Volume 2, 'Political Violence in the Era of Negotiations and Transition, 1990–1994', 584, para 7.

141 TRC Report Volume 2, 'Political Violence in the Era of Negotiations and Transition, 1990–1994', 584–585, paras 8–9. 'In the period immediately following the announcement of an election date, the death toll in the [Pretoria/Johannesburg/Vaal] region rose to four times its previous levels' and 'The Human Rights Committee (HRC) estimates that, between July 1990 and June 1993, an average of 101 people died per month in politically related incidents – a total of 3 653 deaths. In the period

July 1993 to April 1994, conflict steadily intensified, so that by election month it was 2.5 times its previous levels.'

142 TRC Report Volume 2 Chapter 7.
143 Mark Shaw, 'South Africa: Crime in transition', *Institute for Security Studies* (1997): 1, available at https://issafrica.s3.amazonaws.com/site/uploads/Paper_17.pdf.
144 Peter Gastrow and Mark Shaw, 'In Search of Safety: Police Transformation and Public Responses in South Africa', *Daedelus* 130, no. 1 (2000): 259 at 262. See also Ziyanda Stuurman, *Can We Be Safe? The Future of Policing in South Africa* (Cape Town: Tafelberg, 2021).
145 Gastrow and Shaw, 'In Search of Safety', 262.
146 Antony Altbeker, *The Dirty Work of Democracy: A Year on the Streets with SAPS* (Cape Town: Jonathan Ball Publishers, 2005), 261.
147 Altbeker, *The Dirty Work of Democracy*, 261–262. Though Altbeker notes at 263 that a fast-growing budget soon allowed the force to bounce back, growing by approximately a third between 2000 and 2005 to match 1995 personnel levels.
148 *S v Makwanyane*, para 117.
149 *S v Makwanyane*, para 88.
150 Katherine Beckett and Megan Ming Francis, 'The Origins of Mass Incarceration: The Racial Politics of Crime and Punishment in the Post-Civil Rights Era', *Annual Review of Law & Social Science* 16 (2020): 433 at 434 remarks that 'although these terms are sometimes used interchangeably, they do refer to different, if overlapping, phenomena'.
151 Davis, *Are Prisons Obsolete?*, 31–39.
152 Elizabeth Hinton, *From the War on Poverty to the War on Crime: The Making of Mass Incarceration in America* (Boston: Harvard University Press, 2016): 1.
153 Hinton, *From the War on Poverty*, 6.
154 Hinton, *From the War on Poverty*, 1.
155 Lyndon Johnson, 'Special Message to the Congress on Law Enforcement and the Administration of Justice', 8 March 1965, Public Papers of the Presidents 1965/Part 1 (Washington, GPO: 1966), available at https://policing.umhistorylabs.lsa.umich.edu/s/detroitunderfire/item/4536 [https://perma.cc/HX4E-Z84Y], accessed on 26 November 2024).
156 Hinton, *From the War on Poverty*, 2–3 and 13.
157 Richard Nixon Foundation, 'Public enemy number one: A pragmatic approach to America's drug problem' 29 June 2016, available at https://www.nixonfoundation.org/2016/06/26404/ [https://perma.cc/E6XA-RRVS].
158 Hinton, *From the War on Poverty*, 2–3.
159 Hinton, *From the War on Poverty*, 2–3 and 17.
160 Hinton, *From the War on Poverty*, 4.
161 Including that of then Senator Joe Biden, who was staunchly 'tough on crime', as well as, later, that of then Attorney General of California Kamala Harris. See Sheryl

Gay Stolberg and Astead W Herndon, '"Lock the S.O.B.s Up": Joe Biden and the Era of Mass Incarceration', *New York Times*, 25 June 2019, available at https://www.nytimes.com/2019/06/25/us/joe-biden-crime-laws.html, accessed on 5 February 2021. See also Shaila Dewan, 'Kamala Harris and the return of "tough on crime"', *New York Times*, 17 August 2024, available at https://www.nytimes.com/2024/08/17/us/kamala-harris-prosecutor-criminal-justice-reform.html, accessed on 26 November 2024.

162 See Chapter 5 on prison abolition.

163 Hinton, *From the War on Poverty*, 8. Hinton notes that: '[T]he Republican coalition that emerged in the postwar period did not engineer the War on Crime and the rise of the carceral state. As the product of one of the most ambitious liberal welfare programs in American history, the rise of punitive federal policy over the last fifty years is a thoroughly bipartisan story. Built by a consensus of liberals and conservatives who privileged punitive responses to urban problems as a reaction to the civil rights movement, over time, the carceral state and the network of programs it encompassed came to dominate government responses to American inequality.' Quoted in Humanities New York, 'Excerpt: Making Mass Incarceration', 5 March 2018, available at https://humanitiesny.org/making-mass-incarceration/.

164 See Tim Arango, 'Frustrated Californians May Be Ready for a Tougher Approach to Crime', *New York Times*, 23 July 2024, available at https://www.nytimes.com/2024/07/23/us/frustrated-californians-may-be-ready-for-a-tougher-approach-to-crime.html?unlocked_article_code=1.9U0.jpXb.bU65iIoaDx-z&smid=wa-share. Notably, President Trump in December 2018 signed the Formerly Incarcerated Reenter Society Transformed Safely Transitioning Every Person Act ('First Step Act'), a bipartisan criminal justice statute.

165 Culminating in the 1961 Single Convention on Narcotic Drugs, and domestic legislation in the many countries that ratified the convention. See Ann Fordham, 'How the United States fueled a global drug war, and why it must end', Open Societies Foundation, 29 June 2021, available at https://www.opensocietyfoundations.org/voices/how-the-united-states-fueled-a-global-drug-war-and-why-it-must-end [https://perma.cc/LTD6-F7PE], accessed on 26 November 2024.

166 Hinton, *From the War on Poverty*, 5.

167 Wendy Sawyer and Peter Wagner, 'Mass incarceration: The Whole Pie 2024', Prison Policy Initiative, 14 March 2024, available at https://www.prisonpolicy.org/reports/pie2024.html, accessed on 26 November 2024.

168 Sawyer and Wagner, 'Mass incarceration'.

169 See the evidence of Mr Golden Miles Bhudu before the TRC, delivered in 1997, available at https://www.justice.gov.za/Trc/special/prison/bhudu.htm [https://perma.cc/NUS8-Q7KR]. Mr Bhudu testified that: 'Government and the Department of Correctional Services in 1996 and 1997, this year, have [suggested] the idea of a

general amnesty for prisoners, nothing has come however of this promise, and we are calling on the TRC to seriously revisit that public statement.'

170 See discussions on social crime prevention in David Bruce and Chandré Gould, 'The war against the causes of crime: Advocacy for social crime prevention in the face of tougher law enforcement', *SA Crime Quarterly* 30 (2009):13 at 14–15. They mention, for example, the Action for a Safe South Africa initiative, which considers investing in early childhood programmes, reducing domestic violence, improving parenting, providing quality after-school care and reducing the sale of alcohol. They also discuss 'developmental crime prevention'.

171 Shaw, 'South Africa: Crime in Transition', 4.

172 Bruce and Gould, 'The war against the causes of crime', 15.

173 Address by President Mandela at the Opening of the second session of democratic Parliament, 17 February 1995, available at https://www.gov.za/news/speeches/president-nelson-mandela-opening-second-session-democratic-parliament-17-feb-1995 [https://perma.cc/RCN2-3ETU], accessed on 8 December 2024.

174 Janine Rauch, 'The 1996 National Crime Prevention Strategy', Centre for the Study of Violence and Reconciliation (2001): 10, available at http://www.csvr.org.za/docs/urbansafety/1996nationalcrime.pdf [https://perma.cc/L7ZA-TWUR], accessed on 27 November 2024.

175 Lukas Muntingh and Gwen Dereymaeker, 'Understanding impunity in South African law enforcement agencies', *Civil Society Prison Reform Initiative* (2013): 25–27.

176 Lukas Muntingh, 'Punishment and deterrence: don't expect prisons to reduce crime', *SA Crime Quarterly*, no. 26 (2008): 3–9.

177 See Criminal Procedure Amendment Act 1995, section 4(f) of the Criminal Procedure Second Amendment Act 85 of 1997 and section 60 of the Criminal Procedure Act 51 of 1977. The Constitutional Court upheld the amendments in *S v Dlamini* 1999 (4) SA 623 (CC).

178 Section 73(6)(b)(iv) of the Correctional Services Act 111 of 1998 provides that persons sentenced to life imprisonment become eligible for release on parole only after serving at least 25 years. Section 73(6)(b)(v), later repealed, provided that persons serving minimum sentences must serve at least four-fifths of their sentences before becoming eligible for parole. See *Phaahla v Minister of Justice and Correctional Services and Another (Tlhakanye Intervening)* [2019] ZACC 18; 2019 (2) SACR 88 (CC); 2019 (7) BCLR 795 (CC) (3 May 2019).

179 The Magistrates Amendment Act 66 of 1998.

180 Guy Lamb, 'Police Militarisation and the "War on Crime" in South Africa', *Journal of Southern African Studies* 44, no. 5 (2018): 933 at 939–940.

181 Lamb, 'Police Militarisation and the "War on Crime" in South Africa', 940, referring to speech by the Minister of Police, EN Mthethwa MP, on the occasion of the budget vote nos. 24 and 22, Parliament, Cape Town, 6 May 2010, available at

https://www.gov.za/news/speeches/speech-minister-police-en-mthethwa-mp-occasion-budget-vote-no-24-and-22-parliament [https://perma.cc/Z397-KSN6].

182 Lamb, 'Police Militarisation and the "War on Crime" in South Africa', 939–940, referring to the SAPS Annual Report 2010/2011: 21, available at https://www.saps.gov.za/about/stratframework/annual_report/2010_2011/_work/Annual_Report_2010-2011_part_1.pdf [https://perma.cc/H2JU-6YGE].

183 Lukas Muntingh, 'An analytical study of South African prison reform after 1994' (LLD diss., University of the Western Cape, 2012): 129–131.

184 Muntingh, 'An analytical study of South African prison reform after 1994', 131; and Amanda Dissel, 'Tracking Transformation in South African Prisons', *Track Two* 11, no. 1 (2002): 12.

185 Muntingh, 'An analytical study of South African prison reform after 1994', 106–107, 112–113, and 131–133.

186 We acknowledge more recent positive developments, including the Constitutional Court's judgment in *Minister of Justice and Constitutional Development v Prince (Clarke and Others Intervening); National Director of Public Prosecutions v Rubin; National Director of Public Prosecutions v Acton* [2018] ZACC 30; 2018 (6) SA 393 (CC); 2018 (10) BCLR 1220 (CC) (18 September 2018), in which it confirmed an order of the High Court declaring legislation criminalising the private use, possession, purchase and cultivation of cannabis unconstitutional. On 28 May 2024, President Cyril Ramaphosa signed into law the Cannabis for Private Purposes Act 7 of 2024, which regulates the cultivation, possession and use of cannabis by adults in private, while continuing to prohibit dealing in cannabis.

187 JICS Annual Report 2023/2024, 13, available at http://www.jics.gov.za/wp-content/uploads/2024/10/JICS-ANNUAL-REPORT-2023-2024.pdf [https://perma.cc/KJ2A-85NB].

188 See World Prison Brief, 'Highest to Lowest – Prison Population Total – Entire world', available at https://www.prisonstudies.org/highest-to-lowest/prison-population-total?field_region_taxonomy_tid=All and World Prison Brief, 'Highest to Lowest – Prison Population Total – Africa', available at https://www.prisonstudies.org/highest-to-lowest/prison-population-total?field_region_taxonomy_tid=15.

189 On terminology, we note the distinction between 'mandatory' and 'minimum' sentencing regimes. In *S v Malgas* [2001] ZASCA 30; [2001] 3 All SA 220 (A), the Supreme Court of Appeal explained that: 'What is rightly regarded as an unjustifiable intrusion by the legislature upon the legitimate domain of the courts, is legislation which is so prescriptive in its terms that it leaves a court effectively with no sentencing discretion whatsoever and obliges it to pass a specific sentence which, judged by all normal and well-established sentencing criteria, could be manifestly unjust in the circumstances of a particular case. Such a sentencing provision can accurately be described as a mandatory provision in the pejorative sense intended by opponents of legislative incursions into this area. A provision which leaves the

courts free to exercise a substantial measure of judicial discretion is not, in my opinion, properly described as a mandatory provision in that sense. As I see it, this case is concerned with such a provision' (para 3). However, with rare exceptions, our minimum sentences *in effect* operate as mandatory sentences. So we use 'mandatory minimum sentences', 'mandatory sentences' and 'minimum sentences' interchangeably.

190 *S v Gibson* 1974 (4) SA 478 (A) at 481H–482B; *S v Mpetha* 1985 (3) SA 702 (A) at 706H (Corbett JA) and 710D-E (Van Heerden JA). See also the Viljoen Commission from the 1970s, which was critical of minimum sentencing.

191 105 of 1997.

192 Dirk van Zyl Smit and Catherine Appleton, *Life Imprisonment: A Global Human Rights Analysis* (Boston: Harvard University Press, 2019): 154. See also JD Mujuzi, 'The Changing Face of Life Imprisonment in South Africa', *Civil Society Prison Reform Initiative* (2008), available at https://dullahomarinstitute.org.za/acjr/resource-centre/The%20Changing%20Face%20of%20Life%20Imprisonment%20in%20South%20Africa.pdf [https://perma.cc/KPJ9-G232].

193 Hansard, Debates of the National Assembly, 16 November 1997, 608.

194 Van Zyl Smit, 'Swimming against the tide', 239.

195 Criminal Law (Sentencing) Amendment Act 38 of 2007. With minor amendments to the 1997 sentences.

196 *S v Dodo* [2001] ZACC 16; 2001 (3) SA 382 (CC); 2001 (5) BCLR 423 (CC), paras 10–11, endorsing *S v Malgas* (n 190 above).

197 *Centre for Child Law v Minister of Justice and Constitutional Development* [2009] ZACC 18; 2009 (6) 632 (CC); 2009 (11) BCLR 1105 (CC), para 28.

198 *Centre for Child Law v Minister of Justice and Constitutional Development* [2009] ZACC 18; 2009 (6) 632 (CC); 2009 (11) BCLR 1105 (CC), paras 24–29.

199 *Centre for Child Law v Minister of Justice and Constitutional Development* [2009] ZACC 18; 2009 (6) 632 (CC); 2009 (11) BCLR 1105 (CC), paras 31–32. Interestingly, the judgment was handed down in 2009 and the Constitutional Court noted at para 19 that it was 'beyond question' that the minimum sentences have bitten hard, both in the courts' approach to sentencing, and in outcome, with more offenders sent to prison for longer.

200 Julia Sloth-Nielsen and Louise Ehlers, 'Assessing the impact: Mandatory and minimum sentences in South Africa', *SA Crime Quarterly* 14 (2005): 8–9.

201 Authors developed this graph based on helpful numbers from DCS in March 2021 (on file with the authors).

202 Sloth-Nielsen and Ehlers, 'Assessing the impact: Mandatory and minimum sentences in South Africa', 9, quoting figures from Inspecting Judge Fagan.

203 Chris Giffard and Lukas Muntingh, 'The effect of sentencing on the size of the South African prison population', Report commissioned by the Open Society Foundation for South Africa (2006): 2, available at: https://dullahomarinstitute.org.

za/acjr/resource-centre/The%20impact%20of%20sentencing%20on%20the%20
size%20of%20the%20prison%20population.pdf [perma link did not work].

204 Giffard and Muntingh, 'The effect of sentencing on the size of the South African
prison population', 3.

205 As we note in Chapter 6, the new Minister for Corrections, Dr Pieter Groenewald,
has not alleviated the problem: he approved only a tiny fraction of lifers – a bare 27
out of 599 – whom the National Council on Correctional Services (NCCS) recommended for parole, this after completing its exhaustive processes. See https://www.
politicsweb.co.za/politics/lifer-paroles-conclude-well-ahead-of-deadline--pie?utm_
source=Politicsweb+Daily+Headlines&utm_campaign=4d8ad7d0e9-EMAIL_
CAMPAIGN_2024_10_15_08_09&utm_medium=email&utm_term=0_-4d8ad-
7d0e9-%5BLIST_EMAIL_ID%5D [https://perma.cc/3HNS-Y5CL]. The minister's
office proudly reported that 'All profiles, including the inherited backlog of 495
cases and 104 new cases, a total of 599, have been concluded by the Minister as of 3
October 2024. The Minister approved 23 parole applications and has granted one
case of day parole. Three individuals serving life sentences have been granted parole
and are subject to deportation, two of whom are citizens of Mozambique and one of
whom is a citizen of Zimbabwe.'

206 JICS Annual Report 2023/2024, 30.

207 Muntingh, 'Punishment and deterrence', at 3, explains that 'imprisonment had no
visible impact on the rate of violent crime'.

208 The Sentencing Project, 'How Mandatory Minimums Perpetuate Mass Incarceration
and What to do About It', February 2024, available at https://www.sentencingproject.
org/fact-sheet/how-mandatory-minimums-perpetuate-mass-incarceration-and-
what-to-do-about-it/ [https://perma.cc/JZ6H-JF53] and citing Jeremy Travis, Bruce
Western, and F Stevens Redburn, 'The growth of incarceration in the United States:
Exploring causes and consequences' (2014). See also Michael Tonry, 'Judges and
sentencing policy – the American experience' in *Sentencing, Judicial Discretion and
Judicial Training*, eds. Colin Munro and Martin Wasik (Sweet & Maxwell, 1992):
152: 'The evidence is clear and weighty, that enactment of mandatory penalty laws
has either no deterrent effect or a modest deterrent effect that soon wastes away.'

209 For South Africa, see Van Zyl Smit, 'Swimming against the tides', 248, where he
explains that there is 'no evidence, empirical or even anecdotal' to suggest that the
increase in the length of sentence discourages individuals from committing a crime.
Van Zyl Smit cites Andrew von Hirsch et al, *Criminal Deterrence and Sentence
Severity: An Analysis of Recent Research* (Cambridge: University of Cambridge
Institute of Criminology,1999). See also SS Terblanche, *A Guide to Sentencing in
South Africa* 3rd edition (LexisNexis, 2016): 90. Terblanche explains that: 'There is
no evidence of a consistent drop in crime rates . . . and, therefore, no indication that
it has had any useful deterrent effect.' See also Sloth-Nielsen and Ehlers, 'Assessing
the impact', 17: 'there is little reliable evidence that the new sentencing law has

reduced crime in general, or that specific offences targeted by this law have been curbed.' See further *The Guardian*, 'Do long jail sentences stop crime? We ask the expert', 19 November 2021, available at https://www.theguardian.com/lifeandstyle/2021/nov/19/do-long-jail-sentences-stop-we-ask-the-expert [https://perma.cc/ERB3-RFVK], accessed on 29 November 2024.

210 See Oliver Roeder, Lauren-Brooke Eisen, and Julia Bowling, 'What Caused the Crime Decline?' Brennan Center for Justice at New York University of Law (2015), available at https://www.brennancenter.org/sites/default/files/analysis/What_Caused_The_Crime_Decline.pdf [https://perma.cc/3HK6-6J47], accessed on 27 November 2024, and Anthony N Doob, Cheryl Marie Webster, and Rosemary Gartner, 'Issues related to Harsh Sentences and Mandatory Minimum Sentences: General Deterrence and Incapacitation', *Criminological Highlights* (2014): A-2 to A-3, available at https://www.crimsl.utoronto.ca/sites/crimsl.utoronto.ca/files/Issues%20related%20to%20Harsh%20Sentences%20and%20Mandatory%20Minimum%20Sentences%20General%20Deterrence%20and%20Incapacitation.pdf [https://perma.cc/MVL4-N9KH], accessed on 27 November 2024.

211 Van Zyl Smit, 'Swimming against the tides', 248.

212 See David A Anderson, 'The Deterrence Hypothesis and Picking Pockets at the Pickpocket's Hanging', *American Law and Economics Review* 4 (2002): 293–313.

213 SAPS Annual Report 2023/2024, 112, available at https://www.saps.gov.za/about/stratframework/annual_report/2023_2024/SAPS_Annual%20Report_2023-24.pdf [https://perma.cc/BR2P-GLGT], accessed on 3 December 2024.

214 National Prosecuting Authority Annual Report 2023/24, 49, available at https://www.npa.gov.za/sites/default/files/uploads/NPA%202024%20Annual%20Report_web_2.pdf, accessed on 3 December 2024.

215 See 'Aging Out' (report summary, 2017). Vera Institute found that 'recidivism research demonstrates that arrest rates drop to just more than 2 percent in people ages 50 to 65 years old and to almost zero percent for those older than 65', available at https://vera-institute.files.svdcdn.com/production/downloads/publications/Using-Compassionate-Release-to-Address-the-Growth-of-Aging-and-Infirm-Prison-Populations%E2%80%94Fact-Sheet.pdf [https://perma.cc/7ERF-JXYU], accessed on 27 November 2024.

216 Sloth-Nielsen and Ehlers, 'Assessing the impact', 17. In the first of her Reith Lectures, Dr Gwen Adshead observes however that it is not homicide perpetrators who struggle in prison with mental disorders and distress, but usually the non-violent majority who are serving short sentences, available at https://www.bbc.co.uk/sounds/play/m0025cmg [https://perma.cc/JMF4-AVDZ].

217 Ann Skelton and Mike Batley, 'Restorative justice: A contemporary South African review', *Acta Criminologica: African Journal of Criminology and Victimology* 21 no. 3 (2008): 40, citing Lawrence W Sherman and Heather Strang, *Restorative Justice: The Evidence* (Smith Institute, 2007), explains that: '[Sherman and Strang]

analyzed the results of 36 studies from Australia, New Zealand, the US, Canada and the UK, which all measured the effectiveness of restorative justice practices . . . [they] concluded that restorative justice has resulted in substantially reduced repeat offending for some offenders (but not all) and doubled the number of offenders brought to justice as a result of diversion from the criminal justice system, which in turn has reduced the costs of the criminal justice system. The study discovered that restorative justice has reduced recidivism more than imprisonment (for adults) or as well as imprisonment (for youths). Restorative justice was found to have reduced crime victims' post-traumatic stress symptoms and related costs and reduced crime victims' desire for violent revenge against their offenders. It also provided both victims and offenders with more satisfaction with justice than the criminal justice system.' In sum, 'the evidence on restorative justice is more extensive, and more positive, than it has been for many other policies that have been rolled out nationally, and they recommend that it be put to broader use.'

218 SAPS Annual Report 2023/24.
219 Damons and Geffen, 'How bad is South Africa's murder rate', note that in 1995/96 the number of murders were just under 27 000.
220 We supplemented findings by Damons and Geffen with statistics for 2010/2011, 2011/2012 and 2023/2024 from SAPS and Tembisa over the same periods.
221 Claire Ballard, 'The way we punish', *GroundUp*, 22 April 2015, available at https://groundup.org.za/article/way-we-punish_2860/ [https://perma.cc/7XTS-58Q7], accessed on 21 February 2025.
222 Giffard and Muntingh, 'The effect of sentencing on the size of the South African prison population', 2.
223 Fran Buntman and Lukas Muntingh, 'Supermaximum prisons in South Africa', in *The Globalization of Supermax Prisons*, ed. Jeffrey Ian Ross (Rutgers University Press, 2013): 81 and 84–86. See also Gwen Dereymaeker, 'Solitary confinement and super-maximum prisons', Africa Criminal Justice Reform (2017), available at https://acjr.org.za/jics-supermax-presentation-2017.pdf [perma link not working].
224 Buntman and Muntingh, 'Supermaximum prisons in South Africa', 80.
225 Buntman and Muntingh, 'Supermaximum prisons in South Africa', 88.
226 See Stephen C Richards, 'USP Marion – The first federal supermax', *The Prison Journal* 88 no. 1 (2008): 6.
227 Dissel, 'Tracking Transformation in South African Prisons', 12.
228 JICS Report on Solitary Confinement, 'I am a human being', 23 September 2021; JICS Report on the Unannounced Oversight Visit to Ebongweni Super-Maximum Correctional Centre, 'The moral fibre is nowhere to be found', 13 October 2021; JICS Report on Thematic Inspections Conducted at Kgosi-Mampuru II C-Max and Mangaung Public-Private Partnership Correctional Centres, 'Ticking Time Bomb', 13 October 2021; and JICS Report, 'From Security to Cruelty? Supermax Correctional Centres: Ebongweni', 19 December 2019.

229 Rules 43–45 of the United Nations Standard Minimum Rules for the Treatment of Prisoners (the Mandela Rules).
230 Email correspondence dated 29 November 2024.
231 Dirk van Zyl Smit, 'Change and Continuity in South African Prisons', in *Comparing Prison Systems: Toward a Comparative and International Penology*, eds. Robert Weiss and Nigel South (Routledge, 1998): 401. He also stated that: '[T]he monolithic structure of the national prison system remains. It continues to imprison roughly the same number of people drawn from the same social groups as in the past and to hold them in conditions which in practice have not changed significantly.'
232 DCS February unlock totals report 154% occupancy levels.
233 See Daniel Steyn, 'Explainer: why South Africa's prisons are overcrowded', *GroundUp*, 4 December 2024, available at https://groundup.org.za/article/unraveling-south-africas-overcrowded-prisons/ [https://perma.cc/75WJ-JQGT], accessed on 8 December 2024.
234 See Jonny Steinberg, 'Nongoloza's Children: Western Cape Prison Gangs During and After Apartheid', monograph for the Centre for the Study of Violence and Reconciliation, July 2004, available at https://www.csvr.org.za/docs/correctional/nongolozaschildren.pdf [https://perma.cc/7HLG-7W47] and Jonny Steinberg, *The Number: One Man's Search for Identity in the Cape Underworld and Prison Gangs* (Cape Town: Jonathan Ball Publishers, 2004). See further Heinrich Veloen, 'The Numbers Gang in South African Correctional Facilities: Reflections on Structures, Functions and Culture' (MPhil diss., University of Cape Town, 2022) where the author draws on their own experiences of 26 years as a warden in Pollsmoor Prison.
235 JICS Report, 'The Heart of Darkness', Unannounced Oversight Visit to Pollsmoor Medium B, Friday, 29 October 2021.
236 JICS Annual Report 2022/2023, 113.
237 See section 63A of the Criminal Procedure Act 51 of 1977 and section 49G of the Correctional Services Act 111 of 1998.
238 DCS Annual Report 2023/24, 15.
239 Lukas Muntingh and Jean Redpath, 'The socio-economic impact of pre-trial detention in Kenya, Mozambique and Zambia', *Hague Journal on the Rule of Law* 10 (2018): 139–164.
240 The department may spend approximately R64 868 750 a month – that is nearly R70 million – just on remandees who are awaiting trial for longer than two years, as well as remandees unable to afford bail of R1 000 and less.
241 JICS Annual Report 2023/2024, 76.
242 As a result of JICS's urgings, joined eloquently by Advocate Paul Hoffman SC, the National Prosecuting Authority at last re-activated the prosecution of personnel alleged to have murdered a prisoner in Brandvlei in 2015. Advocate Andrew Brown, the author, who is a practising advocate in Cape Town, generously undertook a watching brief, pro bono, on behalf of JICS.

243 *Smith v Minister of Justice and Correctional Services* [2023] ZAGPJHC 1127.
244 *Smith v Minister of Justice and Correctional Services* [2023] ZAGPJHC 1127, para 353.
245 Youth centres accommodate children, juveniles and young adults up to 25 years of age.
246 Cameron, 'Imprisoning the nation', para 62.
247 See Van Zyl Smit, 'Swimming against the tides', 248: '[I]ncreasing the length of sentences is not a carefully thought-out strategy at all. It is, instead, an unstructured response on the part of the legislators and the courts, in which they translate into law the punitive sentiments that they perceive the public to hold in the vague hope that harsher sentences will "send a message to criminals" and thus "do something" about the crime rate.'
248 Steinberg, 'Prison overcrowding and the constitutional right to adequate accommodation in South Africa'.
249 Nancy Gertner and Chiraag Bains, 'Mandatory minimum sentences are cruel and ineffective. Sessions wants them back', *The Washington* Post, 15 May 2017, available at https://www.washingtonpost.com/posteverything/wp/2017/05/15/mandatory-minimum-sentences-are-cruel-and-ineffective-sessions-wants-them-back/, accessed on 10 May 2024: 'A 2014 study by the U.S. Sentencing Commission found that defendants released early (based on sentencing changes not related to mandatory minimums) were not more likely to reoffend than prisoners who served their whole sentences. That is, for drug charges, shorter sentences don't compromise public safety. *Indeed, research shows it is the certainty of punishment — not the severity — that deters crime.*'
250 Cameron, 'The Crisis of Criminal Justice', 49. Also, acknowledging that there are constraints when one focuses on recidivism rates.
251 Lester Kiewit, 'Revolving door of crime and jail', *Mail & Guardian*, 17 January 2020, available at https://mg.co.za/article/2020-01-17-revolving-door-of-crime-and-jail/ [https://perma.cc/K73A-87J7], accessed 19 April 2021.
252 Robin Mcduff, Deanne Pernell and Karen Saunders, 'Open letter to the anti-rape movement' (1977): 11.
253 Andreas von Hirsch, 'Harm and Wrongdoing in Criminalisation Theory', *Crim Law and Philos* 8 (2014): 245–256. We are grateful to Khomotso Moshikaro for this insightful point.
254 Section 1 of the Correctional Services Act.
255 See DCS 2019/20 Annual Report, 27–28, available at http://www.dcs.gov.za/wp-content/uploads/2020/11/DCS-Annual-Report-TABLING-FINAL.pdf [https://perma.cc/XVL5-BEZZ], accessed 14 August 2024. In terms of rehabilitation, 'A net decrease of R76,355 million was mainly under savings realised from item Compensation of Employees and Goods and Services to cover excess expenditure realised under Program Incarceration under Goods and Services for item Operating

Leases for Accommodation Charges.' In terms of social reintegration, 'A net decrease of R10,418 million was mainly due to funds shifted from this program under item Goods and Services to fund Program Administration under item Goods and Services to fund Fleet Services.'

256 See Steinberg, 'Nongoloza's Children' and Steinberg, *The Number*.

257 JICS Annual Report 2023/24, 60.

258 JICS Annual Report 2023/24, 57.

259 The 2022/23 JICS Annual Report explains at 78: 'All deaths in which the cause is not immediately apparent, such as cases where a seemingly healthy inmate collapses and dies suddenly or is found dead in their bed, are initially classified as "unnatural other". This classification is temporary, and the official cause of death is determined once the autopsy report or post-mortem examination results are received. It is through these thorough investigations that the true cause of death can be determined and accurately recorded.'

260 Pamela J Schwikkard, 'Death in Democracy', *Singapore Academy of Law Journal* (Special Issue) (2013): 741–743.

261 Schwikkard, 'Death in Democracy', 743.

CHAPTER 4

262 Andrea Armstrong, 'No Prisoner Left Behind: Enhancing Public Transparency of Public Institutions', *Stanford Law and Policy Review* 25 (2014): 435 at 437.

263 Nelson Mandela, *Long Walk to Freedom* (New York: Little, Brown, 1994), 115.

264 Franz Kafka, *Metamorphosis and Other Stories* (London: Penguin Classics, 2019): 129–156.

265 Michael Mushlin, "'I Am Opposed to This Procedure": How Kafka's In the Penal Colony Illuminates the Current Debate About Solitary Confinement and Oversight of American Prisons', *Oregon Law Review* 93, no. 3 (2015): 626. Mushlin explains that Kafka's story demonstrates 'three critical truths that are relevant to contemporary prison issues. First, awful things can, and will, happen in prisons if they are closed to the public they are supposed to serve. Second, no matter how well-intended and enlightened prison officials are, change cannot occur solely from within. Third, outside oversight is essential if prisons are to be reformed to prevent abuses from occurring.'

266 Michele Deitch, 'But Who Oversees the Overseers? The Status of Prison and Oversight in the United States', *American Journal of Criminal Law* 42 (2020): 217.

267 Michele Deitch, 'Special Populations and the Importance of Prisons Oversight', *American Journal of Criminal Law* 37, no. 3 (2009): 293.

268 *Sonke Gender Justice NPC*, para 17.

269 Stan Stojkovic, 'Prisons Oversight and Prison Leadership', *Pace Law Review* 30, no. 5 (2010): 1486.

270 Deitch, 'But Who Oversees the Overseers?', 223–224.
271 Michele Deitch, 'Distinguishing the Various Functions of Effective Prison Oversight', *Pace Law Review* 30, no. 5 (2010): 1439.
272 Deitch, 'But Who Oversees the Overseers?', 219–223.
273 Eric Stockdale, 'A Short History of Prison Inspection in England,' *The British Journal of Criminology* 23, no. 2 (1983): 209. The bill provided that: 'The Lord Chancellor was to appoint commissioners to inspect the condition of the houses of correction.' Stockdale explains that: 'Unfortunately, Hay's Bill never reached the statute book, although he tried again in 1747.'
274 Stockdale, 'A Short History of Prison Inspection', 209. Stockdale notes that: 'In 1773 Howard was appointed High Sheriff of Bedfordshire.'
275 John Howard, *The State of the Prisons in England and Wales: With Preliminary Observations and an Account of Some Foreign Prisons* (1777) as quoted in Stockdale, 'A Short History of Prison Inspection', 209.
276 31 *Geo. III, c.* 46. Section 5, as quoted in Stockdale, 'A Short History of Prison Inspection', 211, stated that: '[V]isiting justices so respectively appointed shall, either together or singly, personally visit and inspect such prison at least three times in each quarter of a year, and oftener if occasion shall require, and shall examine into the state of the buildings, the behaviour and conduct of the respective officers, and the treatment and condition of the prisoners.'
277 Act of 1835 (5 *and 6 Will. IV, c.* 38). Section 7 of the Act, as quoted in Stockdale, 'A Short History of Prison Inspection', 216, stated that: 'Every person so appointed shall have authority to examine any person holding any office or receiving any salary or emolument in any such gaol, bridewell, house of correction, penitentiary or other place of confinement as aforesaid, and to call for and inspect all books and papers relating thereto, and to inquire into all matters touching and concerning such gaols.'
278 Rory Stewart, 'As prisons minister, I saw how bad things really are on the inside', *The Spectator*, 8 February 2020, available at https://www.spectator.co.uk/article/as-prisons-minister-i-saw-how-bad-things-really-are-on-the-inside/ [https://perma.cc/XKE3-PY74], accessed on 30 November 2024.
279 Ben Leapman, 'Prisons are shameful, says the man who used to run them', *Inside Time*, 2 January 2024, available at https://insidetime.org/comment/prisons-are-shameful-says-the-man-who-used-to-run-them/.
280 *The Economist*, 'How Labour Should Reform Britain's Overstuffed Prisons', 18 July 2024, available at https://www.economist.com/leaders/2024/07/18/how-labour-should-reform-britains-overstuffed-prisons [https://perma.cc/C9F9-BNNM], accessed on 30 November 2024. James Timpson has an impressive track record on prison reform. He is the former Chair of the Prison Reform Trust.
281 Michael Mushlin and Michele Deitch, 'Opening Up a Closed World: What Constitutes Effective Prisons Oversight?', *Pace Law Review* 30, no. 5 (2010): 1392.

282 Stojkovic, 'Prisons Oversight and Prison Leadership',1489.

283 Article 17 of OPCAT requires state parties to maintain, designate or establish 'independent national preventive mechanisms for the prevention of torture' domestically.

284 Article 3 of the OPCAT.

285 See 'About the NPM', available at https://sahrc.org.za/npm/index.php/about-the-npm [https://perma.cc/54GJ-QE67], accessed on 30 November 2024.

286 See the official website of the Office of the Inspectorate https://inspectorate. corrections.govt.nz/#:~:text=The%20Office%20of%20the%20Inspectorate%20 works%20to%20ensure%20that%20all,from%20offenders%20in%20the%20 community.

287 See the official page of the Office of the Correctional Investigator https://oci-bec. gc.ca/en.

288 See section 59(25) of the Prisons Act (1894). See also The Commonwealth Human Rights Initiative 'Prison Visiting System', available at https://www. humanrightsinitiative.org/content/prison-visiting-system [https://perma.cc/HXB5-8DY3], accessed on 8 December 2024. However, the Commonwealth Human Rights Initiative expresses concerns that 'the mechanism has since then become mostly defunct because of lack of intent and transparency despite constant recognition by Indian courts'.

289 The Inspectorate of Prisons derives its mandate from Chapter 17, Section 169 of the Constitution of Malawi.

290 See sections 123–129 of the Zambian Prisons Act, 1965.

291 Deitch, 'But Who Oversees the Overseers?', 223.

292 CANY official website accessible here: https://www.correctionalassociation.org/ our-history.

293 Office of the Inspector General official website accessible here: https://www.oig. ca.gov/.

294 See the Federal Prisons Oversight Act (S.1401), which was introduced in the Senate but not passed. The statute was referred to the Senate Judiciary Committee, where at the time of writing (November 2024) it remains: see https://www.congress.gov/bill/ 118th-congress/senate-bill/1401. See further Elizabeth Weill-Greenberg, 'Congress seeks to create new independent federal prisons oversight body', The Appeal, 27 April 2023, available at https://theappeal.org/federal-prison-oversight-act-congress-bop/ [https://perma.cc/KR4L-76ZE], accessed on 30 November 2024. We thank Alexis Birge, JD candidate at Columbia Law School, for her research assistance.

295 Barend van Niekerk, 'Judicial Visits to Prisons: The End of a Myth', *South African Law Journal* 98 (1981): 416. The 'Gulag Archipelagos' also refers to the title of a series of books by the Russian author Aleksandr Solzhenitsyn.

296 See 'ICRC report on the visit to "Robbeneiland" (Robben Island) Prison on the

1st May, 1964, by Mr G. Hoffmann, Delegate General of the International Committee of the Red Cross in Africa', *International Review of the Red Cross* 98, no. 3 (2016): 1067–1077, available at https://international-review.icrc.org/sites/default/files/ irrc-903-18.pdf [https://perma.cc/DAQ9-3VYE], accessed on 30 November 2024. See further 'Prison conditions in South Africa', Human Rights Watch (1994), available at https://www.hrw.org/reports/pdfs/s/safrica/safrica942.pdf [https://perma. cc/82XT-7YTD], accessed on 30 November 2024.

297 Chloë McGrath and Elrena van der Spuy, 'Looking Back: Insider Views on the Judicial Inspectorate for Correctional Services', *SA Crime Quarterly* 48 (2014): 41: 'The Prison Regulations of the Republic of South Africa extended prison visiting rights to all members of parliament regardless of political persuasion, and provided access to judges of the Supreme Court to any correctional facility in the country. Magistrates were given access to prisons within their jurisdiction.'

298 Van Niekerk, 'Judicial Visits to Prisons', 417.

299 Saras Jagwanth, 'A Review of the Judicial Inspectorate of Prisons of South Africa', CSPRI Research Paper Series no. 4 (2004): 5–6, available at https://dullahomarinsti- tute.org.za/acjr/resource-centre/A%20Review%20of%20the%20Judicial%20 Inspectorate%20of%20Prisons%20of%20South%20Africa%20%28Research %20Paper%20No.%207%29.pdf [https://perma.cc/G73A-CHXN], accessed on 30 November 2024.

300 Jagwanth, 'A Review of the Judicial Inspectorate of Prisons of South Africa', 6.

301 Gideon Morris, in 'Roundtable Discussion on Oversight Over the Prison System', CSPRI, August 2009, available at https://acjr.org.za/resource-centre/Roundtable%20 discussion%20on%20oversight%20over%20the%20prison%20system.pdf [https:// perma.cc/M698-KE9G], accessed on 30 November 2024.

302 Jagwanth, 'A Review of the Judicial Inspectorate of Prisons of South Africa', 8.

303 Dirk van Zyl Smit explained this to the Jali Commission of Inquiry into Alleged Incidents of Corruption, Maladministration, Violence or Intimidation in the Department of Correctional Services (2005), available at https://www.gov.za/sites/default/files/gcis_ document/201409/jalicommfull0.pdf [https://perma.cc/6B9Z-UPCB], 567–568.

304 Inspecting Judges since JICS was established: J Trengove (1998–1999), H Fagan (1999–2006), N Erasmus (2006–2007), J Yekiso (2007–2008), D van Zyl (2008– 2011), V Tshabalala (2011–2015), T Skweyiya (2015), J van der Westhuizen (2016–2019), E Cameron (2019–present). See JICS website, available at http:// www.jics.gov.za/previous-judges-2/ [https://perma.cc/75H3-V3LU].

305 McGrath and Van der Spuy, 'Looking Back', 46.

306 See Correctional Services Act, chapters IX and X.

307 Established by the Constitution section 184 and operating under the SAHRC Act 40 of 2013, which empowers the commission to investigate and report on observance of human rights and to secure appropriate redress where human rights have been violated.

308 The Independent Police Investigative Directorate Act 1 of 2011 provides for the establishment of an independent investigative directorate as an independent police complaints body to investigate any alleged complaint of misconduct or offence committed by a member of the police.

309 The Office of the Military Ombud was established under the Military Ombud Act 4 of 2012. Its mandate is to investigate complaints by members or former members of the SANDF or members of the public regarding the official conduct of a member of the SANDF.

310 The Office of the Health Ombud (OHO) is an independent body established by the National Health Amendment Act of 2013 within the Office of Health Standards Compliance (OHSC); it reports to and is accountable to the Minister of Health.

311 See section 95D of the Correctional Services Amendment Act 14 of 2023.

312 See section 93(3) of the CSA.

313 See section 93 of the CSA.

314 Section 30(7) of the CSA.

315 *Sonke Gender Justice NPC*, para 91.

316 *Sonke Gender Justice NPC*, challenging sections 88A(1)(b), 88A(4) and 91 of the CSA.

317 *Sonke Gender Justice NPC*, para 52, reaffirming principles emanating from the majority judgment in *Glenister v President of the RSA* [2011] ZACC 6; 2011 (3) SA 347 (CC); 2011 (7) BCLR 651 (CC) (*Glenister II*).

318 *Sonke Gender Justice NPC*, para 53.

319 *Sonke Gender Justice NPC*, para 28.

320 *Sonke Gender Justice NPC*, para 125.

321 For an account of the Bill, see Edwin Cameron, 'Prisons watchdog needs sharper teeth – JICS is struggling for independence', *GroundUp*, 28 November 2022, available at https://groundup.org.za/article/prisons-watchdog-needs-sharper-teeth/ [https://perma.cc/8653-QSNX], accessed on 30 November 2024.

322 Section 99 of the CSA ('Access to correctional centres') provides:

'(1) A judge of the Constitutional Court, Supreme Court of Appeal or High Court, and a magistrate within his or her area of jurisdiction, may visit a correctional centre at any time.

(2) A judge and a magistrate referred to in subsection (1) must be allowed access to any part of a correctional centre and any documentary record, and may interview any inmate and bring any matter to the attention of the National Commissioner, the Minister, the National Council or the Inspecting Judge.

(3) (a) Members of the parliamentary Portfolio Committee on Correctional Services and the relevant committee of the National Council of Provinces and members of the National Council may visit any correctional centre at any time.

(b) Members referred to in paragraph (a) must be allowed access to any part of a correctional centre and any documentary record.

(4) A Sheriff or Deputy Sheriff must be allowed access to any inmate when this is necessary in the performance of official duties.

(5) The National Commissioner may permit any person other than those mentioned in subsections (1) to (4) to visit an inmate, a correctional centre or any specific section of a correctional centre for any special or general purpose.'

323 In her Reith Lectures, Dr Gwen Adshead conceives sentencing as the social condemnation of violence deriving from the social contract that, when one of us is injured, we all are.

324 See Dr Amelia Kleijn, Ariane Nevin and Zia Wasserman from Sonke Gender Justice, *One Judge, One Jail – A Guide for Inspecting and Reporting on Places of Detention in South Africa*, available at https://www.saferspaces.org.za/uploads/files/ One_Judge_One_Jail_-_A_Guide_for_Inspecting__Reporting_on_Places_of_ Detention_in_SA.pdf [https://perma.cc/J83V-C4Q3], accessed 27 July 2024.

325 See 'Constitutional Court Judges' Prison Visits', available at https://www.concourt. org.za/index.php/judges/prison-visits [https://perma.cc/TPM5-67CP], accessed on 30 November 2024.

326 Chandni Gopal, Elizabeth Maushart, Tess Peacock and Yana van Leeve.

327 Constitutional Court of South Africa, Justice Edwin Cameron, Report: Pollsmoor Correctional Centre – Remand Centre and Women's Centre (2015) https://www. concourt.org.za/images/phocadownload/prison_visits/cameron/Pollsmoor-Prison-Report-23-April-2015-Justice-Edwin-Cameron-FINAL-for-web.pdf.pdf [https:// perma.cc/2X73-8BJE], accessed 30 July 2024.

328 Confirmed in a personal communication to me on 8 April 2024.

329 See Sonke Gender Justice Campaign video: https://genderjustice.org.za/video/ pollsmoor-remand-treated-us-like-animals/ [https://perma.cc/48LD-ST4Z].

330 Sonke Gender Justice, 'Court Order in Pollsmoor Remand Overcrowding Case', available at https://genderjustice.org.za/publication/court-order-in-pollsmoor-re-mand-overcrowding-case/ [https://perma.cc/CNA6-C634], accessed on 4 February 2024.

331 We note in Cameron, 'The Crisis of Criminal Justice in South Africa', at 46: 'As a result, the Department of Correctional Services transferred a significant number of prisoners from Pollsmoor to other centres. But, grievously, this seems merely to have transferred the problem elsewhere. The then Judicial Inspector of Correctional Services, retired Justice Johann van der Westhuizen, noted that "although [the court order] alleviated the overcrowding crisis at Pollsmoor, it caused other unintended challenges, for example, exacerbating overcrowding elsewhere, especially at smaller centres". He cautioned that overcrowding in the Western Cape is still at 90 per cent or more.'

332 David Luban, 'Complicity and Lesser Evils – A Tale of Two Lawyers', *Georgetown Journal of Legal Ethics* 34, no. 3, at 613, posits four conditions for when continuing to work within an iniquitous system, on the premise this is a 'lesser evil', is unsustainable:

(a) The official can't do any good by staying, so continued association is unmitigated participation in evil [JICS does accomplish productive work and achieve progress in improvements];

(b) Quitting in protest would do some good, perhaps inspiring others to do so [JICS has helped bring sentencing and prison reform back into public discussion];

(c) If you don't quit, your judgment will be corrupted [JICS acts autonomously and independently and is highly critical of DCS]; and

(d) Staying on the job is complicity by consorting, and it contributes to the moral breakdown of those around you [JICS has used its voice and moral power to shine light on problems and protect rights – on Friday 14 January 2022, JICS released to the Parliamentary Portfolio Committee on Justice and Correctional Services four reports condemning solitary confinement; after its last presentation, the chair invited JICS to organise a workshop, with the committee, on sentencing reform, though that has yet to occur].

333 *New York Times*, 'Michel Foucault, on the Role of Prisons', *New York Times*, 5 August 1975, available at https://www.nytimes.com/1975/08/05/archives/michel-foucault-on-the-role-of-prisons.html.

334 Foucault, 'Alternatives to the Prison', 24.

335 *Phaahla* (n 179 above).

336 Jali Commission Report, 575–576.

337 See, for example, Jagwanth, 'A Review of the Judicial Inspectorate of Prisons of South Africa'; McGrath and Van der Spuy, 'Looking Back'; Emily Nagisa Keehn, Nomonde Nyembe and Tanya Sukhija, 'Evaluation of South Africa's Judicial Inspectorate for Correctional Services', July 2013, available at SSRN: https://ssrn. com/abstract=2791848; and Amanda Dissel, 'A review of civilian oversight over correctional services in the last decade', CSPRI (2003), available at https:// dullahomarinstitute.org.za/acjr/resource-centre/A%20Review%20of%20Civilian %20Oversight%20over%20Correctional%20Services%20in%20the%20Last%20 Decade%20%28Research%20Paper%20No.%204%29.pdf [https://perma.cc/ 88LA-L9KM].

338 See Keehn, Nyembe and Sukhija, 'Evaluation of South Africa's Judicial Inspectorate for Correctional Services'.

339 McGrath and Van der Spuy, 'Looking Back', 44.

340 Michele Deitch, 'Independent Oversight Is Essential for a Safe and Healthy Prison System', 3 November 2021, available at https://www.brennancenter.org/our-work/ analysis-opinion/independent-oversight-essential-safe-and-healthy-prison-system [https://perma.cc/7BHY-ML2H], accessed on 30 November 2024.

341 The report on solitary confinement titled 'I am a human being' can be accessed here: Sonia A Rao, 'Prisoners are being held for years in solitary confinement', *GroundUp*, 6 September 2023, available at https://www.groundup.org.za/article/prisoners-being-

held-for-years-in-solitary-confinement/ [https://perma.cc/CLA2-SPNV], accessed on 30 November 2024.
342 JICS Quarterly Report July–September 2021, 9, available at http://www.jics.gov.za/wp-content/uploads/2024/04/JICS-QR2-2021-Jul-Sept-Final.pdf [https://perma.cc/GEN3-F2SV], accessed on 30 November 2024: 'Since JICS's visit to Ebongweni Super-Maximum Correctional Centre on 11–12 May 2021, 81 inmates who were initially transferred to Ebongweni based on minor disciplinary infringements were transferred back to their centres of origin.'
343 Rebecca Gore, 'Abortion behind bars: women in prisons have extra obstacles to overcome', *GroundUp*, 8 June 2022, available at https://www.groundup.org.za/article/abortion-behind-bars-women-in-prisons-have-extra-obstacles-to-overcome/ [https://perma.cc/U3QT-SK5V], accessed on 30 November 2024.
344 Letter from the Acting Commissioner to the Inspecting Judge in September 2022 (on record with the authors).
345 The State of Disaster regulations and directives initially excluded JICS and its ICCVs from the definition of 'essential services'. JICS was thus excluded from entering correctional facilities (see Annexure D of the Department of Co-Operative Governance and Traditional Affairs Regulations issued in terms of Section 27(2) of the Disaster Management Act, 2002, dated 29 April 2020). JICS approached Minister Lamola with a request for the resumption of ICCV duties, which was conceded.
346 Although the department should be commended for taking serious measures and containing the Covid-19 pandemic in prisons, some of their strategies had a harsh impact. The department's approach to contain the pandemic was to segregate inmates suspected of contracting Covid-19. Segregations had a serious impact on the wellbeing of detained and incarcerated persons (prisons advocate Clare Ballard explained that lockdowns in prisons were akin to solitary confinement). In addition, lockdowns within prisons meant that education and recreational programmes were put on hold. There were not enough officials in station, and visits from loved ones were suspended.
347 *Minister of Justice and Constitutional Development v Ntuli (Judicial Inspectorate for Correctional Services as amicus curiae)* [2023] ZASCA 146.
348 CCT 322/23 *Minister of Justice and Correctional Services and Others v Mbalenhle Sidney Ntuli.*
349 The CallSafe device operates as a public telephone but on the mobile network with rechargeable battery. On record with the authors.
350 The Bill of Rights in section 35(2)(f) provides pertinently that every detained person has the right 'to communicate with, and be visited by, that person's (i) spouse or partner; (ii) next of kin; (iii) chosen religious counsellor; and (iv) chosen medical practitioner'.
351 Helpful summary by Corruption Watch can be found here: https://www.corruption-watch.org.za/wp-content/uploads/2022/05/Zondo-final-report-%E2%80%93-Former-

DCS-bosses-benefited-from-Bosasa-corruption-Zondo-finds.pdf (8 March 2024) [https://perma.cc/8Q87-7BDX], accessed on 2 December 2024.

352 See Rebecca Davis, 'How State Capture led to human rights abuses – the case of Bosasa and the prisons', *Daily Maverick*, 14 March 2022, available at https://www.dailymaverick.co.za/article/2022-03-14-how-state-capture-led-to-human-rights-abuses-the-case-of-bosasa-and-the-prisons/ [https://perma.cc/43M6-6PHV], accessed on 30 November 2024.

353 See Jali Commission Report, 568–575.

354 McGrath and Van der Spuy, 'Looking Back', 44.

355 Under section 85 of the Correctional Services Act. See reasons in Jali Commission Report, 569.

356 Section 90(1) of the Correctional Services Act.

357 See Section 95D of the Correctional Services Amendment Act 14 of 2023, available at https://www.gov.za/sites/default/files/gcis_document/202404/correctionalservicesamendmentact142023.pdf [https://perma.cc/F2P7-627F], accessed on 28 July 2024.

358 https://groundup.org.za/.

359 See, for example, a raid at Johannesburg Correctional Centre (Sun City) in July 2024, which uncovered considerable contraband: https://www.ewn.co.za/2024/07/25/gallery-dagga-flat-screen-tvs-play-station-inside-the-sun-city-prison-raid.

360 See Edwin Cameron opinion pieces: 'Botched bail decisions can be curbed', *The Sunday Times*, 19 January 2020, available at https://www.timeslive.co.za/sunday-times/opinion-and-analysis/2020-01-19-botched-bail-decisions-can-be-curbed/ [https://perma.cc/9BA2-YKLD]; 'Our prisons are failing. They need to become correctional facilities', *GroundUp*, 3 March 2020, available at https://groundup.org.za/article/our-prisons-are-failing-they-need-become-correctional-facilities/ [https://perma.cc/A6ZE-Q952]; 'Covid-19 and the perils of over-incarceration', *GroundUp*, 24 April 2020, available at https://groundup.org.za/article/covid-19-and-perils-over-incarceration/ [https://perma.cc/5DLY-NTFT]; 'A visit to "Sun City" prison: nightmare to manage the virus in confined spaces', *News24*, 14 May 2020, available at https://www.news24.com/News24/edwin-cameron-a-visit-to-sun-city-prison-nightmare-to-manage-the-virus-in-confined-spaces-20200514; 'Enemies of the nation: How the "war on drugs" has failed South Africa', *GroundUp*, 19 August 2020, available at https://groundup.org.za/article/enemies-of-the-nation-how-the-war-on-drugs-has-failed-south-africa/ [https://perma.cc/P39B-9K3D]; 'Violence in prisons in increasing, and the prisons watchdog needs more power to stop it', *Daily Maverick*, 4 September 2020, available at https://www.dailymaverick.co.za/article/2020-09-04-violence-in-prisons-is-increasing-and-the-prisons-watchdog-needs-more-power-to-stop-it/ [https://perma.cc/24NT-ZMLW]; 'To enforce the COVID lockdown, did we wage war on the people of South Africa?' *News24*, 6 March 2021, available at https://www.news24.com/news24/edwin-cameron-to-

enforce-the-covid-lockdown-did-we-wage-a-war-on-the-people-of-south-africa-20210306; 'Why we need to vaccinate prisoners now', *GroundUp*, 25 May 2021, available at https://groundup.org.za/article/why-we-need-vaccinate-prisoners-now/ [https://perma.cc/WTW8-GC2H]; 'Harsh prison terms won't solve the crisis of gender-based violence', *GroundUp*, 9 August 2021, available at https://groundup. org.za/article/why-a-carceral-state-wont-solve-the-crisis-of-gender-based-violence/ [https://perma.cc/4YFF-ASSW]; 'Our faulty approach to life sentences is catching up with us', *GroundUp*, 10 November 2021, available at https://groundup.org.za/ article/our-faulty-approach-life-sentences-catching-us/ [https://perma.cc/BNL3-QVPN]; 'Solitary confinement is illegal: So why is it happening in South African prisons', *GroundUp*, 23 February 2022, available at https://groundup.org.za/article/ solitary-confinement-illegal-so-why-it-happening-in-south-african-prisons/ [https:// perma.cc/JP24-MGHJ]; 'Why independent healthcare inside prisons is vital', *GroundUp*, 25 May 2022, available at https://groundup.org.za/article/why-independent-healthcare-inside-prisons-vital/ [https://perma.cc/HHC2-ZCKW]; 'Prisons watchdog needs sharper teeth', *GroundUp*, 28 November 2022, available at https:// groundup.org.za/article/prisons-watchdog-needs-sharper-teeth/ [https://perma.cc/ D56H-66QS]; 'Sex work: where criminal law has no place', *GroundUp*, 24 January 2023, available at https://groundup.org.za/article/where-the-criminal-law-has-no-place-sex-work/ [https://perma.cc/SLX7-YLDC]; and 'Our prisons are falling apart, says inspector', *GroundUp*, 28 July 2023, available at https://groundup.org. za/article/what-if-our-prisons-tumble-down/ [https://perma.cc/CR2T-8CUU].
361 Michele Deitch and Michael B Mushlin, 'What's Going On in Our Prisons?' *New York Times*, 4 January 2016, available at https://www.nytimes.com/2016/01/04/ opinion/whats-going-on-in-our-prisons.html [perma link did not work].
362 Exco Minutes dated 8 March 2021 ('Still in the process of getting information as to which court and prosecutor is handling the matter. The detective in charge of the matter has not been available for the last week of January 2021. Further enquiries were made during February 2021 via telephone and details were left for the detective to contact JICS'). A glimpse into obstacles JICS and the father face in seeking to activate the department and the SAPS is provided by JICS's executive minutes.
363 Bryan Stevenson, *Just Mercy: A Story of Justice and Redemption* (New York: Random House, 2014): 14.
364 Stevenson, *Just Mercy*, 12.
365 Stevenson, *Just Mercy*, 17–18.

CHAPTER 5

366 Correctional Services Minister Pieter Groenewald is reported to have told Parliament that overcrowding 'means that there is an urgent need to construct a total of

50,000 [new] bed spaces', which 'requires the construction of 100 new Correctional Centres': see Luke Fraser, 'South Africa needs R36 billion to build more prisons', *BusinessTech*, 9 December 2024, available at https://businesstech.co.za/news/government/803512/south-africa-needs-r36-billion-to-build-more-prisons/, accessed on 1 January 2025.

367 Andrew Coyle, 'Prison reform efforts around the world: The role of prison administrators', *Pace Law Review* (2004): 8, citing Alexander Paterson, in *Paterson on Prisons: Being the Collected Papers of Sr Alexander Paterson* (Frederick Muller,1951): 26.

368 In her Reith Lectures, Dr Gwen Adshead counsels against the conclusory use of terms like 'irreformable' or 'inherently evil'. People have evil in them – we all do – and may perform evil actions but are best not written off as 'evil'.

369 Annah Moyo-Kupeta, 'Mob Justice is a Language in South Africa', Centre for the Study of Violence and Reconciliation (30 May 2021), available at https://www.csvr.org.za/mob-justice-is-a-language-in-south-africa/ [https://perma.cc/LHG4-9K6D], accessed on 30 November 2024.

370 Karl Kemp, *Why We Kill: Mob Justice and the New Vigilantism in South Africa* (Cape Town: Penguin Random House, 2024): 15. Kemp notes at 16: 'In just over five years, mob justice murders have increased from 849 to 1894 per year – and that's not even mentioning the cases of attempted murder and grievous assault.'

371 SAPS, 'Police recorded crime statistics – First quarter of 2023–2024 financial year' 16; SAPS, 'Police recorded crime statistics – Second quarter of 2023–2024 financial year', 16; and SAPS, 'Police recorded crime statistics – Third quarter of 2023–2024 financial year', 16.

372 Kemp, *Why We Kill*, 16.

373 Anthony Bottoms, in 'The Philosophy and Politics of Punishment and Sentencing', in *The Politics of Sentencing Reform*, eds. Chris Clarkson and Rod Morgan (Oxford: Clarendon Press, 1995), defined 'populist punitiveness' as 'the notion of politicians tapping into, and using for their own purposes, what they believe to be the public's generally punitive stance'. See further the term 'penal populism' in Julian V Roberts et al, *Penal Populism and Public Opinion: Lessons from Five Countries* (Oxford: Oxford University Press, 2002): 4–5.

374 Zelia Gallo, 'Concepts and conditions of penal moderation: Penal policy, public philosophy, and political ideologies. Theoretical reflections from Italy (2010–2018)', *Theoretical Criminology* (2024): 16. We are grateful to David Bruce for sharing this article. Gallo goes on to explain that penal reform is 'a much harder sell when political ideologies, institutions and processes instil a civic pedagogy that reinforces a pathologizing, deterministic view of crime and deviance'.

375 Davis, *Are Prisons Obsolete?*, 16.

376 Jali Commission Report, 394. The commission noted that 'vulnerable, young Prisoners become mere possessions or sex slaves whilst incarcerated. Prison

warders sell them to the highest bidder despite the fact that they are dependent on these very same Prison warders to secure their safety whilst in Prison.'

377 We refer to 'penal moderation' as a concept that operates along a spectrum, as explained by Gallo, 'Concepts and Conditions', 3–4: 'On one end, we place non-punitiveness: in a simplistic articulation, if a policy is not punitive, it is moderate. This side of the spectrum privileges outcomes, such as decreasing incarceration rates; moderation so conceived is a defensive concept. On the other end, we place moderation as a "public philosophy of punishment". Here good outcomes are not sufficient, we also want good intentions: this form of moderation is an aspirational concept. . . . From this perspective, it is not enough for a policy to be non-punitive for it to be an instance of penal moderation: the policy needs to be the outcome of a deliberative process, and be characterized by the reflexive pursuit of parsimony, dignity and restraint.'

378 Alcide De Gasperi, 'Doing Time in Open Prison in Finland', *Journal of Modern Science* (2006): 384. 'By definition open prison is designed for prisoners who are considered to be neither dangerous nor violent. Unless stipulated otherwise by the judge, the prisoners as a rule begin their sentence in a closed prison, from which they may be transferred to an open prison, therefore gaining greater freedom of movement. Prisoners sentenced to less than two years are committed directly to an open prison, where, while serving their sentences, they can continue their daily jobs back in the community.'

379 Doran Larson, 'Why Scandinavian Prisons Are Superior', *The Atlantic*, 24 September 2013, available at https://www.theatlantic.com/international/archive/2013/09/why-scandinavian-prisons-are-superior/279949/ [https://perma.cc/PZ38-GMEJ], accessed on 27 May 2024, explains prisons on Suomenlinna Island.

380 De Gasperi, 'Doing Time in Open Prison in Finland', 385. De Gasperi explains at 393–394 that the Finnish sentencing and prison legislation is based on the following principles: (i) punishment is a mere loss of liberty; (ii) prevention of harm, promoting of placement into society; (iii) normality, the circumstances in a penal institution must be organised so that they correspond to those prevailing in the rest of society; (iv) justness, respect for human dignity and prohibition of discrimination; (v) special needs of juvenile prisoners; and (vi) hearing of prisoner.

381 Rutger Bregman, *Humankind: A Hopeful History* (London: Little, Brown, 2020): 328.

382 Cameron, 'The Crisis of Criminal Justice', 49. Also, acknowledging that there are constraints when one focuses on recidivism rates.

383 See Denis Yukhnenko, Leen Farouki, and Seena Fazel, 'Criminal recidivism rates globally: A 6-year systematic review update', *Journal of Criminal Justice* 88 (2023): 102–115.

384 Bregman, *Humankind*, 329–330. In a 2018 study comparing the US and Norway, economists found that: 'A stay in a Norwegian prison, according to their calcula-

tions, costs on average $60,151 per conviction – almost twice as much as in the US. However, because these ex-convicts go on to commit fewer crimes, they also save Norwegian law enforcement $71,226 apiece. And because more of them find employment, they don't need government assistance and they pay taxes, saving the system on average another $67,086. Last but not least, the number of victims goes down, which is priceless.'

385 Library of Congress, 'Sweden: Supreme Court defines negligent rape', 17 July 2019, available at: https://www.loc.gov/item/global-legal-monitor/2019-07-17/sweden-supreme-court-defines-negligent-rape/ [https://perma.cc/9XQ4-T4YB]. We are grateful to Khomotso Moshikaro for this nuanced point.

386 Simon Robins, 'Improving Africa's Prisons: Prison Policy in Sierra Leone, Tanzania and Zambia', Institute for Security Studies Policy Brief (2009): 2, available at https://issafrica.org/research/policy-brief/improving-africas-prisons-prison-policy-in-sierra-leone-tanzania-and-zambia [https://perma.cc/P6VH-WMJH; and see 'In dialogue with Zambia, experts of the Human Rights Committee Commend the Abolition of the Death Penalty and Measures to Improve Prison Conditions, raises issues concerning violence against women and girls' (3 March 2023), available at https://www.ohchr.org/en/news/2023/03/dialogue-zambia-experts-human-rights-committee-commend-abolition-death-penalty-and. While working on farms as a form of rehabilitation is a positive development, we guard against permitting convict leasing. On whether inmates in South Africa have a right to work see Dirk van Zyl Smit and Frieder Dünkel, *Prison Labour*, 222–237.

387 Larson, 'Why Scandinavian Prisons are Superior', explains that 'throughout Scandinavia, criminal justice policy rarely enters political debate. Decisions about best practices are left to professionals in the field, who are often published criminologists and consult closely with academics. Sustaining the barrier between populist politics and results-based prison policy are media that don't sensationalize crime – if they report it at all.'

388 Foucault, *Discipline and Punish*, 234.

389 Foucault, *Discipline and Punish*, 234–235.

390 Ruby C Tapia, 'Certain failures: Representing the experiences of incarcerated women in the United States', in Solinger et al, *Interrupted Life: Experiences of Incarcerated Women in the United States* (Berkeley: University of California Press, 2010): 3.

391 Davis, *Are Prisons Obsolete?*, 9.

392 See 'Don't reform prisons, abolish them – Ruth Wilson Gilmore', 16 August 2020, available at https://www.youtube.com/watch?v=WZOoP2I1dts, accessed on 27 May 2024.

393 Foucault, 'The Role of Prisons'.

394 See Coyle, 'Prison reform efforts around the world', 831–832. Coyle writes that in 2002, prison administrators from 45 European states met and affirmed that, in their

view, there is rarely any relationship between imprisonment and levels of crime. Instead, their experience was that the use of prisons was a political choice and that where prisons were built the courts would find ways to fill them.

395 Dan Berger, Mariame Kaba and David Stein, 'What abolitionists do', *Jacobin*, 24 August 2017, available at https://jacobin.com/2017/08/prison-abolition-reform-mass-incarceration [https://perma.cc/QJ78-SBKH], accessed on 25 May 2024.

396 Davis, *Are Prisons Obsolete?*, 20.

397 Annotation in the meeting notes of the Statewide Harm Reduction Coalition in Chicopee, MA, 2006. See https://statesofincarceration.org/story/statewide-harm-reduction-coalition-no-new-jails.

398 Berger, Kaba and Stein, 'What abolitionists do'.

399 Berger, Kaba and Stein, 'What abolitionists do'. See Critical Resistance, 'Reformist reforms vs abolitionist steps to end mass imprisonment', available at https://criticalresistance.org/wp-content/uploads/2021/08/CR_abolitioniststeps_antiexpansion_2021_eng.pdf [https://perma.cc/66YW-VCEQ], accessed on 3 May 2024.

400 Foucault, *Discipline and Punish*, 232.

401 Davis, *Are Prisons Obsolete?*, 107.

402 Rachel Kushner, 'Is prison necessary? Ruth Wilson Gilmore might change your mind', *New York Times*, 17 April 2019, available at https://www.nytimes.com/2019/04/17/magazine/prison-abolition-ruth-wilson-gilmore.html [perma link did not work], accessed on 16 October 2020.

403 Davis, *Are Prisons Obsolete?*, 108–110.

404 Berger, Kaba and Stein, 'What abolitionists do'.

405 Berger, Kaba and Stein, 'What abolitionists do'. From 1999, activists in California fought growth of the prisons system: 'While California built and filled twenty-three new prisons between 1983 and 1999, the state has opened only two institutions since (one of them a prison hospital). As the state has shifted tack to emphasize jail construction – partly in response to this organizing – abolitionists have turned their focus to the county level as well.' Abolitionists point to similar successes against more prison and jail capacity in New York, Pennsylvania, Texas, Washington, and elsewhere.

406 Arthur Waskow, quoted in *Instead of Prisons: A Handbook for Abolitionists*, ed. by Fay Honey Knopp et al (Prison Research Education Action Project,1976): 15–16, referenced in Davis, *Are Prisons Obsolete?*, 105.

407 Davis, *Are Prisons Obsolete?*, 108–110 and Kushner, 'Is prison necessary?'.

408 Leigh Goodmark, *Imperfect Victims: Criminalized Survivors and the Promise of Abolition Feminism (Gender and Justice) (Volume 8)* (Berkeley: University of California Press, 2023): 23. Goodmark states that: 'Abolition feminism opposes the use of the carceral system to respond to all kinds of harms, including gender-based violence, and focuses on building structures and institutions that prevent violence,

ensure people's well-being, and use constructive, community-based responses to facilitate active accountability.'

409 See Sohela Surajpal, 'Carceral feminism is not the answer', *Africa is a Country* (2020), calling for reimagining our conceptions of feminist justice in South Africa, since 'putting people in cages is not liberation', available at https://africasacountry. com/2020/09/carceral-feminism-is-not-the-answer [https://perma.cc/6VST-LMQC], accessed on 2 January 2025.

410 Victoria Law, 'Against Carceral Feminism', *Jacobin*, 17 October 2014, available at https://jacobin.com/2014/10/against-carceral-feminism/ [https://perma.cc/BMV6-B2AW], accessed on 2 May 2024.

411 Davis, *Are Prisons Obsolete?*, 108.

412 See Ruth Morris, *Stories of Transformative Justice* (Canadian Scholars' Press, 2000).

413 See Bay Area Transformative Justice Collective, 'Transformative justice and community accountability', available at https://batjc.files.wordpress.com/2014/06/ tj-ca-one-pager.pdf, accessed on 15 May 2024.

414 Section 1 of the Child Justice Act 75 of 2008.

415 See Howard Zehr, *The Little Book of Restorative Justice* (Good Books, 2002).

416 Sherman and Strang, *Restorative Justice*, 4. See Heather Strang et al, 'Restorative Justice Conferencing (RJC) Using Face-to-Face Meetings of Offenders and Victims: Effects on Offender Recidivism and Victim Satisfaction. A Systematic Review' (2013), available at https://restorativejustice.org.uk/sites/default/files/resources/files/ Campbell%20RJ%20review.pdf [https://perma.cc/Y48S-XBYM] (accessed on 6 June 2024). See also Adriaan Lanni, 'Taking Restorative Justice Seriously', *Buffalo Law Review* (2021): 675 at fn 147.

417 Sherman and Strang, *Restorative Justice*, 4.

418 Lanni, 'Taking Restorative Justice Seriously', 637.

419 Lanni, 'Taking Restorative Justice Seriously', 648.

420 See Martha Minow, *When Should Law Forgive?* (New York: W.W. Norton & Company, 2019): 5. 'Research on human health, depression, and family counseling suggests that forgiving others, after being hurt by their actions or words, can enhance physical, emotional, and spiritual well-being.'

421 Minow, *When Should Law Forgive?*, 162.

422 White Paper on Corrections (2016) at 40. See also Correctional Services Act sections 38(1)(j) and 52(1)(g).

423 DCS Annual Report 2023/24, 33.

424 DCS Annual Report 2022/23, 41.

425 See Liz McGregor's account in *Unforgiven: Face to Face with My Father's Killer* (Cape Town: Jonathan Ball Publishers, 2022), excerpted by the author in 'Meeting murderers: Tormented by my father's killing, my quest for answers begins', available at https://www.dailymaverick.co.za/article/2022-04-13-meeting-murderers-

a-womans-quest-for-answers-and-restorative-justice-after-her-fathers-killing/ [https://perma.cc/K5B4-2NHT], accessed on 8 August 2024.

426 See also Annette van der Merwe, 'A new role for crime victims? An evaluation of restorative justice procedures in the Child Justice Act 2008', *De Jure* (2013), 1022.

427 See chapters 8 and 10 of the Child Justice Act.

428 *S v M* [2007] ZACC 18; 2008 (3) SA 232 (CC); 2007 (12) BCLR 1312 (CC).

429 *S v M*, para 62. *S v S* [2011] ZACC 7; 2011 (2) SACR 88 (CC); 2011 (7) BCLR 740 (CC), paras 62–63, creates a partial counterpoint. The majority of the court namely affirmed that *S v M* 'revolutionised sentencing in cases where the person convicted is the primary caregiver of young children', by reasserting the 'central role of the interests of young children as an independent consideration in the sentencing process'. Yet the later court held that it would be 'wrong to apply *S v M* in cases that lie beyond its ambit', pointing out that the mother in *S v M* was a single parent, and was almost exclusively burdened with the care of her children. No other parent could, without disruption, step in during her absence to nurture the children, and provide care. That was not so, the court found, in the case before it, where the mother was not the children's sole caregiver. The father, their co-resident parent, was willing to care for them and could make appropriate provision while she was in prison. Since a custodial sentence would not compromise the children's best interests, the mother's appeal against her short term of imprisonment was dismissed.

430 Alexander, *The New Jim Crow*, 11. Alexander notes that since slavery and segregation, the prison has become 'the primary vehicle of racialized social control in the United States'.

431 Alexander, *The New Jim Crow*, 192.

432 Alexander, *The New Jim Crow*, 156–158.

433 John Braithwaite, *Crime, Shame and Reintegration* (Cambridge: Cambridge University Press, 1989), 13–15.

434 John Braithwaite et al, 'Shame, Restorative Justice, and Crime', in *Taking Stock: The Status of Criminological Theory*, eds. Francis T Cullen, John Paul Wright and Kristie R Blevins, (Routledge, 2009), 397.

435 John Braithwaite, 'Reintegrative Shaming', Lecture at Australian National University, 1.

436 John Braithwaite, 'Restorative Justice and Reintegrative Shaming', 296.

437 Edwin Cameron, 'How we internalise stigma and shame', *GroundUp*, 4 December 2019, available at https://www.groundup.news/article/how-we-internalise-stigma-and-shame/ [https://perma.cc/FR8N-UWL7], accessed on 18 June 2024.

438 Casper Lötter, 'Gentle Justice Reduces Recidivism and Incarceration: Can South Africa Benefit from the Finnish Experience?' UNISA Press (2023): 7. See further Casper Lötter, 'Nine out of 10 South African criminals reoffend, while in Finland it's 1 in 3. This is why.' *The Conversation*, 3 December 2023, available at https://

theconversation.com/nine-out-of-10-south-african-criminals-reoffend-while-in-finland-its-1-in-3-this-is-why-218131 [https://perma.cc/T56F-DUCP], accessed on 19 June 2024.

439 Sima Kotecha, 'Why Starmer hired key-cutting boss as prisons minister', *BBC,* available at https://www.bbc.com/news/articles/cp08y5p52e2o [https://perma.cc/5YNV-Q2K3], accessed on 28 July 2024.

CHAPTER 6

440 See Max du Preez, 'Intelligence? What intelligence?', *Vrye Weekblad,* 2 August 2024, available at https://www.vryeweekblad.com/en/news-and-politics/2024-08-02-intelligence-what-intelligence/ [https://perma.cc/X8KU-E7EB], accessed on 2 August 2024.

441 See Caryn Dolley's recent book *Man Alone: Mandela's Top Cop – Exposing South Africa's Ceaseless Sabotage* (Cape Town: Maverick 451, 2024). She has authored other books, including *Clash of the Cartels: Unmasking the Global Drug Kingpins Stalking South Africa* (Kindle Unlimited, 2022), *To the Wolves: How Traitor Cops Crafted South Africa's Underworld* (Cape Town: Maverick 451, 2021) and *The Enforcers: Inside Cape Town's Deadly Nightclub Battles* (Cape Town: Jonathan Ball Publishers, 2019).

442 Daily Maverick Webinar, 'How the state colludes with SA's underworld in hidden web of organised crime – an expert view', available at https://www.dailymaverick.co.za/article/2024-10-18-how-the-state-colludes-with-sas-underworld-in-hidden-web-of-organised-crime-an-expert-view/ [https://perma.cc/T7NA-384Y], accessed on 2 December 2024.

443 See Marius Roodt and Terence Corrigan, 'Crime: the violent seizure of South Africa's growth prospects', available at https://www.politicsweb.co.za/opinion/the-violent-seizure-of-south-africas-growth-prospe?utm_source=Politicsweb+Daily+-Headlines&utm_campaign=5e87e6b402-EMAIL_CAMPAIGN_2024_12_18_11_04&utm_medium=email&utm_term=0_-5e87e6b402-130030197, accessed on 2 January 2025, urging restructuring but also improving policing; giving provinces and metropolitan councils better control over policing; and greater private sector involvement in crime control.

444 Mark Shaw, 'What to do about extortion syndicates' challenge to state legitimacy', *Business Live,* 28 August 2024, available at https://www.businesslive.co.za/bd/opinion/2024-08-28-mark-shaw-what-to-do-about-extortion-syndicates-challenge-to-state-legitimacy/ [https://perma.cc/T5XT-8JXA], accessed on 2 December 2024.

445 See Commission of Inquiry into State Capture: Report on State Security Agency, Crime intelligence and Policing, available at https://www.statecapture.org.za/site/files/announcements/667/OCR_version_-_State_Capture_Commission_Report_Part_V_Vol_I_-_SSA.pdf.

446 Global Initiative against Transnational Organized Crime, 'Strategic Organized Crime

Risk Assessment South Africa', GI-TOC, September 2022, available at https://globalinitiative.net/analysis/assessing-south-africa-organized-crime-risk/ [https://perma.cc/B5TH-CVKF], accessed on 5 July 2024.

447 GI-TOC, 'Risk Assessment', 4–8.

448 GI-TOC, 'Risk Assessment', 9.

449 Nokulunga Majola, 'Two years after Phoenix violence, anger at government inaction', *GroundUp*, 26 July 2023, available at https://groundup.org.za/article/july-2021-unrest-two-years-later-families-and-community-hold-commemorate-victims/#:~:text=In%20Phoenix%2C%20community%20members%20armed,a%20memorial%20in%20their%20honour [https://perma.cc/2CQY-9USE], accessed on 16 July 2024.

450 For incisive criticism of the SAHRC's dismally inconclusive report, see Rebecca Davis, 'How the reports into the July unrest let South Africa down', *Daily Maverick*, 30 January 2024, available at https://www.dailymaverick.co.za/article/2024-01-30-how-the-reports-into-the-july-2021-unrest-let-south-africa-down/ [https://perma.cc/5HUN-VMZ], accessed on 16 July 2024.

451 Sandy Africa, Silumko Sokupa and Mojankunyane Gumbi, Report of the Expert Panel into the July 2021 Civil Unrest, 29 November 2021, paras 2.16–2.17, available at https://www.thepresidency.gov.za/sites/default/files/2022-05/Report%20of%20the%20Expert%20Panel%20into%20the%20July%202021%20Civil%20Unrest.pdf [https://perma.cc/U6CD-TDZ7].

452 Africa, Sokupa and Gumbi, Report of the Expert Panel, para 2.26.

453 Jonny Steinberg, 'Rates of murder tell the sorry tale of SA', *Business Live*, 18 August 2022, available at https://www.businesslive.co.za/bd/opinion/columnists/2022-08-18-jonny-steinberg-rates-of-murder-tell-the-sorry-tale-of-sa/ [https://perma.cc/87QX-GHWA], accessed on 7 July 2024.

454 SAPS Annual Report 2011/12, available at https://www.gov.za/sites/default/files/gcis_document/201409/sapsanrep11-12.pdf.

455 GI-TOC, 'Risk Assessment', 14. The report mentions a shocking example: 'In June 2016, senior police officer Colonel Christian Lodewyk Prinsloo admitted in court to being part of a network that had supplied at least 2 400 firearms to criminal groups in the Western Cape, causing gang violence to surge from 2009 onwards. Investigators were able to link 900 of these firearms to 1 060 murders, while Prinsloo also admitted that his network had been involved in supplying firearms taken from police stores to people involved in taxi conflicts in KwaZulu-Natal'.

456 Lizette Lancaster, 'Without a clear reduction strategy, violence crime is expected to spiral across South Africa', *Daily Maverick*, 14 June 2021, available at https://www.dailymaverick.co.za/article/2021-06-14-without-a-clear-reduction-strategy-violent-crime-is-expected-to-spiral-across-south-africa/ [https://perma.cc/CT9Q-SN3C], accessed on 7 July 2024.

457 DA Shadow Minister of Police, 15 October 2023, available at https://www.da.org.

za/2023/10/detective-crisis-saps-sheds-more-than-8000-detectives-in-6-years [https://
perma.cc/3ZW7-3YZB], accessed on 30 November 2024.

458 GI-TOC, 'Risk Assessment', 27.

459 Steinberg, 'Rates of murder'.

460 Gareth Newham, 'How can South Africa's minister of police improve policing',
ISS, 13 May 2024, available at https://issafrica.org/iss-today/how-can-south-africa-
s-minister-of-police-improve-policing [https://perma.cc/N826-9GN9], accessed on
7 July 2024.

461 Jane Duncan, 'Why SAPS Crime Intelligence is a Hot Mess', *Daily Maverick*,
1 February 2021, available at https://www.dailymaverick.co.za/article/2021-02-01-
why-saps-crime-intelligence-is-a-hot-mess/ [https://perma.cc/CSP2-FS5X],
accessed on 16 July 2024.

462 Darly Swanepoel and Roelf Meyer, 'South Africa's crime intelligence is politicised,
riddled with nepotism and factionalism – and broken', *Daily Maverick*, 5 September
2021, available at https://www.dailymaverick.co.za/article/2021-09-05-south-af-
ricas-crime-intelligence-is-politicised-riddled-with-nepotism-and-factionalism-
and-broken/ [https://perma.cc/9HYC-GD9E], accessed on 16 July 2024.

463 Elizabeth Bernstein, 'The Sexual Politics of the "New Abolition"', *Differences: Journal
of Feminist Cultural Studies* 18 (2007): 143, explaining that there has been a 'drift from
the welfare state to the carceral state as the enforcement apparatus for feminist goals'.

464 National Strategic Plan on Gender-Based Violence and Femicide (2020), available
at https://www.justice.gov.za/vg/gbv/nsp-gbvf-final-doc-04-05.pdf [https://perma.
cc/8H27-6ECX]. At 49 its Emergency Response Action Plan includes: 'Amendment
of legislation related to GBVF in areas, including but not limited to, (a) bail
provisions of the Criminal Procedure Act 51 of 1977; (b) sentencing laws to provide
harsher sentences and restrict parole to offenders imprisoned for certain cases of
GBVF; (c) tighten provisions of the National Register for Sex Offenders to ensure
that it expands its scope and addresses the question of making it public.'

465 See Abrahams, 'Research Brief'.

466 Surajpal, 'Carceral Feminism is not the Answer'.

467 See, for example, People Opposing Women Abuse (POWA), Memorandum calling
for the criminal justice system to provide greater support for gender-based violence
survivors, November 2020.

468 Leigh Goodmark, *Imperfect Victims*, at 12–13, coins the term 'criminalized survivor'
to refer to women 'whose punitive encounters with the criminal legal system are
directly linked to their own gender-based victimization'. In cases involving women
who kill their abusers, Rebecca Gore, 'Rethinking Crime and Punishment: Women
Who Kill Their Abusers', *Michigan Journal of Gender and Law* 31, no. 2 (2024) at
254, explains that 'advocating for the carceral approach to circumvent such violence
overlooks a group of women caught up in the criminal justice system – women who
kill their abusers. This produces a paradox wherein the laws tailored to punish
abusers also punish the *abused*.'

469 Sasha Gear, 'Behind the Bars of Masculinity: Male Rape and Homophobia in and about South African Men's Prisons', *Sexualities* 10, no. 2 (2007): 216–218.

470 See Abrahams, 'Research Brief' and Kai Barron et al, 'Alcohol, Violence, and Injury-Induced Mortality: Evidence from a Modern-Day Prohibition', *The Review of Economics and Statistics* 106, no. 4 (2024): 938–955. See also two recent judgments of the Eastern Cape High Court noting the role of alcohol in intimate partner violence, *S v Manyathi* [2025] ZAECMKHC 5 and *S v Williams* [2025] ZAECGHC 7. In *S v Manyathi*, Govindjee J notes: 'Low-income worker + alcohol + a trigger for domestic violence = brutality + intimate femicide. The facts of this matter rehash, like a recurring nightmare, the tragic equation that all too frequently summarises the plight of women in South Africa.' Both judgments suggest that the Minister of Health consider requiring that alcohol labels highlight the link between alcohol and gender-based violence.

471 National Shelter Movement of South Africa, 'Gauteng's underspending on social development stymies efforts to stem GBVF: Shelters are in crisis amid unspent R554 million', 8 October 2024, available at https://www.nsmsa.org.za/2024/10/08/gautengs-underspending-on-social-development-stymies-efforts-to-stem-gbvf-shelters-are-in-crisis-amid-unspent-r554-million/ [https://perma.cc/Z8KK-UUC8], accessed on 9 December 2024.

472 See Aya Gruber, *The Feminist War on Crime: The Unexpected Role of Women's Liberation in Mass Incarceration* (Berkeley: University of California Press, 2020) and Leigh Goodmark, *Decriminalizing Domestic Violence: A Balanced Approach to Intimate Partner Violence* (Berkeley: University of California Press, 2018).

473 Report on Visit to Johannesburg Correctional Centre, Diepkloof, 28 June 2019, available at https://www.concourt.org.za/images/phocadownload/prison_visits/cameron/Prisons%20-%20Diepkloof%20Report%20FOR%20CIRCULATION%209%20September%202019.pdf, accessed on 30 June 2024, with law research clerks Nicholas Mayieka, Dasantha Pillay and Michelle Sithole.

474 Report on Visit to Johannesburg Correctional Centre, Diepkloof, para 24.

475 Report on Visit to Johannesburg Correctional Centre, Diepkloof, para 107.

476 Report on Visit to Johannesburg Correctional Centre, Diepkloof, para 100. See also *TimesLive*, 'Each prisoner costs taxpayers R10 890 a month, but only R475 is spent on food', *TimesLive*, 26 June 2021, available at https://www.timeslive.co.za/news/south-africa/2021-06-26-each-prisoner-costs-taxpayers-r10890-a-month-but-only-r475-is-spent-on-food/ [https://perma.cc/6SW9-3BCK].

477 Determining costs per inmate requires a complicated and imperfect calculation. This is because certain costs remain fixed and do not increase in proportion to the number of inmates (for example, the costs of compensating certain employees and certain infrastructure costs), while other costs may be influenced by inmate numbers, but not in an easily calculatable way (for instance, the costs of administration, utilities and additional maintenance to address damage caused by overcrowding).

478 See JICS Annual Report 2003/04 at 22, which states that: '[F]ixing of bail at an unaffordable amount. Once a court has decided that an accused can await his trial outside prison, it should not thwart its own intention by fixing bail at a sum the accused cannot afford. . . . There are about 13 000 prisoners who cannot afford the bail set and are being held in prison only because of their poverty.' Judge Fagan had courageously spoken out against the injustices of unaffordable bail amounts, detention and overcrowding: in various platforms, see also *The Advocate*, available at https://www.gcbsa.co.za/law-journals/2000/fourthterm/2000-fourth-term-vol013-no4-pp20-22.pdf [https://perma.cc/5BPQ-P3VL], accessed on 3 December 2024.

479 See JICS Annual Report 2020/21, 9.

480 JICS Annual Report 2023/24, 87.

481 DCS Annual Report 2023/24, 76, available at https://www.gov.za/sites/default/files/gcis_document/202411/dcs-annnual-report-2023-24.pdf [https://perma.cc/J5BU-VP6Z].

482 From the DCS Annual Report 2022/23, 15.

483 For a comparative study of cash bail and the emergence of bail funds see Harvard Law School's student practice organisation, HLS's Advocates for Human Rights Research Report, 'Developing a Bail Fund in South Africa: A Comparative Analysis' (2023) [forthcoming publication].

484 See 'Electronic monitoring system for the Department of Correctional Services', CSIR, available at https://www.csir.co.za/electronic-monitoring-system-department-correctional-services-dcs [https://perma.cc/DT28-4C2L], accessed on 23 July 2024. A message asking more information via the portal on this website remains unanswered.

485 Claire Ballard and Ram Subramanian, 'Lessons from the past: Remand detention and pre-trial services', *SA Crime Quarterly* (2013), 15–16.

486 With the support of the Bertha Centre for Social Innovation and Entrepreneurship at the Graduate School of Business at the University of Cape Town, in particular, Monica Rossi and Kirsten Amsterdam. We acknowledge the support, passion and care from Robert Brozin, Prison Chaplain Rabbi Michael Katz, Laura Horwitz and Solange Rosa.

487 However, some may recall the office of the 'Prisoner's Friend' at Magistrate's Courts. We thank Paul Hoffman and Stephan van Nieuwenhuizen for these helpful insights. More research into the origins and demise of the Prisoner's Friend may be instructive to current efforts toward a bail fund.

488 See Harvard Law School, Advocates for Human Rights Research Report.

489 Robin Steinberg, Lillian Kalish and Ezra Ritchin, 'Freedom Should Be Free: A Brief History of Bail Funds in the United States', *UCLA Criminal Justice Law Review* (2018), 81. Steinberg is the chief executive officer of the Bail Project in the United States. See further Robin Steinberg, TED Talk, April 2018, available at https://www.

ted.com/talks/robin_steinberg_what_if_we_ended_the_injustice_of_bail/transcript?-subtitle=en [https://perma.cc/G36S-9CFX], accessed on 7 January 2025.

490 Private communication to the authors dated 20 September 2024, referencing https://www.justice.gov.za/reportfiles/other/JAF-ANR-2022-23.pdf, accessed on 2 January 2025.

491 Justice Administered Fund Annual Report 2022/23, 4 and 8.

492 Justice Administered Fund Annual Report 2022/23, 31.

493 JICS Annual Report 2023/24, 30. See figure 7.

494 In *S v Dodo* (n 197), the Constitutional Court approved mandatory minimum sentences, in the absence of substantial and compelling circumstances, as constitutionally valid.

495 Julia Sloth-Nielsen and Louise Ehlers, 'A Pyrrhic victory? Mandatory and minimum sentences in South Africa', ISS Paper 111 (2005), 12–13, available at https://issafrica.s3.amazonaws.com/site/uploads/PAPER111.PDF [https://perma.cc/DH54-LAFE]. In addition, Terblanche in *A Guide to Sentencing in South Africa*, 91, the 'inequality inherent in the application of the legislation'.

496 South African Law Reform Commission Report (Project 82), 'Sentencing (A New Sentencing Framework)', November 2000, available at https://www.justice.gov.za/salrc/reports/r_prj82_sentencing%20_2000dec.pdf [https://perma.cc/2Y6Z-GNTD]. See also South African Law Reform Commission Discussion Paper 91 (Project 82), 'Sentencing (A New Sentencing Framework)', 2000, available at https://www.justice.gov.za/salrc/dpapers/dp91.pdf [https://perma.cc/TT4B-3YAF].

497 South African Law Reform Commission Report, 6.

498 South African Law Reform Commission Report, 27.

499 South African Law Reform Commission Report, 46–47.

500 Nancy Gertner, 'A Short History of American Sentencing: Too Little Law, too Much Law, Or Just Right', *Journal of Criminal Law and Criminology* 100 (2010), 691. She explains that: 'Sentencing is, after all, a system; sentencing institutions work in relation to, and not independent of, one another.'

501 See SS Terblanche, 'The Sentence', in *Criminal Procedure Handbook* 13th edn., ed. JJ Joubert (2020) at 394–397.

502 *S v R* 1993 (1) SA 476 (A), 478.

503 *S v Williams* [1995] ZACC 6; 1995 (3) SA 632; 1995 (7) BCLR 861 (CC) (9 June 1995), para 67.

504 Terblanche, *A Guide to Sentencing in South Africa*, 318, 347: '[T]he biggest threat is the judiciary's lack of trust in the Department of Correctional Services' will and capacity to implement sentences effectively.'

505 DCS Annual Report 2022/23, 21.

506 DCS Annual Report 2022/23. DCS reports that: 'There are currently 218 community corrections offices nationally, serving communities and offenders under the system of community corrections.' Furthermore, DCS reports on a number of measures it

has taken to strengthen these programmes. The 'wide range of support services and programmes' available to parolees include a Restorative Justice Program, which saw 'an increase of 18 121 victims and 5 545 offenders, probationers and parolees' participating in the 2022/23 financial year after DCS appointed 88 Social Auxiliary Workers to assist in the tracing of victims. DCS has also developed guidelines for the prevention, management and tracing of absconders and a parole revocation tool to allow decision-makers to better assess risk. Finally, DCS reports that it has 'formalised partnerships with the Business Sector, Local Government, Inter-Departmental Sector and NPOs to encourage them to consider parolees, probationers and ex-offenders for employment opportunities. Parolees are encouraged to form Co-ops and to employ other parolees in their small businesses (farming, making of furniture, making of clothes, taxi industry etc). In its efforts to curb or minimise the reoffending, 875 economic opportunities were facilitated by the Department resulting in the employment of 943 parolees and probationers . . . . Finding stable employment has been identified as one of the best predicators of post release success among parolees.'

507 See *S v M* 2008 (3) SA 232 (CC) when sentencing a primary caregiver.

508 It is critical to note that life imprisonment 'is now imposed for offences that would not have attracted the death penalty, except in the rarest of circumstances'. These include (as one would expect) premeditated murder, murder committed alongside a robbery with aggravating circumstances, rape of a person under the age of sixteen years or of a person physically or mentally disabled, or where the survivor was raped more than once (whether by the perpetrator or a co-perpetrator or accomplice ('gang rape')). But, surprisingly, the list also includes cases where the rapist knows they have HIV, *regardless of whether there is transmission or even any risk of it*. In addition, life is mandatory for trafficking in persons and for offences related to terrorism – plus genocide and crimes against humanity.

509 JICS Annual Report 2023/24, 30.

510 Van Zyl Smit and Appleton, *Life Imprisonment*, 98.

511 Lukas Muntingh, 'Op-Ed: Rethinking Life Imprisonment', *Daily Maverick*, 2 March 2017, available at https://www.dailymaverick.co.za/article/2017-03-02-op-ed-rethinking-life-imprisonment/ [https://perma.cc/7AE9-FGZD], accessed on 30 June 2024.

512 *Phaahla* (n 179 above).

513 Van Zyl Smit and Appleton, *Life Imprisonment*, 193 and 196.

514 *Vinter and Others v the United Kingdom* Application nos. 66069/09, 130/10 and 3896/10 (2013). In the context of life imprisonment without parole.

515 *Vinter and Others v the United Kingdom*, concurring opinion of Judge Power-Forde.

516 See Grobler, 'SA's parole system is dysfunctional'.

517 Section 78 of the CSA.

518 Section 75 of the CSA.

519 A breakdown of the statistics provided to JICS reflects that in addressing the backlog, the minister approved only 24 parole applications (including one day parole application) out of 385, a 6% approval rate. See 'Minister Pieter Groenewald concludes lifer paroles well ahead of deadline', 15 October 2024, available at: https://www. gov.za/news/media-statements/minister-pieter-groenewald-concludes-lifer-paroles-well-ahead-deadline-15-oct [https://perma.cc/CV78-3542], accessed on 2 January 2025.

520 The vast majority of lifers applying for parole currently are those who benefited from more lenient parole provisions, before 2004, that allow them to apply for parole after 15 or 20 years. See JICS Annual Report 2023/2024, 31. Further, of the 385 parole applications the minister recently considered, only one was sentenced in terms of the new, stricter provisions.

521 The 8 March Principles for a Human Rights-Based Approach to Criminal Law Proscribing Conduct Associated with Sex, Reproduction, Drug Use, HIV, Homelessness and Poverty (March 2023), available at https://icj2.wpenginepowered.com/wp-content/uploads/2023/03/Principles-ReportEnglish28Apr024.pdf) [https://perma.cc/M3KF-85LK], accessed on 4 December 2024.

522 See Cathi Albertyn, 'Drugs and moral panic', in *Crime & Power in South Africa* , eds. Dennis Davis and Mana Slabbert (Cape Town: David Philip Publisher, 1985), 106.

523 This point was made in Edwin Cameron, 'Enemies of the nation: How the "war on drugs" has failed South Africa', *GroundUp*, 19 August 2020, available at https://groundup.org.za/article/enemies-of-the-nation-how-the-war-on-drugs-has-failed-south-africa/, accessed on 30 June 2024.

524 See Jali Commission Report, 353.

525 See statements and speeches from the Office of the High Commissioner for Human Rights (dated 14 March 2024), available at https://www.ohchr.org/en/statements-and-speeches/2024/03/turk-urges-transformative-change-global-drug-policy, accessed on 7 July 2024.

526 Office of the United Nations High Commissioner for Human Rights, Report, 'Human rights challenges in addressing and countering all aspects of the world drug problem', 15 August 2023, A/HRC/54/53, available at https://documents.un.org/doc/undoc/gen/g23/156/03/pdf/g2315603.pdf [https://perma.cc/WX4V-N5ZN].

527 Office of UN High Commissioner for Human Rights Report, 17–19.

528 Office of UN High Commissioner for Human Rights Report, paras 23–24. Noting that: 'According to UNODC, of the 3.1 million individuals arrested for drug offences globally, an estimated 61 per cent were arrested for possession of drugs, while 78 per cent of the 2.5 million people in prison for drug offences – who account for some 20 per cent of the total global prison population – were sentenced for drug trafficking. In many instances, however, people were merely in possession of drugs but sentenced for drug trafficking.'

529 Office of UN High Commissioner for Human Rights Report, para 27.

530 Office of UN High Commissioner for Human Rights Report, para 68.

531 *Minister of Justice and Constitutional Development v Prince* (n 187 above), overturning the court's previous contrary decision in *Prince*.

532 National Drug Master Plan, 4th edition, 2019 to 2024, 50, available at https://www.gov.za/sites/default/files/gcis_document/202006/drug-master-plan.pdf [https://perma.cc/AL45-52TF].

533 National Drug Master Plan, 14.

534 Former President Motlanthe was among the large cohort of distinguished former heads of state and heads of government who issued 'Time to End Prohibition', (2021), a Report of the Global Commission on Drugs, available at https://www.globalcommissionondrugs.org/wp-content/uploads/2021/12/Time_to_end_prohibition_EN_2021_report.pdf [https://perma.cc/838U-RBZJ], accessed 24 July 2024, which urged abandonment of the drug war and opting for decriminalisation instead.

535 *The Lancet*, 'Drug decriminalization: grounding policy in evidence', Editorial, *The Lancet*, 402, no. 10416 (25 November 2023): 1941.

536 Portugal continues to report one of the lowest drug-induced mortality rates in Europe. See the European Monitoring Centre for Drugs and Drug Addiction's European Drug Report 2023, 26–29.

537 Anthony Faiola, 'Once hailed for decriminalizing drugs, Portugal is now having doubts', *Washington Post*, June 2023, available at https://www.washingtonpost.com/world/2023/07/07/portugal-drugs-decriminalization-heroin-crack/ [perma link did not work], accessed on 20 June 2024.

538 Faiola, 'Once hailed for decriminalizing drugs'. In addition, *The Lancet*, Editorial, explains that: 'When the use of illicit drugs in the country began to rise in recent years, critics leapt on the reversal as evidence of the policy's failure. But the increase in drug use coincided with a fall in funding for Portugal's drug treatment programme – an essential part of the policy.'

539 Nicholas Kristof, 'How to Win the War on Drugs', *New York Times*, 22 September 2017, available at https://www.nytimes.com/2017/09/22/opinion/sunday/portugal-drug-decriminalization.html?smid=url-share, accessed on 20 June 2024.

540 German Lopez, 'America's Embrace of Marijuana', *New York Times*, 24 October 2024, available at https://www.nytimes.com/2024/10/24/briefing/americas-embrace-of-marijuana.html [perma link did not work], accessed on 6 December 2024.

541 German Lopez, 'From Portugal to Portland', *New York Times*, 4 August 2023, available at https://www.nytimes.com/2023/08/04/briefing/portugal-portland-decriminalization-overdoses.html, accessed on 20 June 2024.

542 Keith Humphreys and Rob Bovett, 'Why Oregon's Drug Decriminalization Failed', *The Atlantic*, 17 March 2024, available at https://www.theatlantic.com/ideas/archive/2024/03/oregon-drug-decriminalization-failed/677678/?utm_source=pocket_reader [https://perma.cc/8DZ5-P9DQ], accessed on 20 June 2024.

543 OPB, 'Oregon's drug decriminalization aimed to make police a gateway to rehab, not jail. State leaders failed to make it work', 14 February 2024, available at https://www.opb.org/article/2024/02/14/oregon-drug-decriminalization-plan-measure-110-leadership-failures/, accessed on 20 June 2024.

544 Lopez, 'America's Embrace of Marijuana'. Although Oregon did impose a fine of $100 for people using drugs, they could easily avoid or ignore the fines.

545 Humphreys and Bovett, 'Why Oregon's Drug Decriminalization Failed'.

546 'Decriminalising of people who use drugs in BC' details the exemption, which came into effect at the end of January 2023, available at https://www2.gov.bc.ca/gov/content/overdose/decriminalization.

547 Leyland Cecco, 'British Columbia drops decriminalization of drugs in public', *The Guardian*, 24 April 2024, available at https://www.theguardian.com/world/2024/apr/29/british-columbia-drug-decriminalization [https://perma.cc/S25A-6WCP], accessed on 5 December 2024.

548 See Jesse Copelyn, 'SA is facing a fast-escalating heroin crisis – and it's being misunderstood', *Spotlight*, 17 April 2024, available at https://www.spotlightnsp.co.za/2024/04/17/sa-is-facing-a-fast-escalating-heroin-crisis-and-its-being-misunderstood/, indicating that stricter policing and border enforcement may inflict harm, and showing weaknesses in our public addiction services; for instance, OST or methadone (best practice for treating addiction) is currently unavailable in state health facilities: 'Clinical trials have repeatedly shown that rehabilitation programmes that rely on OST for at least six months are more effective than abstinence-based approaches. It's thus no surprise that South Africa's Drug Master Plan states that OST is an "evidence-based intervention for individuals who are opiate dependent".'
Yet heroin users reliant on government services cannot access medically assisted rehabilitation – obtaining methadone for at most about a week (an OST programme in Tshwane, funded by the municipality).

549 See Andrew Scheibe et al, 'Harm reduction in practice – The Community Oriented Substance Use Programme in Tshwane', *African Journal of Primary Health Care and Family Medicine* 12, no. 1 (2020). Other programmes include the Belhaven Centre in eThekwini, the TBHIV Care Step Up Project and SAHARA in George.

550 Shaun Shelly, 'Drugs are not the problem. The way we think about them is', *GroundUp*, 7 June 2021, available at https://groundup.org.za/article/drugs-are-not-problem-way-we-think-about-them/ [https://perma.cc/3SA9-MG29], accessed 24 June 2024.

551 See Emily Widra, 'Addicted to punishment: Jails and prisons punish drug use far more than they treat it', available at https://www.prisonpolicy.org/blog/2024/01/30/punishing-drug-use/ [https://perma.cc/AVB8-TJ6B]. Also, noting that: 'Not every person who uses substances needs or wants treatment, but it is imperative that evidence-based, quality healthcare options be made available for those who do – regardless of their involvement in the criminal legal system.'

552 ISSUP, 'Drug Use and COVID-19 in Prisons: First Clinic Dedicated to the Treatment of People Living in Prisons with Opioid Use Disorders in Kenya', available at https://www.issup.net/knowledge-share/resources/2020-06/drug-use-and-covid-19-prisons-first-clinic-dedicated-treatment [https://perma.cc/MGP2-G3RA] (June 2020).

553 UNODC, 'Nelson Mandela International Day: Spotlight on Kenya's first methadone dispensing clinic in prison compound', July 2020, available at https://www.unodc.org/easternafrica/en/Stories/nelson-mandela-day-2020-spotlight.html [https://perma.cc/7QTN-2AEZ], accessed on 22 June 2024.

554 See Lynzi Armstrong, '"I Can Lead the Life That I Want to Lead": Social Harm, Human Needs and the Decriminalisation of Sex Work in Aotearoa/New Zealand', *Sex Res Social Policy* 18, no. 4 (2021), 941–951.

555 Elsa Oliveira, '"I Am More than Just a Sex Worker but You Have to Also Know That I Sell Sex and It's Okay": Lived Experiences of Migrant Sex Workers in Inner-City Johannesburg, South Africa', *Urban Forum* 28, no. 1 (2017): 43–57; Elsa Oliveira, '"You Might Not Think so but I Value Me Because I Provide for My Family": Reflections of a Zimbabwean Sex Worker', *ITCH – The Creative Journal* (2015); Rebecca Walker, 'Selling Sex, Mothering and "Keeping Well" in the City: Reflecting on the Everyday Experiences of Cross-Border Migrant Women Who Sell Sex in Johannesburg', *Urban Forum* 28 (2017), 59–73.

556 Tammy Pietersen, 'Advocacy group demands justice for murdered Cape Town sex worker', *News24*, 4 February 2016, available at https://www.news24.com/news24/advocacy-group-demands-justice-for-murdered-cape-town-sex-worker-20160204.

557 Cameron, 'Sex work: where criminal law has no place. See also Marlise Richter and Pamela Chakuvinga, 'Being pimped out – How South Africa's AIDS response fails sex workers', *Agenda: Empowering women for gender equity* 26, no. 2 (2012), 65–79.

558 Human Rights Watch, 'Why Sex Work Should Be Decriminalised In South Africa' (2019), available at https://www.hrw.org/sites/default/files/report_pdf/southafrica0819_web_0.pdf [https://perma.cc/KV47-C7C5], accessed on 21 June 2024; Ilse Pauw and Loren Brener, '"You are just whores – you can't be raped": barriers to safer sex practices among women street sex workers in Cape Town', *Culture, Health and Sexuality* 5, no. 6 (2003), 465–481; Donna Evans and Rebecca Walker, '"Even though the man raped me and stole my cell phone, I am more frightened of the police than I am of that man": The Policing Of Sex Work In South Africa: A Research Report On The Human Rights Challenges Across Two South African Provinces', Sonke Gender Justice and SWEAT (2017), available at https://genderjustice.org.za/publication/the-policing-of-sex-work-in-south-africa/ [https://perma.cc/4Q57-2TFM], accessed 4 January 2025; Nicole Fick, 'Policing and the sex industry: Sex workers speak out', *SA Crime Quarterly* (2006), 13–18.

559 Elsabé Brits, 'Study finds extreme levels of violence against sex workers', *GroundUp*, 27 August 2021, available at https://www.groundup.org.za/article/study-finds-

exceptionally-high-levels-violence-against-sex-workers/ [https://perma.cc/XC2Y-ENCB], accessed 24 July 2024. See the study by Rachel Jewkes et al, 'Sexual IPV and non-partner rape of female sex workers: Findings of a cross-sectional community-centric national study in South Africa', *SSM – Mental Health* 1 (2021), 100012.

560 Women's Legal Centre, 'Police Abuse of Sex Workers: Data from cases reported by the Women's Legal Centre between 2011 and 2015' (April 2016), available at https://wlce.co.za/wp-content/uploads/2017/02/Police-abuse-of-sex-workers.pdf [https://perma.cc/Z6L3-TRKB] at 18; and see, on the death of sex worker Robyn Montsumi in Mowbray police cells during lockdown, Sandisiwe Shoba, '"She was found hanging in the police cell" – sex worker dies in police custody', *Daily Maverick*, 5 June 2020, available at https://www.dailymaverick.co.za/article/2020-06-05-she-was-found-hanging-in-the-police-cell-sex-worker-dies-in-police-custody/ [https://perma.cc/ALH2-WSZ6], accessed 4 January 2025.

561 See Zia Wasserman, *Analysis of the Criminal Records Expungement Process in South Africa* (2021), available at https://genderjustice.org.za/publication/analysis-of-the-criminal-records-expungement-process-in-south-africa/ [https://perma.cc/Q8NT-W479], accessed on 4 January 2025.

562 See Global Network of Sex Work Projects, Policy Brief: 'The Decriminalisation of Third Parties' (2016), available at https://www.nswp.org/sites/default/files/Policy%20Brief%20The%20Decriminalisation%20of%20Third%20Parties%2C%20NSWP%20-%202016.pdf [https://perma.cc/UNK6-D2FG], accessed on 4 January 2025.

563 See Global Network of Sex Work Projects, Policy Brief: 'The Impact of "End Demand" Legislation on Women Sex Workers', (2018), available at https://www.nswp.org/sites/default/files/pb_impact_of_end_demand_on_women_sws_nswp_-_2018.pdf [https://perma.cc/5FGG-BXW8] (accessed 4 January 2025).

564 Martha Nussbaum contrasts the opprobrium attached to sex work with the acceptance of the work of a consenting person who for reward allows medical research on her colon. See Martha C Nussbaum, '"Whether From Reason Or Prejudice": Taking Money For Bodily Services', *The Journal of Legal Studies* 27, no. S2 (1998), 693–723.

565 Based on consultations with sex workers by UN Working Group on Discrimination against Women and Girls in the Guidance Document titled 'Eliminating discrimination against sex workers and securing their human rights', 7 December 2023, available at https://documents.un.org/doc/undoc/gen/g23/241/61/pdf/g2324161.pdf [https://perma.cc/6RLZ-EJKN] para 13. See further Global Network of Sex Work Projects, 'The impact of "end demand" legislation on women sex workers', which found that: 'The reality is that women are made more vulnerable to violence, discrimination and exploitation.'

566 For a synopsis, see https://x.com/GlobalSexWork/status/1804174787276578971, accessed on 4 January 2025.

567 UN Working Group, 'Eliminating Discrimination', para 31.

568 Criminal Law (Sexual Offences and Related Matters) Amendment Bill, available at https://www.gov.za/news/media-statements/minister-ronald-lamola-criminal-law-amendment-bill-2022-decriminalisation-sex, accessed on 4 January 2025.

569 Liezl Human, '"Tough blow" for sex workers as decrim bill delayed', *GroundUp*, 7 June 2023, available at https://groundup.org.za/article/sex-work-decriminalisation-bill-heads-back-to-the-drawing-board/ [https://perma.cc/BRX8-69HK], accessed on 24 June 2024.

570 For itemisation in one year of female and transgender sex workers' murders (2018–2019), and a situational analysis of sex work, violence and death, see Nosipho Vidima, Ruvimbo Tenga and Marlise Richter, '#SayHerName Female and Transwomxn Sex Worker Deaths in South Africa', SWEAT (2020), available at https://sweat.org.za/wp-content/uploads/2024/09/Sweat-2020-Say-Her-Name_final-low-res-1.pdf, accessed on 4 January 2025.

571 Tania Broughton, 'Court bid to decriminalise sex work', *GroundUp*, 10 October 2024, available at https://groundup.org.za/article/bid-to-decriminalise-sex-work/ [https://perma.cc/28XC-BDPU].

572 See application, paras 60–61.

573 See Chesa Boudin and Marlise Richter, 'Adult, consensual sex work in South Africa: The cautionary message of criminal law and sexual morality', *SA Journal on Human Rights* 25 (2009), 179–197.

574 See Louise Edwards, 'Africa: A Regional Campaign to Decriminalise Petty Offences', available at https://www.prisonstudies.org/news/africa-regional-campaign-decriminalise-petty-offences [https://perma.cc/YC7Q-CRZ7], accessed on 5 December 2024.

575 Available at https://achpr.au.int/en/node/846, accessed 2 January 2025.

576 African Court on Human and Peoples' Rights, *Advisory Opinion, No. 001/2018*, 4 December 2020, para 41.

577 The case was brought by the NGO AdvocAid: *AdvocAid Limited v Republic of Sierra Leone*, Judgment No. ECW/CCJ/JUD/33/24, 7 November 2024. The ECOWAS Court ordered the state to amend, modify or repeal these loitering laws.

578 SALC, 'ECOWAS Court orders Sierra Leone to repeal loitering laws', 11 November 2024, available at https://www.southernafricalitigationcentre.org/ecowas-court-orders-sierra-leone-to-repeal-loitering-laws/ [https://perma.cc/Q5Y2-SEH4], accessed on 9 December 2024.

579 Rules 43–45 of the UN Standard Minimum Rules for the Treatment of Prisoners (the Nelson Mandela Rules) and see Interim Report of the Special Rapporteur of the Human Rights Council on torture and other cruel, inhuman or degrading treatment or punishment, 'Solitary Confinement', 5 August 2011, A/66/268.

580 TRC Prisons Report, 212, para 45, quoting Murthie Naidoo.

581 As quoted in the Jali Commission Report, 334.

582 TRC Prisons Report, 212, para 43.

583 In *Minister of Justice v Hofmeyr* 1993 (3) SA 131 (A), the Appellate Division, predecessor of the Supreme Court of Appeal, insightfully noted that 'any enforced and prolonged isolation' cannot be called punishment: 'It is a form of torment without physical violence.'

584 Jali Commission Report, 337.

585 See section 30 of the Correctional Services Act.

586 In December 2019, the former Inspecting Judge, Justice Van der Westhuizen, submitted a report titled 'From Security to Cruelty? Supermax Correctional Centres: Ebongweni'.

587 Report on the Thematic Inspection conducted at Ebongweni Super-Maximum Correctional Centre (11–12 May 2021, titled 'The moral fibre is nowhere to be found'; Report on the Thematic Inspections conducted at Kgosi Mampuru II C-Max and Mangaung Public Private Partnership Correctional Centres, 29 June and 1 July 2021, titled 'Ticking time bomb'; and the report on solitary confinement, 23 September 2021, titled 'I am a human being'.

588 Jali Commission Report, 351.

589 See Mapping Solitary Confinement Project, available at https://www. solitaryconfinement.org/map/south-africa [https://perma.cc/82ZP-7MZT], accessed on 9 December 2024. See Cameron, 'Solitary confinement is illegal: So why is it happening in South African prisons?', *GroundUp*, 23 February 2022, available at https://groundup.org.za/article/solitary-confinement-illegal-so-why-it-happening-in-south-african-prisons/ [https://perma.cc/JP24-MGHJ].

590 UN Commission on Human Rights, Human Rights Council, Interim Report of the Special Rapporteur on torture and other cruel, inhuman or degrading treatment or punishment, 'Solitary Confinement', paras 62–63.

591 Kayla James and Elena Vanko, 'The Impacts of Solitary Confinement', Vera Institute (2021), available at https://www.vera.org/downloads/publications/ the-impacts-of-solitary-confinement.pdf [https://perma.cc/A87Q-3QL9].

592 UN Commission on Human Rights, Human Rights Council, Interim Report of the Special Rapporteur, 'Solitary Confinement', paras 64–65.

593 James and Vanko, 'The Impacts of Solitary Confinement', 35.

594 Samantha Naidoo, Danielle Jade Roberts, and Sandhiya Singh, 'Behind Bars and Beyond: A Glimpse into the Mental Well-being of the Incarcerated and Guards at Ebongweni Correctional Centre in South Africa', 2024. During a meeting with the Management Committee of the Department of Correctional Services on 24 June 2024, while we were writing this book, officials levelled criticism at the report for its small study sample; JICS was happy to accept these points as well directed – the study's findings simply replicated those comprehensively and authoritatively established in other, larger studies elsewhere in the world; the JICS study was meant to localise those findings, for local advocacy purposes, and did exactly that.

595 It was striking to us how closely the issues of New Zealand's Prisoners of Extreme

Risk Unit (PERU) in Auckland prison echo those JICS seeks to combat locally: see https://inspectorate.corrections.govt.nz/news/news_items/inspection_report_for_prisoners_of_extreme_risk_unit_released [https://perma.cc/D9KF-NBGL]. Chief Inspector Janis Adair acknowledged 'that these men need additional measures to be managed safely', but, despite this, 'found conditions in the PERU to be overly and unnecessarily restrictive'. She found that all the men spent most of their time alone in their cells, with no mixing with any other prisoners, with 'very few interventions that offered meaningful human interaction or constructive activities'. Some of the men had spent months or years in these conditions, which the Chief Inspector said 'likely amounted to prolonged solitary confinement': 'We found the isolation and hopelessness experienced by the men was raised as a concern by mental health clinicians.'

596 Gwen Dereymaeker, 'Solitary confinement and super-maximum prisons', Africa Criminal Justice Reform and Dullah Omar Institute, 7 September 2017, available at https://dullahomarinstitute.org.za/acjr/jics-supermax-presentation-2017.pdf [https://perma.cc/65Q5-Y27F].

597 Jali Commission Report, 365, quotes: 'Successful control depends on people rather than infrastructure.'

598 See Human Rights Council on Torture, Interim Report of the Special Rapporteur, 'Solitary Confinement', paras 64–65.

599 Sharon Shalev, *A Sourcebook on Solitary Confinement* (2008), 23, available at https://www.solitaryconfinement.org/_files/ugd/SolitaryConfinementSourcebookPrint.pdf [https://perma.cc/8WAU-858G], accessed on 14 July 2024.

600 Atul Gawande, 'Hellhole', *The New Yorker*, 23 March 2009, available at https://www.newyorker.com/magazine/2009/03/30/hellhole, accessed on 14 July 2024.

601 Kimberley Brownlee, 'A Human Right against Social Deprivation' *The Philosophical Quarterly* 63, no. 251 (2013) and Kimberley Brownlee, 'The Lonely Heart Breaks: On the Right to be a Social Contributor', *The Aristotelian Society* (2016). We are grateful to Khomotso Moshikaro for sharing Brownlee's work.

602 Brownlee, 'The Lonely Heart Breaks', 35, and referring to Shalev, *A Sourcebook on Solitary Confinement*.

603 Kimberley Brownlee, 'Don't Call People "Rapists": On the Social Contribution Injustice of Punishment', 16.

604 JICS Annual Report 2023/24, 9.

605 See Edwin Cameron, 'Why independent healthcare inside prisons is vital', *GroundUp*, 25 May 2022, available at https://groundup.org.za/article/why-independent-healthcare-inside-prisons-vital/ [https://perma.cc/HHC2-ZCKW]. An indignant response from within the ministry, published under a nom de plume, can be found at Liberia Salasa, 'Prison Healthcare is better than it was before and here are 5 reasons why', *News24*, 23 July 2022, available at https://www.news24.com/news24/opinions/columnists/guestcolumn/opinion-liberia-salasa-prison-healthcare-is-better-than-it-was-before-and-here-are-5-reasons-why-20220723.

606 Zodwa Sibutha, JICS's head of regions, assembled a survey of inmates with disabilities in January 2025. This reflected the totals of those with disabilities (which ranged from sight disablement to amputations, mental unwellness and, in rare cases, paraplegia) as 396 sentenced and 34 unsentenced.

607 Mandela Rules, Rule 24. See Rick Lines, 'From equivalence of standards to equivalence of objectives: The entitlement of prisoners to health care standards higher than those outside prisons', *International Journal of Prisoners Health* 2, no. 4 (2006): 269–280. The 'equivalence of care' principle ought to be a minimum threshold. We should be focusing on equivalent healthcare objectives in prisons – equivalent outcomes, not means.

608 See Cameron et al, 'Who is "everyone" in s 35(2)?', 47.5.5. See also Adila Hassim, 'The "5 star" prison hotel? The right of access to ARV treatment for HIV positive prisoners in South Africa', *International Journal of Prisoner Health* 2, no. 3 (2006): 168–171.

609 See 'Health Services' of the Department of Correctional Services, available at http:// www.dcs.gov.za/?page_id=323 [https://perma.cc/9F46-KUJU], accessed on 6 August 2024.

610 See Takudzwa Pongweni, '"We just want to work" – unemployed healthcare workers appeal to Union Buildings', *Daily Maverick*, 26 February 2024, available at https:// www.dailymaverick.co.za/article/2024-02-26-we-just-want-to-work-unemployed-healthcare-workers-appeal-to-union-buildings/ [https://perma.cc/4Z2Z-W9C4], accessed on 13 July 2024.

611 17 of 2002.

612 See, for example, Sibusiso Sifunda et al, 'Access point analysis on the state of health care services in South African prisons: A qualitative exploration of correctional health care workers' and inmates' perspectives in KwaZulu-Natal and Mpumalanga', *Social Science and Medicine* 63 (2006): 2301 at 2304: 'We found strong evidence of prison being a strategic point to increase access to health services for offenders.'

613 Solomon Benatar, 'The state of our prisons and what this reveals about our society', *South African Medical Journal* 104, no. 9 (2014): 613–614.

614 *Smith v Minister of Justice and Correctional Services* [2023] ZAGPJHC 1127.

615 *Smith v Minister of Justice and Correctional Services* [2023] ZAGPJHC 1127, para 336.

616 TRC Report Volume 5, 'Safeguards for Vulnerable Health Professionals', 335.

617 Rule 25 of the Mandela Rules: 'full clinical independence'.

618 United Nations Office on Drugs and Crime and World Health Organization Regional Office for Europe, 'Good governance for prison health in the 21st century: A policy brief on the organisation of prison health' (2013), vii and 9, available at https:// www.unodc.org/documents/justice-and-prison-reform/WHO_Europe.pdf [https:// perma.cc/6NKM-9U23]. 'Health personnel in prisons should act in their professional capacity completely independent of prison authorities.'

619 Association for the Prevention of Torture, 'Detention Focus Database: Health care staff', available at https://www.apt.ch/knowledge-hub/dfd/health-care-staff#reading [https://perma.cc/FP5B-W6EJ].

620 Benatar, 'The state of our prisons'.

621 Roy Walmsley, 'World Female Imprisonment List', 4th edn, World Prison Brief and Institute for Criminal Policy Research (2022), available at https://www.prison-studies.org/sites/default/files/resources/downloads/world_female_prison_4th_edn_v4_web.pdf [https://perma.cc/M52N-Y7TR].

622 Walmsley, 'World Female Imprisonment List', 13.

623 Penal Reform International, 'Key facts', available at https://www.penalreform.org/issues/women/key-facts/ [https://perma.cc/74NW-HFGV].

624 World Prison Brief, available at https://www.prisonstudies.org/country/south-africa, accessed on 25 July 2024, records that, in 2000, South Africa imprisoned 3 966 female inmates and 4 649 female inmates in 2023. So the proportion has slightly increased (2.5% in 2000 against 3% in 2023), though the female prison population rate (per 100 000 of the national population) has decreased from 9,2% to 7,6%.

625 See Bianca Parry, 'Pathways and penalties: exploring experiences of agency among incarcerated women in South Africa', *Feminism & Psychology* 31, no. 2 (2021), 252–269.

626 Lillian Artz, Yonina Hoffman-Wanderer and Kelley Moult, *Hard Time(s): Women's Pathways to Crime and Incarceration*, Gender, Health and Justice Research Unit: University of Cape Town (2012), xiii. See also Sadiyya Haffejee, Lisa Vetten and Mike Greyling, 'Exploring violence in the lives of women and girls incarcerated at three prisons in Gauteng Province, South Africa', *Agenda* 19:66 (2005).

627 Parry, 'Pathways and penalties'.

628 Gore, 'Rethinking Crime and Punishment: Women Who Kill Their Abusers'.

629 Nokonwaba Z Mnguni and Mahlogonolo S Thobane, 'Factors contributing to women being used as drug mules: A phenomenological study of female offenders incarcerated at the Johannesburg and Kgoši Mampuru II Correctional Centres in South Africa', *Cogent Social Sciences* 8, no. 2 (2022), 4.

630 As explained earlier, the number of women who are incarcerated for sex work is hard to ascertain and seems low.

631 See Parry, 'Pathways and penalties'.

632 See Parry, 'Pathways and penalties', 252–269.

633 JICS Annual Report 2023/24, 29.

634 Sibulelo Qhogwana and Puleng Segalo, 'Rehab for South Africa's female inmates focuses on domestic chores – instead of finding good work', *The Conversation*, 13 September 2023, available at https://theconversation.com/rehab-for-south-af-ricas-female-inmates-focuses-on-domestic-chores-instead-of-finding-good-work-210391 [https://perma.cc/NR76-WGU7], accessed on 3 December 2024.

635 See Rebecca Gore, 'Carceral period poverty', *African Law Matters*, 27 September

2024, available at https://www.africanlawmatters.com/blog/carceral-period-poverty-in-south-african-prisons [https://perma.cc/P8KJ-4UN9], accessed on 3 December 2024.

636 JICS Annual Report 2023/24, 81.

637 DCS Annual Report 2023/24, 72, reports that there are 2 052 women awaiting trial and 2 589 women who have been sentenced.

638 See further Caroline Agboola et al, 'Unpacking Women-to-Women Rape Within Correctional Centres in South Africa: Empirical Lenses', *African Journal of Criminology and Victimology* Vol. 33, Issue 2 (2020).

639 In January 2024, Dr Ramiah helped once more, when JICS intervened on behalf of an inmate at Groenpunt whose cancer was being insufficiently managed.

640 Rule 5 of the Bangkok Rules.

641 See UNODC ROSAF, 'Launch of a gender responsive correctional centre for incarcerated women in South Africa', 12 December 2022, available at https://www.unodc.org/rosaf/stories/2022/December/launch-of-a-gender-responsive-correctional-centre.html.

642 UN Commission on Human Rights, Human Rights Council, Report of the Special Rapporteur, 'Study on the phenomena of torture, cruel, inhuman or degrading treatment or punishment in the world, including an assessment of conditions of detention', 5 February 2010, A/HRC/13/3/Add.59, para 231.

643 National Centre for Transgender Equality, 'LGBTQ people behind bars: A guide to understanding the issues facing transgender prisoners and their legal rights' (2018), 5–6.

644 Principle 9, 'The right to treatment with humanity while in detention', of the Yogyakarta Principles (2007).

645 49 of 2003.

646 *September v Subramoney* [2019] ZAEQC 4, 23 September 2019.

647 *Nthabiseng Mokoena v Head of Correctional Centre, Johannesburg Medium B*, proceedings lodged on 25 June 2024 in the Johannesburg High Court sitting as the Equality Court under case number 2024-070075 – personal communication from Lawyers for Human Rights.

648 *Mapodile v Minister of Correctional Services* [2016] ZAGPJHC 174, 24 June 2016.

649 Adam Gopnik, 'Should We Abolish Prisons', *The New Yorker*, 22 July 2024, available at https://www.newyorker.com/magazine/2024/07/29/abolition-labor-the-fight-to-end-prison-slavery-book-review-until-we-reckon-violence-mass-incarceration-and-a-road-to-repair [perma link did not work], accessed on 30 November 2024.

650 Echoing Judge Power-Forde in *Vinter and Others v The United Kingdom*.

651 Kimberley Brownlee, 'Punishment and Precious Emotions: A Hope Standard for Punishment', *Oxford Journal of Legal Studies* 41, Issue 3 (2021): 590.

CHAPTER 7

652 Yet again, we draw strength and wisdom from Dr Gwen Adshead's recent Reith Lectures.

653 Centre for the Study of Violence and Reconciliation (CSVR Report), 'The Violent Nature of Crime in South Africa: A Concept Paper for the Justice, Crime Prevention and Security Cluster', 25 June 2007, 161.

654 Bill Dixon, 'Introduction: Justice Gained? Crime, Crime Control and Criminology in Transition', in *Justice Gained? Crime and Crime Control in South Africa's Transition*, eds. Bill Dixon and Elrena van der Spuy, xxv.

655 CSVR Report, 161–175.

656 CSVR Report, 173: 'Criminal justice officials themselves may reinforce the culture of violence. Police brutality is not as endemic as it was under apartheid, but there is still a substantial problem of police violence, spurred on in part by more generalised anger about crime. Police violence is part of, and reinforces, the normalisation of violence, and undermines respect for the law. Correctional officials also reflect societal attitudes that are hostile towards offenders in allowing an environment of violence to flourish within prisons, as they do not regard prison inmates as being worthy of protection against violence.'

657 CSVR Report, 171.

Bibliography

Abrahams, Naeemah. 'Research brief: 20 years of femicide research in South Africa'. South African Medical Research Council, 2024. https://www.samrc.ac.za/policy-briefs/20-years-femicide-research-south-africa [perma.cc/2S6B-466B].

Adshead, Gwen. Reith Lectures. https://www.bbc.co.uk/sounds/play/m0025cmg [https://perma.cc/JMF4-AVDZ].

Africa, Sandy, Silumko Sokupa and Mojankunyane Gumbi. Report of the Expert Panel into the July 2021 Civil Unrest. 29 November 2021. https://www.thepresidency.gov.za/sites/default/files/2022-05/Report%20of%20the%20Expert%20Panel%20into%20the%20July%202021%20Civil%20Unrest.pdf [https://perma.cc/U6CD-TDZ7].

African Court on Human and Peoples' Rights. *Advisory Opinion, No. 001/2018*. 4 December 2020.

Agboola, Caroline, Simon Kang'ethe and Boitumelo Joyce Mohapi. 'Unpacking Women-to-Women Rape Within Correctional Centres in South Africa: Empirical Lenses'. *African Journal of Criminology and Victimology* 33, no. 2 (2020): 92–109.

Albertyn, Cathi. 'Drugs and moral panic'. In *Crime & Power in South Africa*, edited by Dennis Davis and Mana Slabbert. Cape Town: David Philip Publisher, 1985.

Alexander, Michelle. *The New Jim Crow: Mass Incarceration in the Age of Colorblindness*. New York: The New Press, 2010.

Altbeker, Antony. *The Dirty Work of Democracy: A Year on the Streets with SAPS*. Cape Town: Jonathan Ball Publishers, 2005.

Anderson, David A. 'The Deterrence Hypothesis and Picking Pockets at the Pickpocket's Hanging'. *American Law and Economics Review* 4, no. 2 (2002): 293–319.

Arango, Tim. 'Frustrated Californians May be Ready for a Tougher Approach to Crime'. *New York Times*, 23 July 2024. https://www.nytimes.com/2024/07/23/us/frustrated-californians-may-be-ready-for-a-tougher-approach-to-crime.html?unlocked_article_code=1.9U0.jpXb.bU65iIoaDx-z&smid=wa-share.

Armstrong, Andrea. 'No Prisoner Left Behind: Enhancing Public Transparency of Public Institutions'. *Stanford Law and Policy Review* 25 (2014).

Armstrong, Lynzi. '"I Can Lead the Life That I Want to Lead": Social Harm, Human Needs and the Decriminalisation of Sex Work in Aotearoa/New Zealand'. *Sexuality Research and Social Policy* 18, no. 4 (2021): 941–951.

Artz, Lillian, Yonina Hoffman-Wanderer and Kelley Moult. *Hard Time(s): Women's*

Pathways to Crime and Incarceration. Gender, Health and Justice Research Unit: University of Cape Town (2012).

Association for the Prevention of Torture. 'Detention Focus Database: Health care staff'. https://www.apt.ch/knowledge-hub/dfd/health-care-staff#reading.

Baldwin-Ragaven, Laurel, Leslie London and Jeanelle de Gruchy. *An Ambulance of the Wrong Colour: Health Professionals, Human Rights and Ethics in South Africa*. Cape Town: University of Cape Town Press, 1999.

Ballard, Claire. 'The way we punish'. *GroundUp*, 22 April 2015. https://groundup.org.za/article/way-we-punish_2860/ [https://perma.cc/7XTS-58Q7].

Ballard, Claire and Ram Subramanian. 'Lessons from the past: Remand detention and pre-trial services. *SA Crime Quarterly* (2013): 15-24.

Barron, Kai, Charles DH Parry, Debbie Bradshaw, Rob Dorrington, Pam Groenewald, Ria Laubscher and Richard Matzopoulos. 'Alcohol, Violence, and Injury-Induced Mortality: Evidence from a Modern-Day Prohibition'. *The Review of Economics and Statistics* 106, no. 4 (2024): 938–955.

Battersby, John D. 'Hanging Now Routine at Pretoria Prison'. *New York Times*, 1 December 1988. https://www.nytimes.com/1988/12/01/world/hangings-now-the-routine-at-pretoria-prison.html.

Bay Area Transformative Justice Collective. 'Transformative justice and community accountability'. https://batjc.files.wordpress.com/2014/06/tj-ca-one-pager.pdf.

Beckett, Katherine and Megan Ming Francis. 'The Origins of Mass Incarceration: The Racial Politics of Crime and Punishment in the Post-Civil Rights Era'. *Annual Review of Law and Social Science* 16 (2020): 433–452.

Benatar, Solomon. 'The state of our prisons and what this reveals about our society'. *South African Medical Journal* 104, no. 9 (2014): 613–614.

Berger, Dan, Mariame Kaba and David Stein. 'What abolitionists do'. *Jacobin*, 24 August 2017. https://jacobin.com/2017/08/prison-abolition-reform-mass-incarceration.

Bernault, Florence. 'The politics of enclosure in colonial and post-colonial Africa'. In *A History of Prison and Confinement in Africa* (Social History of Africa Series), edited by Florence Bernault, 1. London: Heinemann, 2003.

Bernstein, Elizabeth. 'The Sexual Politics of the "New Abolition"'. *Differences: Journal of Feminist Cultural Studies* 18 (2007): 128–151.

Bottoms, Anthony. 'The Philosophy and Politics of Punishment and Sentencing'. In *The Politics of Sentencing Reform*, edited by Chris Clarkson and Rod Morgan. Oxford: Clarendon Press, 1995.

Boudin, Chesa and Marlise Richter. 'Adult, consensual sex work in South Africa: The cautionary message of criminal law and sexual morality'. *SA Journal on Human Rights* 25 (2009): 179–197.

Braithwaite, John. *Crime, Shame and Reintegration*. Cambridge: Cambridge University Press, 1989.

Braithwaite, John. 'Reintegrative Shaming'. Lecture at Australian National University.

Braithwaite, John, Eliza Ahmed and Valerie Braithwaite. 'Shame, Restorative Justice, and

Crime'. In *Taking Stock: The Status of Criminological Theory*, edited by Francis T Cullen, John Paul Wright and Kristie R Blevins. London: Routledge, 2009.

Bregman, Rutger. *Humankind: A Hopeful History*. London: Little, Brown, 2020.

Brickhill, Jason, Adila Hassim, Michael Bishop and Tembeka Ngcukaitobi, eds. *South African Constitutional Law*. Cape Town: Juta, 2003.

Brits, Elsabé. 'Study finds extreme levels of violence against sex workers'. *GroundUp*, 27 August 2021. https://www.groundup.org.za/article/study-finds-exceptional-ly-high-levels-violence-against-sex-workers/[https://perma.cc/XC2Y-ENCB.

Broughton, Tania. 'Court bid to decriminalise sex work'. *GroundUp*, 10 October 2024. https://groundup.org.za/article/bid-to-decriminalise-sex-work/[https://perma.cc/28XC-BDPU].

Brownlee, Kimberley. 'A Human Right against Social Deprivation'. *The Philosophical Quarterly* 63, no. 251 (April 2013): 199–222.

Brownlee, Kimberley. 'The Lonely Heart Breaks: On the Right to be a Social Contributor'. *The Aristotelian Society* 90, no. 1 (2016): 27–48.

Brownlee, Kimberley. 'Don't Call People "Rapists": On the Social Contribution Injustice of Punishment'. *Current Legal Problems* 69, no. 1 (2016): 327–352.

Brownlee, Kimberley. 'Punishment and Precious Emotions: A Hope Standard for Punishment'. *Oxford Journal of Legal Studies* 41, no. 3 (2021): 589–611.

Bruce, David and Chandré Gould. 'The war against the causes of crime: Advocacy for social crime prevention in the face of tougher law enforcement'. *SA Crime Quarterly* 30 (2009).

Bunting, Sonia. 'The prisons of apartheid'. *Africa South in Exile* 4, no. 4 (1960).

Buntman, Fran and Lukas Muntingh. 'Supermaximum prisons in South Africa'. In *The Globalization of Supermax Prisons*, edited by Jeffrey Ian Ross. New Brunswick: Rutgers University Press, 2013: 84–94.

Cameron, Edwin. 'Imprisoning the nation: Minimum sentences in South Africa'. University of the Western Cape Dean's Distinguished Lecture, 2017. https://www.groundup.org.za/media/uploads/documents/UWCImprisoningThe%20Nation19October2017.pdf [https://perma.cc/PL6G-B6T5].

Cameron, Edwin. 'How we internalise stigma and shame'. *GroundUp*, 4 December 2019. https://www.groundup.news/article/how-we-internalise-stigma-and-shame/ [https://perma.cc/FR8N-UWL7].

Cameron, Edwin. 'The Crisis of Criminal Justice in South Africa'. *South African Law Journal* 137, part 4 (2020).

Cameron, Edwin. 'Botched bail decisions can be curbed'. *Sunday Times*, 19 January 2020. https://www.timeslive.co.za/sunday-times/opinion-and-analysis/2020-01-19-botched-bail-decisions-can-be-curbed/ [https://perma.cc/9BA2-YKLD].

Cameron, Edwin. 'Our prisons are failing. They need to become correctional facilities'. *GroundUp*, 3 March 2020. https://groundup.org.za/article/our-prisons-are-failing-they-need-become-correctional-facilities/ [https://perma.cc/A6ZE-Q952];

Cameron, Edwin. 'Covid-19 and the perils of over-incarceration'. *GroundUp*, 24 April 2020. https://groundup.org.za/article/covid-19-and-perils-over-incarceration/ [https://perma.cc/5DLY-NTFT].

Cameron, Edwin. 'A visit to "Sun City" prison: nightmare to manage the virus in confined spaces', *News24*, 14 May 2020. https://www.news24.com/News24/edwin-cameron-a-visit-to-sun-city-prison-nightmare-to-manage-the-virus-in-confined-spaces-20200514.

Cameron, Edwin. 'Enemies of the nation: How the "war on drugs" has failed South Africa'. *GroundUp*, 19 August 2020. https://groundup.org.za/article/enemies-of-the-nation-how-the-war-on-drugs-has-failed-south-africa/

Cameron, Edwin. 'Violence in prisons in increasing, and the prisons watchdog needs more power to stop it'. *Daily Maverick*, 4 September 2020. https://www.dailymaverick.co.za/article/2020-09-04-violence-in-prisons-is-increasing-and-the-prisons-watchdog-needs-more-power-to-stop-it/ [https://perma.cc/24NT-ZMLW].

Cameron, Edwin. 'To enforce the COVID lockdown, did we wage war on the people of South Africa?' *News24*, 6 March 2021. https://www.news24.com/news24/edwin-cameron-to-enforce-the-covid-lockdown-did-we-wage-a-war-on-the-people-of-south-africa-20210306.

Cameron, Edwin. 'Why we need to vaccinate prisoners now'. *GroundUp*, 25 May 2021. https://groundup.org.za/article/why-we-need-vaccinate-prisoners-now/ [https://perma.cc/WTW8-GC2H].

Cameron, Edwin. 'Harsh prison terms won't solve the crisis of gender-based violence'. *GroundUp*, 9 August 2021. https://groundup.org.za/article/why-a-carceral-state-wont-solve-the-crisis-of-gender-based-violence/ [https://perma.cc/4YFF-ASSW].

Cameron, Edwin. 'Our faulty approach to life sentences is catching up with us'. *GroundUp*, 10 November 2021. https://groundup.org.za/article/our-faulty-approach-life-sentences-catching-us/ [https://perma.cc/BNL3-QVPN].

Cameron, Edwin. 'Solitary confinement is illegal: So why is it happening in South African prisons?'. *GroundUp*, 23 February 2022. https://groundup.org.za/article/solitary-confinement-illegal-so-why-it-happening-in-south-african-prisons/ [https://perma.cc/JP24-MGHJ].

Cameron, Edwin. 'Why independent healthcare inside prisons is vital'. *GroundUp*, 25 May 2022. https://groundup.org.za/article/why-independent-healthcare-inside-prisons-vital/ [https://perma.cc/HHC2-ZCKW].

Cameron, Edwin. 'Prisons watchdog needs sharper teeth – JICS is struggling for independence'. *GroundUp*, 28 November 2022. https://groundup.org.za/article/prisons-watchdog-needs-sharper-teeth/ [https://perma.cc/8653-QSNX].

Cameron, Edwin. 'Sex work: where criminal law has no place'. *GroundUp*, 24 January 2023. https://groundup.org.za/article/where-the-criminal-law-has-no-place-sex-work/ [https://perma.cc/SLX7-YLDC].

Cameron, Edwin. 'Our prisons are falling apart, says inspector'. *GroundUp*, 28 July 2023. https://groundup.org.za/article/what-if-our-prisons-tumble-down/ [https://perma.cc/CR2T-8CUU].

Cameron, Edwin, Kevin Minofu, Nabeelah Mia, Rebecca Gore and Sohela Surajpal. 'Chapter 47 Rights of incarcerated and detained persons'. In *South African Constitutional Law*, edited by Jason Brickhill, Adila Hassim, Michael Bishop and Tembeka Ngcukaitobi. Cape Town: Juta, 2003.

Cecco, Leyland. 'British Columbia drops decriminalization of drugs in public'. *The Guardian*, 24 April 2024. https://www.theguardian.com/world/2024/apr/29/british-columbia-drug-decriminalization [https://perma.cc/S25A-6WCP].

Centre for the Study of Violence and Reconciliation. 'The Violent Nature of Crime in South Africa: A Concept Paper for the Justice, Crime Prevention and Security Cluster', 25 June 2007.

Charles, Marvin, Jeff Wicks and William Brederode. 'SA's murder rate rises to two-decade high – and cops are powerless'. *News24*, 16 November 2023. https://www.news24.com/news24/southafrica/news/sas-murder-rate-rises-to-two-decade-high-and-cops-are-powerless-20231116.

Commission of Inquiry into State Capture. Report on State Security Agency, Crime intelligence and Policing. https://www.statecapture.org.za/site/files/announce-ments/667/OCR_version_-_State_Capture_Commission_Report_Part_V_Vol_I_-_SSA.pdf.

Constitutional Court of South Africa. Justice Edwin Cameron. Report: Pollsmoor Correctional Centre – Remand Centre and Women's Centre (2015). https://www.concourt.org.za/images/phocadownload/prison_visits/cameron/Pollsmoor-Prison-Report-23-April-2015-Justice-Edwin-Cameron-FINAL-for-web.pdf.pdf [https://perma.cc/2X73-8BJE].

Copelyn, Jesse. 'SA is facing a fast-escalating heroin crisis – and it's being misunder-stood'. *Spotlight*, 17 April 2024. https://www.spotlightnsp.co.za/2024/04/17/sa-is-facing-a-fast-escalating-heroin-crisis-and-its-being-misunderstood/.

Coyle, Andrew G. 'Prisons'. In *Encyclopaedia Brittanica*. https://www.britannica.com/topic/prison [https://perma.cc/EQQ3-CT8L].

Coyle, Andrew. 'Prison reform efforts around the world: The role of prison administrators'. *Pace Law Review* 24, no. 2 (2004): 825–832.

Crampton, Hazel. *Dagga: A Short History*. Johannesburg: Jacana Media, 2015.

Critical Resistance. 'Reformist reforms vs abolitionist steps to end mass imprisonment'. https://criticalresistance.org/wp-content/uploads/2021/08/CR_abolitioniststeps_anti-expansion_2021_eng.pdf [https://perma.cc/66YW-VCEQ].

Cullen, Francis T, John Paul Wright and Kristie R Blevins. *Taking Stock: The Status of Criminological Theory*. London: Routledge, 2009.

Daily Maverick Webinar. 'How the state colludes with SA's underworld in hidden web of organised crime – an expert view'. https://www.dailymaverick.co.za/article/2024-10-18-how-the-state-colludes-with-sas-underworld-in-hidden-web-of-organised-crime-an-expert-view/ [https://perma.cc/T7NA-384Y].

Damons, Marecia and Nathan Geffen. 'How bad is South Africa's murder rate'. *Ground-Up*, 2 June 2023. https://groundup.org.za/article/how-bad-murder-in-south-africa/ [https://perma.cc/YV95-A7EW].

Davis, Angela Y. *Are Prisons Obsolete?* New York: Seven Stories Press, 2003.

Davis, Dennis and Mana Slabbert, eds. *Crime & Power in South Africa*. Cape Town: David Philip Publisher, 1985.

Davis, Rebecca. 'How State Capture led to human rights abuses – the case of Bosasa and the prisons'. *Daily Maverick*, 14 March 2022. https://www.dailymaverick.co.za/article/2022-03-14-how-state-capture-led-to-human-rights-abuses-the-case-of-bosasa-and-the-prisons/ [https://perma.cc/43M6-6PHV].

Davis, Rebecca. 'How the reports into the July unrest let South Africa down'. *Daily Maverick*, 30 January 2024. https://www.dailymaverick.co.za/article/2024-01-30-

how-the-reports-into-the-july-2021-unrest-let-south-africa-down/ [https://perma.
cc/5HUN-VMZ].

DCS Annual Report 2019/20. http://www.dcs.gov.za/wp-content/uploads/2020/11/
DCS-Annual-Report-TABLING-FINAL.pdf [https://perma.cc/XVL5-BEZZ].

DCS Annual Report 2022/23. http://www.dcs.gov.za/wp-content/uploads/2016/08/
DCS-Annual-Report-Ready-for-Tabling.pdf.

DCS Annual Report 2023/24. https://www.gov.za/sites/default/files/gcis_document/
202411/dcs-annnual-report-2023-24.pdf [https://perma.cc/J5BU-VP6Z].

De Gasperi, Alcide. 'Doing Time in Open Prison in Finland'. *Journal of Modern Science*
(2006): 384.

Deitch, Michele. 'Special Populations and the Importance of Prisons Oversight'. *American
Journal of Criminal Law* 37, no. 3 (2009): 293.

Deitch, Michele. 'Distinguishing the Various Functions of Effective Prison Oversight'. *Pace
Law Review* 30, no. 5 (2010): 1439.

Deitch, Michele. 'But Who Oversees the Overseers? The Status of Prison and Oversight
in the United States'. *American Journal of Criminal Law* 42 (2020): 217.

Deitch, Michele. 'Independent Oversight Is Essential for a Safe and Healthy Prison
System'. 3 November 2021. https://www.brennancenter.org/our-work/analysis-
opinion/independent-oversight-essential-safe-and-healthy-prison-system [https://
perma.cc/7BHY-ML2H].

Deitch, Michele and Michael B Mushlin. 'What's Going On in Our Prisons?' *New York
Times*, 4 January 2016. https://www.nytimes.com/2016/01/04/opinion/whats-going-
on-in-our-prisons.html [perma link did not work].

Delaney, Ruth, Ram Subramanian, Alison Shames and Nicholas Turner. 'American History,
Race, and Prison'. https://www.vera.org/reimagining-prison-web-report/american-
history-race-and-prison%20 [https://perma.cc/Z9YT-SALN].

Dereymaeker, Gwen. 'Solitary confinement and super-maximum prisons'. Africa Criminal
Justice Reform and Dullah Omar Institute, 7 September 2017. https://dullahomarinsti-
tute.org.za/acjr/jics-supermax-presentation-2017.pdf [https://perma.cc/65Q5-Y27F].

Dewan, Shaila. 'Kamala Harris and the Return of "tough on crime"'. *New York Times*,
17 August 2024. https://www.nytimes.com/2024/08/17/us/kamala-harris-prosecutor-
criminal-justice-reform.html

Diar, Prakash. *The Sharpeville Six: The South African Trial that Shocked the World*. Toronto:
McClelland & Stewart, 1990.

Dissel, Amanda. 'Tracking Transformation in South African Prisons'. *Track Two* 11, no. 1
(2002).

Dissel, Amanda. 'A review of civilian oversight over correctional services in the last
decade'. CSPRI (2003). https://dullahomarinstitute.org.za/acjr/resource-centre/
A%20Review%20of%20Civilian%20Oversight%20over%20Correctional%20
Services%20in%20the%20Last%20Decade%20%28Research%20Paper%20No.%20
4%29.pdf [https://perma.cc/88LA-L9KM].

Dissel, Amanda and Jody Kollapen. 'Racism and Discrimination in the South African
Penal System'. Report for Penal Reform International and the Centre for the Study of
Violence and Reconciliation, 2022.

Dixon, Bill. 'Introduction: Justice Gained? Crime, Crime Control and Criminology in Transition'. In *Justice Gained? Crime and Crime Control in South Africa's Transition*, edited by Bill Dixon and Elrena van der Spuy. Cape Town: University of Cape Town Press, 2004.

Dixon, Bill and Elrena van der Spuy, eds. *Justice Gained? Crime and Control in South Africa's Transition*. Cape Town: University of Cape Town Press, 2004.

Dolley, Caryn. *Clash of the Cartels: Unmasking the Global Drug Kingpins Stalking South Africa*. Kindle Unlimited, 2022.

Dolley, Caryn. *To the Wolves: How Traitor Cops Crafted South Africa's Underworld*. Cape Town: Maverick 451, 2021.

Dolley, Caryn. *The Enforcers: Inside Cape Town's Deadly Nightclub Battles*. Cape Town: Jonathan Ball Publishers, 2019.

Dolley, Caryn. *Man Alone: Mandela's Top Cop – Exposing South Africa's Ceaseless Sabotage*. Cape Town: Maverick 451, 2024.

Doob, Anthony N, Cheryl Marie Webster and Rosemary Gartner. 'Issues related to Harsh Sentences and Mandatory Minimum Sentences: General Deterrence and Incapacitation'. *Criminological Highlights* (2014): A-2 to A-3. https://www.crimsl.utoronto.ca/sites/crimsl.utoronto.ca/files/Issues%20related%20to%20Harsh%20Sentences%20and%20Mandatory%20Minimum%20Sentences%20General%20Deterrence%20and%20Incapacitation.pdf [https://perma.cc/MVL4-N9KH]

Du Preez, Max. 'Intelligence? What intelligence?'. *Vrye Weekblad*, 2 August 2024. https://www.vryeweekblad.com/en/news-and-politics/2024-08-02-intelligence-what-intelligence/ [https://perma.cc/X8KU-E7EB].

Dugard, John. 'Should Judges Resign – A Reply to Professor Wacks'. *South African Law Journal* 101, no. 2 (1984).

Dullah Omar Institute. White Paper on the Policy of the Department of Correctional Services in the New South Africa. https://dullahomarinstitute.org.za/acjr/resource-centre/White%20Paper%20on%20Corrections%20in%20South%20Africa.pdf [https://perma.cc/M4FJ-32MD].

Dullah Omar Institute. White Paper on Corrections in South Africa. https://dullahomarinstitute.org.za/acjr/resource-centre/White%20Paper%20on%20Corrections%20in%20South%20Africa.pdf [https://perma.cc/M4FJ-32MD].

Duncan, Jane. 'Why SAPS Crime Intelligence is a Hot Mess'. *Daily Maverick*, 1 February 2021. https://www.dailymaverick.co.za/article/2021-02-01-why-saps-crime-intelligence-is-a-hot-mess/ [https://perma.cc/CSP2-FS5X].

Edwards, Louise. 'Africa: A Regional Campaign to Decriminalise Petty Offences'. https://www.prisonstudies.org/news/africa-regional-campaign-decriminalise-petty-offences [https://perma.cc/YC7Q-CRZ7].

Evans, Donna and Rebecca Walker. '"Even though the man raped me and stole my cell phone, I am more frightened of the police than I am of that man": The Policing Of Sex Work In South Africa: A Research Report On The Human Rights Challenges Across Two South African Provinces'. Sonke Gender Justice and SWEAT (2017). https://genderjustice.org.za/publication/the-policing-of-sex-work-in-south-africa/ [https://perma.cc/4Q57-2TFM].

Faiola, Anthony. 'Once hailed for decriminalizing drugs, Portugal is now having doubts'. *Washington Post*, June 2023. https://www.washingtonpost.com/world/2023/07/07/portugal-drugs-decriminalization-heroin-crack/.

Fick, Nicole. 'Policing and the sex industry: Sex workers speak out'. *SA Crime Quarterly* 15 (2006): 13–18.

Fordham, Ann. 'How the United States fueled a global drug war and why it must end'. Open Societies Foundation. https://www.opensocietyfoundations.org/voices/ how-the-united-states-fueled-a-global-drug-war-and-why-it-must-end [https://perma. cc/LTD6-F7PE].

Foucault, Michel. *Discipline and Punish: Birth of the Prison*. Translated by Alan Sheridan. New York: Pantheon Books, 1977.

Foucault, Michel. 'Alternatives to Prison – Dissemination or Decline of Social Control'. *Theory, Culture & Society* 26, no. 6 (2009): 15.

Foucault, Michel. *The Punitive Society: Lectures at the Collège de France, 1972–1973*. London: Picador, 2018.

Fraser, Luke. 'South Africa needs R36 billion to build more prisons'. *BusinessTech*, 9 December 2024. https://businesstech.co.za/news/government/803512/south-africa-needs-r36-billion-to-build-more-prisons/.

Gallo, Zelia. 'Concepts and conditions of penal moderation: Penal policy, public philosophy, and political ideologies. Theoretical reflections from Italy (2010–2018)'. *Theoretical Criminology* (2024): 16.

Gastrow, Peter and Mark Shaw. 'In Search of Safety: Police Transformation and Public Responses in South Africa'. *Daedelus* 130, no. 1 (2000): 259–275.

Gawande, Atul. 'Hellhole'. *The New Yorker*, 23 March 2009. https://www.newyorker. com/magazine/2009/03/30/hellhole.

Gear, Sasha. 'Behind the Bars of Masculinity: Male Rape and Homophobia in and about South African Men's Prisons'. *Sexualities* 10, no. 2 (2007): 216–218.

Gertner, Nancy. 'A Short History of American Sentencing: Too Little Law, too Much Law, Or Just Right'. *Journal of Criminal Law and Criminology* 100, no. 3 (2010): 691–707.

Gertner, Nancy and Chiraag Bains. 'Mandatory minimum sentences are cruel and ineffective. Sessions wants them back'. *The Washington Post*, 15 May 2017. https:// www.washingtonpost.com/posteverything/wp/2017/05/15/mandatory-minimum-sentences-are-cruel-and-ineffective-sessions-wants-them-back/.

Giffard, Chris and Lukas Muntingh. 'The effect of sentencing on the size of the South African prison population'. Report commissioned by the Open Society Foundation for South Africa (2006). https://dullahomarinstitute.org.za/acjr/resource-centre/The%20 impact%20of%20sentencing%20on%20the%20size%20of%20the%20prison%20 population.pdf.

Gilmore, Ruth Wilson. 'Don't reform prisons, abolish them'. YouTube, 16 August 2020. https://www.youtube.com/watch?v=WZOoP2I1dts.

Global Commission on Drugs Report. 'Time to End Prohibition' (2021). https://www. globalcommissionondrugs.org/wp-content/uploads/2021/12/Time_to_end_prohibi-tion_EN_2021_report.pdf [https://perma.cc/838U-RBZJ].

Global Initiative Against Transnational Organized Crime. 'Strategic Organized Crime Risk Assessment South Africa'. GI-TOC, September 2022. https://globalinitiative.net/ analysis/assessing-south-africa-organized-crime-risk/ [https://perma.cc/B5TH-CVKF].

Global Network of Sex Work Projects. Policy Brief. 'The Decriminalisation of Third Parties' (2016). https://www.nswp.org/sites/default/files/Policy%20Brief%20The%20

Decriminalisation%20of%20Third%20Parties%2C%20NSWP%20-%202016.pdf [https://perma.cc/UNK6-D2FG].

Global Network of Sex Work Projects. Policy Brief. 'The Impact of "End Demand" Legislation on Women Sex Workers' (2018). https://www.nswp.org/sites/default/files/pb_impact_of_end_demand_on_women_sws_nswp_-_2018.pdf [https://perma.cc/5FGG-BXW8].

Goodmark, Leigh. *Decriminalizing Domestic Violence: A Balanced Approach to Intimate Partner Violence*. Berkeley: University of California Press, 2018.

Goodmark, Leigh. *Imperfect Victims: Criminalized Survivors and the Promise of Abolition Feminism* (Gender and Justice) (Volume 8). Berkeley: University of California Press, 2023.

Gopnik, Adam. 'Should We Abolish Prisons'. *The New Yorker*, 22 July 2024. https://www.newyorker.com/magazine/2024/07/29/abolition-labor-the-fight-to-end-prison-slavery-book-review-until-we-reckon-violence-mass-incarceration-and-a-road-to-repair.

Gore, Rebecca. 'Abortion behind bars: women in prisons have extra obstacles to overcome'. *GroundUp*, 8 June 2022. https://www.groundup.org.za/article/abortion-behind-bars-women-in-prisons-have-extra-obstacles-to-overcome/ [https://perma.cc/U3QT-SK5V].

Gore, Rebecca. 'Rethinking Crime and Punishment: Women Who Kill Their Abusers'. *Michigan Journal of Gender and Law* 31, no. 2 (2024): 229–310.

Gore, Rebecca. 'Carceral period poverty'. *African Law Matters*, 27 September 2024. https://www.africanlawmatters.com/blog/carceral-period-poverty-in-south-african-prisons [https://perma.cc/P8KJ-4UN9].

Grant, Thomas. *The Mandela Brief: Sydney Kentridge and the Trials of Apartheid*. London: John Murray, 2022.

Grobler, Liza. 'SA's parole system is dysfunctional and indigent prisoners are often its victims'. *Daily Maverick*, 29 July 2024. https://www.dailymaverick.co.za/opinionista/2024-07-29-sas-parole-system-is-dysfunctional-and-indigent-prisoners-are-often-its-victims/ [https://perma.cc/K7B4-XQEF].

Gruber, Aya. *The Feminist War on Crime: The Unexpected Role of Women's Liberation in Mass Incarceration*. Berkeley: University of California Press, 2020.

Haffejee, Sadiyya, Lisa Vetten and Mike Greyling. 'Exploring violence in the lives of women and girls incarcerated at three prisons in Gauteng Province, South Africa'. *Agenda* 19, no. 66 (2005): 40–47.

Hansard. Debates of the National Assembly, 16 November 1997.

Hansson, Desirée and Dirk van Zyl Smit, eds. *Towards Justice? Crime and State Control in South Africa*. Oxford: Oxford University Press, 1990.

Harvard Law School. Advocates for Human Rights Research Report. 'Developing a Bail Fund in South Africa: A Comparative Analysis' (2023).

Hassim, Adila. 'The "5 star" prison hotel? The right of access to ARV treatment for HIV positive prisoners in South Africa'. *International Journal of Prisoner Health* 2, no. 3 (2006): 168–171.

Hinton, Elizabeth. *From the War on Poverty to the War on Crime: The Making of Mass Incarceration in America*. Boston: Harvard University Press, 2016.

Howard, John. *The State of the Prisons in England and Wales: With Preliminary Observations and an Account of Some Foreign Prisons* (1777).

Human, Liezl. '"Tough blow" for sex workers as decrim bill delayed'. *GroundUp*, 7 June 2023. https://groundup.org.za/article/sex-work-decriminalisation-bill-heads-back-to-the-drawing-board/ [https://perma.cc/BRX8-69HK].

Human Rights Watch. 'Prison conditions in South Africa' (1994). https://www.hrw.org/reports/pdfs/s/safrica/safrica942.pdf [https://perma.cc/82XT-7YTD].

Human Rights Watch. 'Why Sex Work Should Be Decriminalised In South Africa' (2019). https://www.hrw.org/sites/default/files/report_pdf/southafrica0819_web_0.pdf [https://perma.cc/KV47-C7C5].

Humphreys, Keith and Rob Bovett. 'Why Oregon's Drug Decriminalization Failed'. *The Atlantic*, 17 March 2024. https://www.theatlantic.com/ideas/archive/2024/03/oregon-drug-decriminalization-failed/677678/?utm_source=pocket_reader [https://perma.cc/8DZ5-P9DQ].

ICRC report on the visit to 'Robbeneiland' (Robben Island) Prison on the 1st May, 1964, by Mr G. Hoffmann, Delegate General of the International Committee of the Red Cross in Africa'. *International Review of the Red Cross* 98, no. 3 (2016):1067–1077. https://international-review.icrc.org/sites/default/files/irrc-903-18.pdf [https://perma.cc/DAQ9-3VYE].

ISSUP. 'Drug Use and COVID-19 in Prisons: First Clinic Dedicated to the Treatment of People Living in Prisons with Opioid Use Disorders in Kenya', June 2020. https://www.issup.net/knowledge-share/resources/2020-06/drug-use-and-covid-19-prisons-first-clinic-dedicated-treatment [https://perma.cc/MGP2-G3RA].

Jagwanth, Saras. 'A Review of the Judicial Inspectorate of Prisons of South Africa'. CSPRI Research Paper Series no. 4 (2004): 5–6. https://dullahomarinstitute.org.za/acjr/resource-centre/A%20Review%20of%20the%20Judicial%20Inspectorate%20of%20Prisons%20of%20South%20Africa%20%28Research%20Paper%20No.%207%29.pdf [https://perma.cc/G73A-CHXN].

Jali Commission of Inquiry into Alleged Incidents of Corruption, Maladministration, Violence or Intimidation in the Department of Correctional Services (2005). https://www.gov.za/sites/default/files/gcis_document/201409/jalicommfull0.pdf [https://perma.cc/6B9Z-UPCB].

James, Kayla and Elena Vanko. 'The Impacts of Solitary Confinement'. Vera Institute (2021). https://www.vera.org/downloads/publications/the-impacts-of-solitary-confinement.pdf [https://perma.cc/A87Q-3QL9].

Jewkes, Rachel, Kennedy Otwombe, Kristin Dunkle, Minja Milovanovic, Khuthadzo Hlongwane, Maya Jaffer, Mokgadi Matuludi, Venice Mbowane, Kathryn L Hopkins, Naomi Hill, Glenda Gray and Jenny Coetzee. 'Sexual IPV and non-partner rape of female sex workers: Findings of a cross-sectional community-centric national study in South Africa'. *SSM – Mental Health* 1 (2021), 100012.

JICS Annual Report 2003/04.

JICS Annual Report 2020/21. http://www.jics.gov.za/wp-content/uploads/2021/12/JICS_AR-2020-2021.pdf.

JICS Annual Report 2022/23. http://www.jics.gov.za/wp-content/uploads/2024/05/JICS-AR-2022-2023.pdf.

JICS Annual Report 2023/24. http://www.jics.gov.za/wp-content/uploads/2024/10/JICS-ANNUAL-REPORT-2023-2024.pdf.

JICS Quarterly Report July–September 2021. http://www.jics.gov.za/wp-content/uploads/2024/04/JICS-QR2-2021-Jul-Sept-Final.pdf [https://perma.cc/GEN3-F2SV].

JICS Report. 'From Security to Cruelty? Supermax Correctional Centres: Ebongweni', 19 December 2019.

JICS Report. 'The Heart of Darkness', Unannounced Oversight Visit to Pollsmoor Medium B, Friday, 29 October 2021.

JICS Report on Solitary Confinement. 'I am a human being', 23 September 2021.

JICS Report on the Unannounced Oversight Visit to Ebongweni Super-Maximum Correctional Centre. 'The moral fibre is nowhere to be found', 13 October 2021.

JICS Report on Thematic Inspections Conducted at Kgosi Mampuru II C-Max and Mangaung Public-Private Partnership Correctional Centres. 'Ticking Time Bomb', 13 October 2021.

Johnson, Lyndon. 'Special Message to the Congress on Law Enforcement and the Administration of Justice', 8 March 1965. Public Papers of the Presidents 1965/Part 1 (Washington, GPO: 1966). https://policing.umhistorylabs.lsa.umich.edu/s/detroitunderfire/item/4536 [https://perma.cc/HX4E-Z84Y].

Joubert, JJ. *Criminal Procedure Handbook* 13th edition. Cape Town: Juta, 2020.

Justice Administered Fund Annual Report 2022/23.

Kafka, Franz. *Metamorphosis and Other Stories*. London: Penguin Classics, 2019.

Keehn, Emily Nagisa, Nomonde Nyembe and Tanya Sukhija. 'Evaluation of South Africa's Judicial Inspectorate for Correctional Services'. SSRN (July 2013). https://ssrn.com/abstract=2791848.

Kemp, Karl. *Why We Kill: Mob Justice and the New Vigilantism in South Africa*. Cape Town: Penguin Random House, 2024.

Kiewit, Lester. 'Revolving door of crime and jail'. *Mail & Guardian*, 17 January 2020.

Kleijn, Amelia, Ariane Nevin and Zia Wasserman. *One Judge, One Jail – A Guide for Inspecting and Reporting on Places of Detention in South Africa*. Sonke Gender Justice. https://www.saferspaces.org.za/uploads/files/One_Judge_One_Jail_-_A_Guide_for_Inspecting__Reporting_on_Places_of_Detention_in_SA.pdf [https://perma.cc/J83V-C4Q3].

Knopp, Fay Honey. *Instead of Prisons: A Handbook for Abolitionists*. Prison Research Education Action Project, 1976.

Kotecha, Sima. 'Why Starmer hired key-cutting boss as prisons minister'. BBC. https://www.bbc.com/news/articles/cp08y5p52e2o [https://perma.cc/5YNV-Q2K3].

Kriegler, Anine and Mark Shaw. 'Facts show South Africa has not become more violent since democracy'. *The Conversation*, 21 July 2016. https://theconversation.com/facts-show-south-africa-has-not-become-more-violent-since-democracy-62444 [https://perma.cc/46WY-S9PC].

Kristof, Nicholas. 'How to Win the War on Drugs'. *New York Times*, 22 September 2017. https://www.nytimes.com/2017/09/22/opinion/sunday/portugal-drug-decriminalization.html?smid=url-share,

Kushner, Rachel. 'Is prison necessary? Ruth Wilson Gilmore might change your mind'. *New York Times*, 17 April 2019. https://www.nytimes.com/2019/04/17/magazine/prison-abolition-ruth-wilson-gilmore.html.

Lamb, Guy. 'Police Militarisation and the "War on Crime" in South Africa'. *Journal of Southern African Studies* 44, no. 5 (2018): 933–949.

Lancaster, Lizette. 'Without a clear reduction strategy, violence crime is expected to spiral across South Africa'. *Daily Maverick*, 14 June 2021. https://www.dailymaverick.co.za/article/2021-06-14-without-a-clear-reduction-strategy-violent-crime-is-expected-to-spiral-across-south-africa/ [https://perma.cc/CT9Q-SN3C].

Lang, Hartmut. 'The Population Development of the Rehoboth Basters'. *Anthropos* 93 (1998): 381–391.

Lanni, Adriaan. 'Taking Restorative Justice Seriously'. *Buffalo Law Review* 69, no. 3 (2021): 675 at fn 147.

Lansdowne Commission on Penal and Prison Reform Report (1947).

Larson, Doran. 'Why Scandinavian Prisons Are Superior'. *The Atlantic*, 24 September 2013. https://www.theatlantic.com/international/archive/2013/09/why-scandinavian-prisons-are-superior/279949/ [https://perma.cc/PZ38-GMEJ].

Law, Victoria. 'Against Carceral Feminism'. *Jacobin*, 17 October 2014. https://jacobin.com/2014/10/against-carceral-feminism/ [https://perma.cc/BMV6-B2AW].

Leapman, Ben. 'Prisons are shameful, says the man who used to run them'. *Inside Time*, 2 January 2024. https://insidetime.org/comment/prisons-are-shameful-says-the-man-who-used-to-run-them/.

Lewin, Hugh. *Bandiet Out of Jail: Seven Years in a South African Prison*. Johannesburg: Umuzi, 2000.

Library of Congress. 'Sweden: Supreme Court defines negligent rape', 17 July 2019. https://www.loc.gov/item/global-legal-monitor/2019-07-17/sweden-supreme-court-defines-negligent-rape/ [https://perma.cc/9XQ4-T4YB].

Lichtenstein, Alex. *Twice the Work of Free Labor: The Political Economy of Convict Labor in the New South*. New York: Verso, 1996.

Lines, Rick. 'From equivalence of standards to equivalence of objectives: The entitlement of prisoners to health care standards higher than those outside prisons'. *International Journal of Prisoners Health* 2, no. 4 (2006): 269–280.

Lopez, German. 'From Portugal to Portland'. *New York Times*, 4 August 2023. https://www.nytimes.com/2023/08/04/briefing/portugal-portland-decriminalization-overdoses.html.

Lopez, German. 'America's Embrace of Marijuana'. *New York Times*, 24 October 2024. https://www.nytimes.com/2024/10/24/briefing/americas-embrace-of-marijuana.html.

Lötter, Casper. 'Gentle Justice Reduces Recidivism and Incarceration: Can South Africa Benefit from the Finnish Experience?' Pretoria: UNISA Press, 2023.

Lötter, Casper. 'Nine out of 10 South African criminals reoffend, while in Finland it's 1 in 3. This is why.' *The Conversation*, 3 December 2023. https://theconversation.com/nine-out-of-10-south-african-criminals-reoffend-while-in-finland-its-1-in-3-this-is-why-218131 [https://perma.cc/T56F-DUCP].

Luban, David. 'Complicity and Lesser Evils – A Tale of Two Lawyers'. *Georgetown Journal of Legal Ethics* 34, no. 3: 613.

Majola, Nokulunga. 'Two years after Phoenix violence, anger at government inaction'. *GroundUp*, 26 July 2023. https://groundup.org.za/article/july-2021-unrest-two-years-later-families-and-community-hold-commemorate-victims/#:~:text=In%20Phoenix%2C%20community%20members%20armed,a%20memorial%20in%20their%20honour [https://perma.cc/2CQY-9USE].

Mandela, Nelson. *Long Walk to Freedom*. New York: Little, Brown, 1994.

Mandela, Nelson. Address at the Opening of the second session of democratic Parliament, 17 February 1995. https://www.gov.za/news/speeches/president-nelson-mandela-opening-second-session-democratic-parliament-17-feb-1995 [https://perma.cc/RCN2-3ETU].

Mapping Solitary Confinement Project. https://www.solitaryconfinement.org/map/south-africa [https://perma.cc/82ZP-7MZT].

Mcduff, Robin, Deanne Pernell and Karen Saunders. 'Open letter to the anti-rape movement'. *Second Wave* 5, no. 1 (1977).

McGowen, Randall. 'The well-ordered prison'. In *The Oxford History of the Prison: The Practice of Punishment in Western Society*, edited by Norval Morris and David J Rothman. Oxford: Oxford University Press, 1998.

McGrath, Chloë and Elrena van der Spuy. 'Looking Back: Insider Views on the Judicial Inspectorate for Correctional Services'. *SA Crime Quarterly* 48 (2014): 39–48.

McGregor, Liz. *Unforgiven: Face to Face with My Father's Killer*. Cape Town: Jonathan Ball Publishers, 2022.

McGregor, Liz. 'Meeting murderers: Tormented by my father's killing, my quest for answers begins'. https://www.dailymaverick.co.za/article/2022-04-13-meeting-murderers-a-womans-quest-for-answers-and-restorative-justice-after-her-fathers-killing/ [https://perma.cc/K5B4-2NHT].

Minow, Martha. *When Should Law Forgive?* New York: W.W. Norton & Company, 2019.

Mnguni, Nokonwaba Z and Mahlogonolo S Thobane. 'Factors contributing to women being used as drug mules: A phenomenological study of female offenders incarcerated at the Johannesburg and Kgoši Mampuru II Correctional Centres in South Africa'. *Cogent Social Sciences* 8, no. 1 (2022): 1–17.

Morris, Gideon. 'Roundtable Discussion on Oversight Over the Prison System'. CSPRI, August 2009. https://acjr.org.za/resource-centre/Roundtable%20discussion%20on%20oversight%20over%20the%20prison%20system.pdf [https://perma.cc/M698-KE9G].

Morris, Norval and David J Rothman, eds. *The Oxford History of the Prison: The Practice of Punishment in Western Society*. Oxford: Oxford University Press, 1998.

Morris, Ruth. *Stories of Transformative Justice*. Toronto: Canadian Scholars, 2000.

Moyo-Kupeta, Annah. 'Mob Justice is a Language in South Africa'. Centre for the Study of Violence and Reconciliation (30 May 2021). https://www.csvr.org.za/mob-justice-is-a-language-in-south-africa/ [https://perma.cc/LHG4-9K6D].

Mujuzi, Jamil Ddamulira. 'The Changing Face of Life Imprisonment in South Africa'. Civil Society Prison Reform Initiative, University of the Western Cape (2008).

Muntingh, Lukas. 'Punishment and deterrence: don't expect prisons to reduce crime'. *SA Crime Quarterly*, no. 26 (2008).

Muntingh, Lukas. 'An analytical study of South African prison reform after 1994'. LLD diss., University of the Western Cape, 2012.

Muntingh, Lukas. 'Op-Ed: Rethinking Life Imprisonment'. *Daily Maverick*, 2 March 2017. https://www.dailymaverick.co.za/article/2017-03-02-op-ed-rethinking-life-imprisonment/ [https://perma.cc/7AE9-FGZD].

Muntingh, Lukas and Gwen Dereymaeker. 'Understanding impunity in South African law enforcement agencies'. Civil Society Prison Reform Initiative, University of the Western Cape (2013).

Muntingh, Lukas and Jean Redpath. 'The socio-economic impact of pre-trial detention in Kenya, Mozambique and Zambia'. *Hague Journal on the Rule of Law* 10 (2018): 139–164.

Mushlin, Michael. '"I am opposed to this procedure": How Kafka's In the Penal Colony Illuminates the Current Debate About Solitary Confinement and Oversight of American Prisons'. *Oregon Law Review* 93, no. 3 (2015): 626.

Mushlin, Michael and Michele Deitch. 'Opening Up A Closed World: What Constitutes Effective Prisons Oversight?' *Pace Law Review* 30, no. 5 (2010): 1392.

Naidoo, Samantha, Danielle Jade Roberts and Sandhiya Singh. 'Behind Bars and Beyond: A Glimpse into the Mental Well-being of the Incarcerated and Guards at Ebongweni Correctional Centre in South Africa' (2024).

National Centre for Transgender Equality. 'LGBTQ people behind bars: A guide to understanding the issues facing transgender prisoners and their legal rights' (2018): 5–6.

National Drug Master Plan, 4th edition, 2019 to 2024.

National Prosecuting Authority Annual Report 2023/24. https://www.npa.gov.za/sites/default/files/uploads/NPA%202024%20Annual%20Report_web_2.pdf

National Shelter Movement of South Africa. 'Gauteng's underspending on social development stymies efforts to stem GBVF: Shelters are in crisis amid unspent R554 million'. 8 October 2024. https://www.nsmsa.org.za/2024/10/08/gautengs-underspending-on-social-development-stymies-efforts-to-stem-gbvf-shelters-are-in-crisis-amid-unspent-r554-million/ [https://perma.cc/Z8KK-UUC8].

National Strategic Plan on Gender-Based Violence and Femicide (2020). https://www.justice.gov.za/vg/gbv/nsp-gbvf-final-doc-04-05.pdf [https://perma.cc/8H27-6ECX].

New York Times. 'Michel Foucault, on the Role of Prisons'. *New York Times*, 5 August 1975. https://www.nytimes.com/1975/08/05/archives/michel-foucault-on-the-role-of-prisons.html.

Newham, Gareth. 'How can South Africa's minister of police improve policing'. ISS, 13 May 2024. https://issafrica.org/iss-today/how-can-south-africa-s-minister-of-police-improve-policing [https://perma.cc/N826-9GN9].

Nussbaum, Martha C. '"Whether From Reason Or Prejudice": Taking Money For Bodily Services'. *The Journal of Legal Studies* 27, no. S2 (1998): 693–723.

Office of the United Nations High Commissioner for Human Rights. Report: 'Human rights challenges in addressing and countering all aspects of the world drug problem'. A/HRC/54/53, 15 August 2023. https://documents.un.org/doc/undoc/gen/g23/156/03/pdf/g2315603.pdf [https://perma.cc/WX4V-N5ZN].

Oliveira, Elsa. '"You Might Not Think so But I Value Me Because I Provide for My Family": Reflections of a Zimbabwean Sex Worker'. *ITCH – The Creative Journal* (2015).

Oliveira, Elsa. '"I Am More than Just a Sex Worker but You Have to Also Know That I Sell Sex and It's Okay": Lived Experiences of Migrant Sex Workers in Inner-City Johannesburg, South Africa'. *Urban Forum* 28, no. 1 (2017): 43–57.

OPB. 'Oregon's drug decriminalization aimed to make police a gateway to rehab, not jail. State leaders failed to make it work'. OPB, 14 February 2024. https://www.opb.org/article/2024/02/14/oregon-drug-decriminalization-plan-measure-110-leadership-failures/.

Oswald, Eirwen Elizabeth. 'Writing in hostile spaces: A critical examination of South African prison literature'. PhD diss., University of Johannesburg, 2013.

Parry, Bianca. 'Pathways and penalties: exploring experiences of agency among incarcerated women in South Africa'. *Feminism & Psychology* 31, no. 2 (2021): 252–269.

Paterson, Alexander. *Paterson on Prisons: Being the Collected Papers of Sir Alexander Paterson*. Frederick Muller, 1951.

Pauw, Ilsa and Loren Brener. '"You are just whores – you can't be raped": barriers to safer sex practices among women street sex workers in Cape Town'. *Culture, Health and Sexuality* 5, no. 6 (2003): 465–481.

Penal Reform International. 'Key facts'. https://www.penalreform.org/issues/women/key-facts/ [https://perma.cc/74NW-HFGV].

Peters, Edward M. 'Prison before the prison: the ancient and medieval worlds'. In *The

Oxford History of the Prison: The Practice of Punishment in Western Society, edited by Norval Morris and David J Rothman, 3–23. Oxford: Oxford University Press, 1998.

Pietersen, Tammy. 'Advocacy group demands justice for murdered Cape Town sex worker'. *News24*, 4 February 2016. https://www.news24.com/news24/advocacy-group-demands-justice-for-murdered-cape-town-sex-worker-20160204.

Pongweni, Takudzwa. '"We just want to work" – unemployed healthcare workers appeal to Union Buildings'. *Daily Maverick*, 26 February 2024. https://www.dailymaverick.co.za/article/2024-02-26-we-just-want-to-work-unemployed-healthcare-workers-appeal-to-union-buildings/ [https://perma.cc/4Z2Z-W9C4].

Qhogwana, Sibulelo and Puleng Segalo. 'Rehab for South Africa's female inmates focuses on domestic chores – instead of finding good work'. *The Conversation*, 13 September 2023. https://theconversation.com/rehab-for-south-africas-female-inmates-focuses-on-domestic-chores-instead-of-finding-good-work-210391 [https://perma.cc/NR76-WGU7].

Rao, Sonia A. 'Prisoners are being held for years in solitary confinement'. *GroundUp*, 6 September 2023. https://www.groundup.org.za/article/prisoners-being-held-for-years-in-solitary-confinement/ [https://perma.cc/CLA2-SPNV].

Rauch, Janine. 'The 1996 National Crime Prevention Strategy'. Centre for the Study of Violence and Reconciliation (2001).

Report by JICS on Visit to Johannesburg Correctional Centre, Diepkloof, 28 June 2019.

Richard Nixon Foundation. 'Public enemy number one: a pragmatic approach to America's drug problem'. https://www.nixonfoundation.org/2016/06/26404/ [https://perma.cc/E6XA-RRVS].

Richards, Stephen C. 'USP Marion – The first federal supermax'. *The Prison Journal* 88 no. 1 (2008): 6–22.

Richter, Marlise and Pamela Chakuvinga. 'Being pimped out – How South Africa's AIDS response fails sex workers'. *Agenda: Empowering women for gender equity* 26, no. 2 (2012): 65–79.

Robben Island Museum. 'Imprisonment: 1730–1879'. https://www.robben-island.org.za/imprisonment-1730-1879/#:~:text=The%20black%20men%20imprisoned%20for,1869%20(right) [https://perma.cc/Y8Y3-6SAQ].

Roberts, Julian V, Loretta J Stalans, David Indermaur and Mike Hough. *Penal Populism and Public Opinion: Lessons from Five Countries*. Oxford: Oxford University Press, 2002.

Robins, Simon. 'Improving Africa's Prisons: Prison Policy in Sierra Leone, Tanzania and Zambia'. Institute for Security Studies Policy Brief (2009): 2. https://issafrica.org/research/policy-brief/improving-africas-prisons-prison-policy-in-sierra-leone-tanzania-and-zambia [https://perma.cc/P6VH-WMJH.

Roeder, Oliver, Lauren-Brooke Eisen and Julia Bowling. 'What Caused the Crime Decline?' Brennan Center for Justice at New York University of Law (2015). https://www.brennancenter.org/sites/default/files/analysis/What_Caused_The_Crime_Decline.pdf [https://perma.cc/3HK6-6J47]

Roodt, Marius and Terence Corrigan. 'Crime: the violent seizure of South Africa's growth prospects'. https://www.politicsweb.co.za/opinion/the-violent-seizure-of-south-africas-growth-prospe?utm_source=Politicsweb+Daily+Headlines&utm_campaign=5e87e6b402-EMAIL_CAMPAIGN_2024_12_18_11_04&utm_medium=email&utm_term=0_-5e87e6b402-130030197.

Salasa, Liberia. 'Prison Healthcare is better than it was before and here are 5 reasons why'. *News24*, 23 July 2022. https://www.news24.com/news24/opinions/columnists/guestcolumn/opinion-liberia-salasa-prison-healthcare-is-better-than-it-was-before-and-here-are-5-reasons-why-20220723.

SALC. 'ECOWAS Court orders Sierra Leone to repeal loitering laws', 11 November 2024. https://www.southernafricalitigationcentre.org/ecowas-court-orders-sierra-leone-to-repeal-loitering-laws/ [https://perma.cc/Q5Y2-SEH4].

SAPS Annual Report 2011/2012. https://www.gov.za/sites/default/files/gcis_document/201409/sapsanrep11-12.pdf [https://perma.cc/MC4L-UHYH].

SAPS Annual Report 2023/2024. https://www.saps.gov.za/about/stratframework/annual_report/2023_2024/SAPS_Annual%20Report_2023-24.pdf [https://perma.cc/BR2P-GLGT]

SAPS. 'Police recorded crime statistics – First quarter of 2023–2024 financial year'.

SAPS. 'Police recorded crime statistics – Second quarter of 2023–2024 financial year'.

SAPS. 'Police recorded crime statistics – Third quarter of 2023–2024 financial year'.

Sarkin, Jeremy. 'Prisons in Africa: An evaluation from a human rights perspective'. *Sur – International Journal on Human Rights* 9 (2009): 2.

Sawyer, Wendy and Peter Wagner. 'Mass incarceration: The Whole Pie 2024'. Prison Policy Initiative, 14 March 2024. https://www.prisonpolicy.org/reports/pie2024.html.

Scheibe, Andrew, Shaun Shelly, Johannes Hugo, Matilda Mohale, Sasha Lalla, Wayne Renkin, Natasha Gloeck, Senzo Khambule, Lorinda Kroucamp, Urvisha Bhoora and Tessa S Marcus. 'Harm reduction in practice – The Community Oriented Substance Use Programme in Tshwane'. *African Journal of Primary Health Care and Family Medicine* 12, no. 1 (2020).

Shalev, Sharon. 'A sourcebook on solitary confinement' (2008): 23. https://www.solitaryconfinement.org/_files/ugd/SolitaryConfinementSourcebookPrint.pdf [https://perma.cc/8WAU-858G].

Shelly, Shaun. 'Drugs are not the problem. The way we think about them is'. *GroundUp*, 7 June 2021. https://groundup.org.za/article/drugs-are-not-problem-way-we-think-about-them/ [https://perma.cc/3SA9-MG29].

Schwikkard, Pamela J. 'Death in Democracy'. *Singapore Academy of Law Journal* (Special Issue) (2013): 741–743.

Shaw, Mark. 'South Africa: Crime in transition'. Institute for Security Studies (1997): 1–13.

Shaw, Mark. 'What to do about extortion syndicates' challenge to state legitimacy'. *Business Live*, 28 August 2024. https://www.businesslive.co.za/bd/opinion/2024-08-28-mark-shaw-what-to-do-about-extortion-syndicates-challenge-to-state-legitimacy/ [https://perma.cc/T5XT-8JXA].

Sherman, Lawrence W and Heather Strang. *Restorative Justice: The Evidence*. Smith Institute, 2007.

Shoba, Sandisiwe. '"She was found hanging in the police cell" – sex worker dies in police custody'. *Daily Maverick*, 5 June 2020. https://www.dailymaverick.co.za/article/2020-06-05-she-was-found-hanging-in-the-police-cell-sex-worker-dies-in-police-custody/ [https://perma.cc/ALH2-WSZ6].

Sifunda, Sibusiso, Priscilla S Reddy, Ron Braithwaite, Torrance Stephens, Rob AC Ruiter and Bart Van den Borne. 'Access point analysis on the state of health care services in South African prisons: A qualitative exploration of correctional health care workers' and inmates' perspectives in KwaZulu-Natal and Mpumalanga'. *Social Science and Medicine* 63, no. 9 (2006): 2301–2309.

Singh, Shanta. 'The Historical Development of Prisons in South Africa: A penological perspective'. *New Contree* 50 (2005): 18.

Skelton, Ann and Mike Batley. 'Restorative justice: A contemporary South African review'. *Acta Criminologica: African Journal of Criminology and Victimology* 21, no. 3 (2008): 40.

Sloth-Nielsen, Julia and Louise Ehlers. 'Assessing the impact: mandatory and minimum sentences in South Africa'. *SA Crime Quarterly* 14 (2005): 8–9.

Sloth-Nielsen, Julia and Louise Ehlers. 'A Pyrrhic victory? Mandatory and minimum sentences in South Africa'. ISS Paper 111 (2005), 12–13. https://issafrica.s3.amazonaws.com/site/uploads/PAPER111.PDF [https://perma.cc/DH54-LAFE].

Smith, Peter Scharff. 'The Effects of Solitary Confinement on Prison Inmates: A Brief History and Review of the Literature. *Crime and Justice: A Review of Research* 34 (2006): 441–458.

Snyckers, Frank and Jolandi le Roux. 'Criminal procedure: rights of arrested, detained and accused persons'. In *Constitutional Law of South Africa* 2nd edition, edited by Stuart Woolman and Michael Bishop, 50–51. Cape Town: Juta, 2013.

Solinger, Rickie, Paula C Johnson, Martha L Raimon, Tina Reynolds and Ruby Tapia. *Interrupted Life: Experiences of Incarcerated Women in the United States*. Berkeley: University of California Press, 2010.

Sonke Gender Justice NPC.

South African History Online. 'End Conscription Campaign (ECC)'. https://www.sahistory.org.za/article/end-conscription-campaign-ecc [https://perma.cc/TLP7-FD2N].

South African History Online. 'David Bruce'. https://www.sahistory.org.za/people/david-bruce [https://perma.cc/2U2V-ZRDW].

South African Law Reform Commission. Discussion Paper 91 (Project 82). 'Sentencing (A New Sentencing Framework)', 2000. https://www.justice.gov.za/salrc/dpapers/dp91.pdf [https://perma.cc/TT4B-3YAF].

South African Law Reform Commission Report (Project 82). 'Sentencing (A New Sentencing Framework)', November 2000. https://www.justice.gov.za/salrc/reports/r_prj82_sentencing%20_2000dec.pdf [https://perma.cc/2Y6Z-GNTD].

Statewide Harm Reduction Coalition. Annotation in the meeting notes (2006). https://statesofincarceration.org/story/statewide-harm-reduction-coalition-no-new-jails.

Steinberg, Jonny. 'Nongoloza's Children: Western Cape Prison Gangs During and After Apartheid'. Monograph for the Centre for the Study of Violence and Reconciliation (July 2004). https://www.csvr.org.za/docs/correctional/nongolozaschildren.pdf [https://perma.cc/7HLG-7W47]

Steinberg, Jonny. *The Number: One Man's Search for Identity in the Cape Underworld and Prison Gangs*. Cape Town: Jonathan Ball Publishers, 2004.

Steinberg, Jonny. 'Rates of murder tell the sorry tale of SA'. *Business Live*, 18 August 2022. https://www.businesslive.co.za/bd/opinion/columnists/2022-08-18-jonny-steinberg-rates-of-murder-tell-the-sorry-tale-of-sa/ [https://perma.cc/87QX-GHWA].

Steinberg, Jonny. 'Prison Overcrowding and the Constitutional Right to Adequate Accommodation in South Africa'. www.csvr.org.za/docs/correctional/prisoncover-crowding.pdf [https://perma.cc/B5U5-YSPE].

Steinberg, Robin, Lillian Kalish and Ezra Ritchin. 'Freedom Should Be Free: A Brief History of Bail Funds in the United States'. *UCLA Criminal Justice Law Review* (2018): 81.

Steinberg, Robin. TED Talk, April 2018. https://www.ted.com/talks/robin_steinberg_what_if_we_ended_the_injustice_of_bail/transcript?subtitle=en [https://perma.cc/G36S-9CFX].

Stevenson, Bryan. *Just Mercy: A Story of Justice and Redemption*. New York: Random House, 2014.

Stevenson, Bryan. 'Slavery Gave America a Fear of Black People and a Taste for Violent Punishment. Both Still Define our Criminal-Justice System'. *New York Times*, 14 August 2019. https://www.nytimes.com/interactive/2019/08/14/magazine/prison-industrial-complex-slavery-racism.html [https://perma.cc/XL9F-YCKN].

Stewart, Rory. 'As prisons minister, I saw how bad things really are on the inside'. *The Spectator*, 8 February 2020. https://www.spectator.co.uk/article/as-prisons-minister-i-saw-how-bad-things-really-are-on-the-inside/ [https://perma.cc/XKE3-PY74].

Steyn, Daniel. 'Explainer: why South Africa's prisons are overcrowded'. *GroundUp*, 4 December 2024. https://groundup.org.za/article/unraveling-south-africas-overcrowded-prisons/ [https://perma.cc/75WJ-JQGT].

Stockdale, Eric. 'A Short History of Prison Inspection in England'. *The British Journal of Criminology* 23, no. 3 (1983): 209–228.

Stojkovic, Stan. 'Prisons Oversight and Prison Leadership'. *Pace Law Review* 30, no. 5 (2010): 1486.

Stolberg, Sheryl Gay and Astead W Herndon. '"Lock the S.O.B.s Up": Joe Biden and the Era of Mass Incarceration'. *New York Times*, 25 June 2019. https://www.nytimes.com/2019/06/25/us/joe-biden-crime-laws.html.

Strang, Heather, Lawrence W Sherman, Evan Mayo-Wilson, Daniel Woods and Barak Ariel. 'Restorative Justice Conferencing (RJC) Using Face-to-Face Meetings of Offenders and Victims: Effects on Offender Recidivism and Victim Satisfaction. A Systematic Review' (2013). https://restorativejustice.org.uk/sites/default/files/resources/files/Campbell%20RJ%20review.pdf [https://perma.cc/Y48S-XBYM].

Stuurman, Ziyanda. *Can We Be Safe? The Future of Policing in South Africa*. Cape Town: Tafelberg, 2021.

Surajpal, Sohela. 'Carceral feminism is not the answer'. *Africa is a Country* (2020). https://africasacountry.com/2020/09/carceral-feminism-is-not-the-answer. [https://perma.cc/6VST-LMQC].

Swanepoel, Darly and Roelf Meyer. 'South Africa's crime intelligence is politicised, riddled with nepotism and factionalism – and broken'. *Daily Maverick*, 5 September 2021. https://www.dailymaverick.co.za/article/2021-09-05-south-africas-crime-intelligence-is-politicised-riddled-with-nepotism-and-factionalism-and-broken/ [https://perma.cc/9HYC-GD9E].

Tapia, Ruby C. 'Certain failures: Representing the experiences of incarcerated women in the United States'. In *Interrupted Life: Experiences of Incarcerated Women in the United States*, edited by Rickie Solinger, Paula C Johnson, Martha L Raimon, Tina Reynolds and Ruby Tapia, 3. Berkeley: University of California Press, 2010.

Terblanche, SS. *A Guide to Sentencing in South Africa*, 3rd edition. LexisNexis, 2016.

Terblanche, SS. 'The Sentence'. In *Criminal Procedure Handbook* 13th edition, edited by JJ Joubert. Cape Town: Juta, 2020.

The 8 March Principles for a Human Rights-Based Approach to Criminal Law Proscribing Conduct Associated with Sex, Reproduction, Drug Use, HIV, Homelessness and Poverty (March 2023). https://icj2.wpenginepowered.com/wp-content/uploads/2023/03/Principles-ReportEnglish28Apr024.pdf) [https://perma.cc/M3KF-85LK].

The Advocate. https://www.gcbsa.co.za/law-journals/2000/fourthterm/2000-fourthterm-vol013-no4-pp20-22.pdf [https://perma.cc/5BPQ-P3VL].

The Economist. 'How Labour Should Reform Britain's Overstuffed Prisons', 18 July 2024. https://www.economist.com/leaders/2024/07/18/how-labour-should-reform-britains-overstuffed-prisons [https://perma.cc/C9F9-BNNM].

The European Monitoring Centre for Drugs and Drug Addiction's European Drug Report 2023.

The Guardian. 'Do long jail sentences stop crime? We ask the expert', 19 November 2021. https://www.theguardian.com/lifeandstyle/2021/nov/19/do-long-jail-sentences-stop-we-ask-the-expert [https://perma.cc/ERB3-RFVK].

The Lancet. 'Drug decriminalization: grounding policy in evidence'. Editorial, *The Lancet*, 402, no. 10416 (25 November 2023).

The Sentencing Project. 'How Mandatory Minimums Perpetuate Mass Incarceration and What to do About It' (February 2024). https://www.sentencingproject.org/fact-sheet/how-mandatory-minimums-perpetuate-mass-incarceration-and-what-to-do-about-it/ [https://perma.cc/JZ6H-JF53].

TimesLive. 'Each prisoner costs taxpayers R10 890 a month, but only R475 is spent on food'. *TimesLive*, 26 June 2021. https://www.timeslive.co.za/news/south-africa/2021-06-26-each-prisoner-costs-taxpayers-r10890-a-month-but-only-r475-is-spent-on-food/ [https://perma.cc/6SW9-3BCK].

Tonry, Michael. 'Judges and sentencing policy – the American experience'. In *Sentencing, Judicial Discretion and Judicial Training*, edited by Colin Munro and Martin Wasik. Sweet & Maxwell, 1992.

Travis, Jeremy, Bruce Western and F Steven Redburn. 'The growth of incarceration in the United States: Exploring causes and consequences' (2014). https://www.sentencing-project.org/fact-sheet/how-mandatory-minimums-perpetuate-mass-incarceration-and-what-to-do-about-it/ [https://perma.cc/JZ6H-JF53].

TRC Report Volume 2 Chapter 7. 'Political Violence in the Era of Negotiations and Transition, 1990–1994'.

TRC Report Volume 3 Chapter 2. 'Regional Profile: Eastern Cape'.

TRC Report Volume 4 Chapter 5. 'Institutional Hearing: The Health Sector'.

TRC Report Volume 4 Chapter 7. 'Institutional Hearings: Prisons'.

TRC Report Volume 5. 'Safeguards for Vulnerable Health Professionals'.

UN Commission on Human Rights. Human Rights Council. Interim Report of the Special Rapporteur on torture and other cruel, inhuman or degrading treatment or punishment. 'Solitary Confinement', 5 August 2011, A/66/268.

UN Commission on Human Rights. Human Rights Council. Report of the Special Rapporteur on torture and other cruel, inhuman or degrading treatment or punishment. 'Study on the phenomena of torture, cruel, inhuman or degrading treatment or punishment in the world, including an assessment of conditions of detention', 5 February 2010, A/HRC/13/3/.

UN Office on Drugs and Crime and World Health Organization Regional Office for Europe. 'Good governance for prison health in the 21st century: A policy brief on the organisation of prison health' (2013). https://www.unodc.org/documents/justice-and-prison-reform/WHO_Europe.pdf [https://perma.cc/6NKM-9U23].

UN Working Group on Discrimination against Women and Girls. 'Eliminating discrimination against sex workers and securing their human rights', 7 December 2023. https://documents.un.org/doc/undoc/gen/g23/241/61/pdf/g2324161.pdf [https://perma.cc/6RLZ-EJKN].

UNICEF. 'Time to protect children from violence and save lives now'. https://www.unicef.org/southafrica/press-releases/time-protect-children-violence-and-save-lives-now.

UNODC. 'Nelson Mandela International Day: Spotlight on Kenya's first methadone dispensing clinic in prison compound', July 2020. https://www.unodc.org/easternafrica/en/Stories/nelson-mandela-day-2020-spotlight.html [https://perma.cc/7QTN-2AEZ].

UNODC ROSAF. 'Launch of a gender responsive correctional centre for incarcerated women in South Africa', 12 December 2022. https://www.unodc.org/rosaf/stories/2022/December/launch-of-a-gender-responsive-correctional-centre.html.

Van der Merwe, Annette. 'A new role for crime victims? An evaluation of restorative justice procedures in the Child Justice Act 2008'. De Jure (2013): 1022.

Van Niekerk, Barend. 'Judicial Visits to Prisons: The End of a Myth'. South African Law Journal 98 (1981): 416.

Van Zyl Smit, Dirk. 'Public Policy and the Punishment of Crime in a Divided Society: A Historical Perspective on the South African Penal System'. Crime and Social Justice 21/22 (1988): 146–162.

Van Zyl Smit, Dirk. 'Contextualising criminology in contemporary South Africa'. In Towards Justice? Crime and State Control in South Africa, edited by Desirée Hansson and Dirk van Zyl Smit. Oxford: Oxford University Press, 1990.

Van Zyl Smit, Dirk. South African Prison Law and Practice. Butterworths, 1992.

Van Zyl Smit, Dirk. 'Change and continuity in South African prisons'. In Comparing Prison Systems: Toward a Comparative and International Penology, edited by Robert Weiss and Nigel South. London: Routledge, 1998.

Van Zyl Smit, Dirk. 'Swimming against the tides: controlling the size of the prison population in the new South Africa'. In Justice Gained? Crime and Control in South Africa's Transition, edited by Bill Dixon and Elrena van der Spuy. Cape Town: University of Cape Town Press, 2004.

Van Zyl Smit, Dirk and Catherine Appleton. Life Imprisonment: A Global Human Rights Analysis. Boston: Harvard University Press, 2019.

Van Zyl Smit, Dirk and Frieder Dünkel, eds. Prison Labour: Salvation or Slavery? International Perspectives. Ashgate Pub Ltd, 1999, reissued 2018.

Veloen, Heinrich. 'The Numbers Gang in South African Correctional Facilities: Reflections on Structures, Functions and Culture'. MPhil diss., University of Cape Town, 2022.

Vera Institute. 'Ageing Out'. https://vera-institute.files.svdcdn.com/production/downloads/publications/Using-Compassionate-Release-to-Address-the-Growth-of-Aging-and-Infirm-Prison-Populations%E2%80%94Fact-Sheet.pdf [https://perma.cc/7ERF-JXYU].

Vidima, Nosipho, Ruvimbo Tenga and Marlise Richter. '#SayHerName Female and Transwomxn Sex Worker Deaths in South Africa'. SWEAT (2020). https://sweat.org.za/wp-content/uploads/2024/09/Sweat-2020-Say-Her-Name_final-low-res-1.pdf.

Von Hirsch, Andreas. 'Harm and Wrongdoing in Criminalisation Theory'. Crim Law and Philos 8 (2014): 245–256.

Von Hirsch, Andrew, Anthony Bottoms, Elizabeth Burney and PO Wilkstrom. *Criminal Deterrence and Sentence Severity: An Analysis of Recent Research*. Cambridge: University of Cambridge Institute of Criminology, 1999.

Waetjen, Tembisa. 'Apartheid's 1971 Drug Law: Between Cannabis and Control in South Africa'. *The Social History of Alcohol and Drugs* 36, no. 2 (2022): 164–200.

Walker, Rebecca. 'Selling Sex, Mothering and "Keeping Well" in the City: Reflecting on the Everyday Experiences of Cross-Border Migrant Women Who Sell Sex in Johannesburg'. *Urban Forum* 28 (2017): 59–73.

Walmsley, Roy. 'World Female Imprisonment List', 4th editon. World Prison Brief and Institute for Criminal Policy Research (2022). https://www.prisonstudies.org/sites/default/files/resources/downloads/world_female_prison_4th_edn_v4_web.pdf [https://perma.cc/M52N-Y7TR].

Wasserman, Zia. *Analysis of the Criminal Records Expungement Process in South Africa* (2021). https://genderjustice.org.za/publication/analysis-of-the-criminal-records-expungement-process-in-south-africa/ [https://perma.cc/Q8NT-W479].

Weill-Greenberg, Elizabeth. 'Congress seeks to create new independent federal prisons oversight body'. The Appeal, 27 April 2023. https://theappeal.org/federal-prison-oversight-act-congress-bop/ [https://perma.cc/KR4L-76ZE].

Weiss, Robert and Nigel South, eds. *Comparing Prison Systems: Toward a Comparative and International Penology*. London: Routledge, 1998.

Weschler, Lawrence. 'An Afrikaner Dante'. *The New Yorker*, 8 November 1993.

Widra, Emily. 'Addicted to punishment: Jails and prisons punish drug use far more than they treat it'. https://www.prisonpolicy.org/blog/2024/01/30/punishing-drug-use/ [https://perma.cc/AVB8-TJ6B].

Women's Legal Centre. 'Police Abuse of Sex Workers: Data from cases reported by the Women's Legal Centre between 2011 and 2015' (April 2016). https://wlce.co.za/wp-content/uploads/2017/02/Police-abuse-of-sex-workers.pdf [https://perma.cc/Z6L3-TRKB].

Woolman, Stuart and Michael Bishop, eds. *Constitutional Law of South Africa*, 2nd edition. Cape Town: Juta, 2013.

World Population Review. Femicide rates by country 2024. https://worldpopulationreview.com/country-rankings/femicide-rates-by-country [https://perma.cc/P6J9-82MS].

World Prison Brief. 'Highest to Lowest – Prison Population Total – Entire world'. https://www.prisonstudies.org/highest-to-lowest/prison-population-total?field_region_taxonomy_tid=All.

World Prison Brief. 'Highest to Lowest – Prison Population Total – Africa'. https://www.prisonstudies.org/highest-to-lowest/prison-population-total?field_region_taxonomy_tid=15.

Yukhnenko, Denis, Leen Farouki, and Seena Fazel. 'Criminal recidivism rates globally: A 6-year systematic review update'. *Journal of Criminal Justice* 88 (2023): 102–115.

Zehr, Howard. *The Little Book of Restorative Justice*. Good Books, 2002.

Index

282

Finland 126–127, 130, 237, 241
firearms 117, 143–144, 148, 198, 243
Firearms Control Act of 2000 144
firing squad 37
Fischer, Bram 52
flogging 33, 37
food, diet, nutrition 17–18, 30, 38–41, 44,
52, 83, 97, 104, 171, 180–181, 184, 213
force, excessive use of 65, 90, 99
forced removals 17
Formerly Incarcerated Reenter Society
Transformed Safely Transitioning
Every Person Act 217
Fortuin, Chantel (judge) 193–194
Foucault, Michel 33–34, 86, 106, 110,
128–129, 131, 207
Francis, Ellem 85, 185

G4S 115–117
Gaga, Nengeni 45
Gallo, Zelia 236
gallows in Pretoria 51
gangs in prisons 5, 38, 50, 67–68, 75, 82,
84, 86, 88–90, 110, 126, 138, 140,
142, 144–146, 154, 160, 165–166,
169, 177, 187, 198, 210, 243, 248
Gaura, Doreen 7
Gawande, Atul 179
gay persons 17, 192, 194–195
GBVF see gender-based violence;
femicide
Gear, Sasha 7
gender-based violence 73, 133, 146–148,
170, 187, 239, 244–245
see also femicide
General Law Amendment Act 37 of 1963
48
Gericke, Justine 7
Gertner, Nancy 85, 157
Glenister v President of the RSA (*Glenister
II*) 101, 203
Glen (rehabilitated former prisoner) 29–30
Global Initiative against Transnational
Organized Crime (GI-TOC) 143
Global Peace Index 57
Goldberg v Minister of Prisons 203
Goodmark, Leigh 239, 244

Gore, Rebecca 5, 244
government of national unity (GNU) 163,
172–173
Grahamstown Legal Resources Centre 51
grievous bodily harm (GBH) 153
Grobler, Liza 162
Groenewald, Pieter 163, 220, 235
Grootvlei Correctional Centre 103, 113
GroundUp 116
Gqeberha 75

Haffejee, Hoosen 47
Halden (Norway) 127
Hamakwayo , James 45
Hanekom, Derek 18–19
Hanekom, Trish 18–19
Hannibal Lecter 16
harm-reduction, -prevention 167–169, 237
Harm Reduction International 7, 169
Haron, Abdullah 46
Harris, Kamala 216
hate crimes 132
Hausler, Harry 7
Hay, William 94–95, 227
Health Care Act 183
healthcare, free 133
healthcare in correctional centres 104,
111–112, 133, 140, 170, 180–186,
188–189, 192, 194, 199, 213, 257
Health Ombud, Office of, Act 230
Helderstroom Correctional Centre 193
hepatitis 119
heroin 167–168, 251
High Court 10, 29, 104–105, 108, 113,
136, 185, 195, 219, 230
hijackings 144
Hinton, Elizabeth 217
History of prisons 32-44
HIV/Aids 7, 119, 138, 164, 170–171,
181–182, 184, 199, 248
Hoffman, Paul 154, 224, 246
Hogan, Barbara 18–19
Holomisa, Phathekile 119
homelessness 164, 173, 199, 249
hope (for parole, release) 160–161
Hopkins, Anthony 16
Horwitz, Laura 246

Nchabaleng, Peter 47
Ndondo, Batandwa 47
Ndzanga, Lawrence 46
Ndzumo, Saul 47
necklacing 124
Nel, Mary 119
Newham, Gareth 146
New Jim Crow, The 35, 137
New Yorker, The 196, 228
Ngema, Thembelihle 7
Ngwenya, Lungile 7
Ngudle, 'Looksmart' 45
NICRO *see* National Institute for Crime Prevention and the Reintegration of Offenders
Niehaus, Carl 18–19
Nixon, Richard 12, 63, 68
Non-custodial Measures for Women Offenders (Bangkok Rules) 189–190, 192, 259
Non-white terminology 11
Nordic prisons model 126–127, 171–172
Norval Foundation 82
Norway 127, 237
NPA *see* National Prosecuting Authority
NPM *see* National Preventive Mechanism
Ntshuntsha, Nabaoth 46
Number, The 90
Nunn, Dorsey 137
Nussbaum, Martha 253

Office of Health Standards Compliance (OHSC) 230
Office of the Correctional Investigator, Canada 96
Office of the High Commissioner for Human Rights (OHCHR) 164, 166
Office of the Inspectorate, New Zealand 96
Office of the Inspector General, California 97
officials of Correctional Services 29, 63, 75, 78, 83–87, 90–91, 93–94, 107, 109–110, 114–121, 123, 126, 140, 151, 161, 166, 177–178, 182–183, 185, 188–189, 192, 195–196, 211–213, 226, 233, 255, 260
Official Visitors, Zambia 97

Old Fort 54
Old Testament 89
Omar, Dullah 68, 121, 178
One Judge, One Jail campaign 103
Oos-Randse Administrasieraad v Rikhoto 203
open prisons 126–127
opioid crisis 168–169
opioid substitution therapy (OST) 169
Optional Protocol to the Convention against Torture and Other Cruel, Inhuman or Degrading Treatment or Punishment (OPCAT) 95–96, 227
Oregon 168
organised crime 142–144, 146, 198
origins of prisons 32
overcrowded prisons (correctional centres) 5, 44, 56–57, 79, 81–82, 84, 87, 90, 102, 104–105, 109, 111, 115, 122, 127, 141, 149–151, 154, 156, 158, 166, 173, 180, 182–183, 188–190, 195, 197, 213, 231, 235, 245
over-inclusive prison system 88, 141
    see also under-inclusive prison system
oversight of prisons 5, 54, 92–121, 123, 128, 163, 173, 186, 193, 226
    see also Judicial Inspectorate for Correctional Services (JICS)
Oxford University 10–11, 16–17, 19, 42

palliative inspectorate 105
Pan African Lawyers Union 174
paramilitary policing 66
Parliament 5, 12, 48, 52–53, 61, 65, 68–70, 95, 97, 99, 101–102, 105, 118, 144, 150, 155–158, 163, 176, 210, 229–230, 232, 235
Parliamentary Portfolio Committee on Justice and Correctional Services 99, 102, 118, 150, 176, 230, 232
parole 15, 56, 64–65, 72, 74, 77, 87, 107, 112–113, 118, 130, 136, 141, 152, 156, 158–163, 218, 221, 244, 247–248
parole boards 56, 162
Parry, Bianca 187
pass laws 19, 40-43, 209, 211
passports, handing in of 152

www.ingramcontent.com/pod-product-compliance
Lightning Source LLC
Chambersburg PA
CBHW021614270326

41931CB00008B/700